T0372431

Marketing Fashion

Strategy, Branding and Promotion

Third Edition

Harriet Posner

LAURENCE KING

Contents

↑ A look from the Hacker Project;
see page 43.

Introduction

A great deal has changed since the first edition of *Marketing Fashion* came out in 2011. Social media and e-commerce were then in their infancy, and fashion marketing and promotion were still carried out along largely traditional lines. Consumers were reluctant to shop online, mainly because they were worried about digital security or did not want to forgo the physical experience of shopping. In 2010, between commissioning and publication, both Instagram and Pinterest were launched. By the time the second edition, *Marketing Fashion: Strategy, Branding and Promotion*, was published in 2015, social media, particularly Instagram, was well embedded. The Instagram influencer had made their mark, resulting in the creation of new businesses, such as the influencer agency.

By the time the third edition was commissioned, there was a growing sense of unease about some aspects of fashion. The ethics behind its manufacture were being challenged: who made our clothes, how much were they paid and in what conditions did they live and work? Fashion Revolution's Who Made My Clothes? movement launched in 2017, and the ethics of consumption came under the spotlight when it was revealed that Burberry had incinerated unsold clothes, accessories and perfume worth £28.6m during 2017 in order to protect its brand. Environmental protesters took to the streets for Earth Day in 2019, their message: 'Business as usual costs the Earth.' Then came the pandemic in early 2020, and the cost-of-living crisis in 2021. How do you think about and address fashion marketing and promotion in this context?

These concerns are pressing, but we need to wear clothes, and fashion allows us to dream. It can transport us from the mundane into a magical realm where a garment's shape and proportion become a silhouette, a colour transforms from plain brown into glamorous mocha, and a simple sheath of black fabric becomes a little black dress. How do we keep this passion alive while recognizing the very real challenges the world faces? Fashion is a complex cultural phenomenon, but it is also a global manufacturing and retail industry. It extends from the agricultural, chemical and fibre industries that produce and supply the raw materials for textiles, through to the more glamorous spheres of styling, art direction, photography, advertising, media and digital marketing.

Marketing, branding and promotion play a critical role in the fashion industry today; they are stimulating and exciting disciplines that inform many of the strategic and creative decisions behind the design, production and retailing of fashion. Marketing and branding, for example, bridge the gap between the intangibles of fashion and the concrete realities of business. They can be viewed as part of a holistic system connecting the commercial goals and value system of a business organization with the personal ideas, desires and actual needs of customers. Marketing has been described as both a science and an art, requiring systematic research and analysis as well as creativity, innovation and intuition. It operates at every level of the fashion system and affects the entire supply chain, from product development to retail; it is as relevant to couture, luxury labels and designer brands as it is to independent niche labels.

This new edition of *Marketing Fashion* is written with the premise that marketing, branding and promotion can be used as forces for good. Marketing has always had to reinvent itself in response to external factors. Now it also has the challenge of appealing to new types of customer who want to deal with an industry that contributes positively to a world in turmoil by making an ethical impact.

What is in this book?

Marketing Fashion is a contemporary visual guide to the principles of marketing theory and branding practice. It explains key theoretical concepts, illustrating how these might be applied within the ever-evolving context of the global fashion, retail and e-commerce industry. It will lead you through the marketing process, from initial research to the creation of marketing and branding campaigns. Examples and case studies drawn from a broad range of fashion businesses help to explain key concepts, and suggestions for further reading are provided at the end of the book. *Marketing Fashion* provides many useful tips and inspirational ideas aimed at assisting you to:

> » Study and understand marketing theory and practice

> » Understand how fashion marketing and branding principles are put into action

> » Design fashion products that can be marketed with ease

> » Recognize the importance of research and market analysis

> » Analyse fashion consumers and understand their needs

> » Create exciting and effective marketing and promotional campaigns

How the book is structured

Chapter 1: Marketing Theory introduces the fundamental tools of marketing and marketing strategy. The key concepts are illustrated with examples from the global retail and fashion industry to explain how they are applied in practice.

Chapter 2: The Fashion Market outlines the basic structure of the fashion industry and its seasonal cycles. It explains the different levels of the market and provides information on emerging global fashion markets along with such growing markets as rental fashion, pre-loved fashion and the increasing trend for mend and repair.

Chapter 3: Research & Planning explains the concept of the marketing environment and the areas to be researched and analysed when gathering market and trend intelligence. It gives an overview of marketing research methods, how to monitor the market, and how to use research when planning a marketing strategy.

Chapter 4: Understanding the Customer focuses on research into and analysis of customers. It explores ways in which a business can analyse its customer base so as to understand their requirements and target products, marketing strategies and social-media communication accordingly. Key to this chapter is the concept of the customer journey from first awareness to brand engagement, purchase, loyalty and brand advocacy. It explains the impact of psychology on consumer purchasing behaviour and offers techniques for creating customer profiles.

Chapter 5: Introduction to Branding explains the fundamentals of branding and why brands are such valuable assets. The chapter covers brand strategy and management, shows how brands are created, and explains the importance of brand identity as a strategic tool for building a relationship between a brand and its customers.

Chapter 6: Fashion Promotion covers the main types of promotional activity employed in fashion retail and e-commerce. It covers fashion advertising, sales promotion, PR and social media, as well as how to measure the effectiveness of a campaign. A broad selection of case studies highlights current trends in contemporary fashion promotion.

Who is this book for?

Marketing Fashion is for anyone interested in the world of fashion and how it works. Fashion marketing, branding and promotion are integral to the system, and an essential area of study for all who plan a career in the industry. This book is designed specifically for students of these disciplines, but those studying fashion design or who wish to start their own brand will also benefit. Fashion is never static, and marketing, branding and promotion for fashion do not always conform to standard theoretical formulae. To be successful, you need to build on basic principles and adapt ideas so as to meet the challenges of each new market situation. *Marketing Fashion* aims to educate but also to inspire, and you are encouraged to use the material as a platform for further research and inquiry.

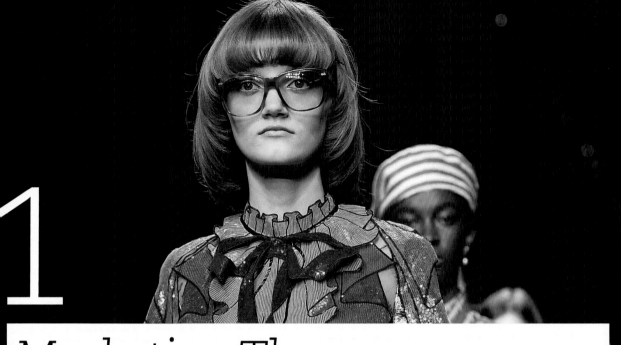

1

Marketing Theory

"Marketing is not the art of finding clever ways to dispose of what you make. Marketing is the art of creating genuine customer value."

Philip Kotler

This chapter introduces you to essential marketing theory and the strategic tools used by marketers. The most fundamental of these are the **Marketing Mix** and the strategic model of **Segmentation**, **Targeting** and **Positioning** known as **STP Marketing Strategy**. In this chapter we will consider what marketing is, and give a range of definitions in an attempt to show as broad a picture as possible, while also explaining the concepts of **Unique Selling Point (USP)**, **Differentiation**, **Added Value** and **Competitive Advantage**. By the end of this chapter you should be able to understand the basics, and then, going forward, it will be possible for you to consider in more detail how the theory might apply in practice to fashion marketing and promotion.

What is marketing?

Marketing is intriguing in that it has been variously described as a business function, business philosophy, and a management or social process. Marketing should really be viewed as a holistic system connecting a business with its customers. Professor Philip Kotler, who has been described as the godfather of modern marketing, believes that what makes a company is its marketing. He considers marketing to be both a science and an art. It is strategic and creative, requiring systematic research and analysis, as well as innovation, intuition and gut instinct.

The range and potential of marketing can be almost limitless; it may start long before any product has been designed, and continue long after a customer has purchased. This scope and multi-dimensional nature could make a clear definition appear elusive. However, the next section will address this by presenting four definitions that capture the essentials and simplify the complexities of marketing. The key points raised by the individual definitions are then examined in more depth.

Marketing definitions

Each of the definitions given below highlights a particular facet of the marketing dynamic. Viewed together, they reveal the broad scope of marketing:

> "Marketing is the management process responsible for identifying, anticipating and satisfying customer requirements profitably." Chartered Institute of Marketing (CIM), UK

> "Marketing is the human activity directed at satisfying needs and wants through an exchange process." Philip Kotler (1980)

> "Marketing is the social and managerial process by which individuals and groups obtain what they need and want through creating and exchanging products of value with others." Philip Kotler (1991)

> "Marketing is the science and art of exploring, creating, and delivering value to satisfy the needs of a target market at a profit." Philip Kotler (2011)

↓ A Vivienne Westwood bag promoted in-store as an exclusive gift at Christmas.

Collectively, these definitions summarize the fundamental elements of marketing as:

> » An understanding of customer requirements
>
> » The ability to create, communicate and deliver value
>
> » A social process
>
> » An exchange process
>
> » A managerial and business process

While the fundamentals of marketing may be similar for any industry, the exact nature of their application will differ from one sector to another. In the following pages we will see how each of these elements of marketing can be applied in the context of fashion, and, in particular, how they relate to the connection between the consumer and their clothing.

An understanding of customer requirements

The definition from the Chartered Institute of Marketing draws attention to the significance of identifying and anticipating the needs of customers. Naturally, this is an important first step in being able to design, produce and deliver merchandise that satisfies or indeed exceeds consumer desires, requirements or expectations. However, it is not just in relation to the product that customer requirements need to be considered. The total experience and service that customers receive as part of their engagement and relationship with a fashion, beauty or lifestyle brand must also be factored in to the marketing equation. This may include a wide range of activities and interactions, among them online product searches, engagement with the brand's social media, visits to a physical store, noticing pop-up adverts or influencer posts, or returning products easily. This means that branded content and all the processes of engagement are as worthy of consideration as the fashion product, and must therefore be viewed as essential to marketing.

An underlying concept of marketing is to produce what people want. It is therefore important to carry out research in order to identify who the consumers are and determine what they might require. While it is true that many professionals within the fashion industry might have an intuitive understanding of their customers, this in itself does not eliminate the need for research. Predicting future fashion, market, societal and economic trends and working to anticipate consumer demand is a significant element of marketing, and key for fashion and the wider creative industries. The time taken between an initial design idea and the manufacture of a product is known as the **lead time**. This can be lengthy, and prototyping or

> "*Marketing should be an ethos (rather than a department) that pervades every facet of a business.*"
>
> Martin Butler

> "Remarkable marketing is the art of building things worth noticing right into your product or service. Not slapping on marketing as a last-minute add-on, but understanding that if your offering itself isn't remarkable, it's invisible."
>
> Seth Godin

↑ LittleMissMatched has a unique take on marketing. The company offers three socks in a pair; while each of the socks coordinates with the others in the set, none of them is an exact match. This novel approach solves the problem of 'the missing sock'.

sampling a new product or seasonal collection may be costly and can also be very wasteful. This puts great pressure on the fashion system. The key is to invest in manufacturing the right products in the right quantity, and this is why anticipating what customers will want is so crucial. Researching the market, undertaking consumer research and forecasting future trends will all be explained in more depth in Chapters 2, 3 and 4.

Creating, communicating and delivering value

Successful business relies on a strong and effective interrelationship between the activities of creating, communicating and delivering. If one of these aspects fails, it will affect the result. It is no good generating engaging content and promoting wonderful products if they are not delivered. Similarly, if the online experience or physical products do not match the quality expected by customers, or service is not up to standard, value will not have been delivered. A disgruntled customer may post a bad online review of the products and services, and this can have a detrimental effect on the brand's reputation.

So, what exactly is value? Value does not just refer to low price or what might be termed 'good value'. In this instance it is used to express a much larger concept and refers to the range of issues that customers might value, care about or connect with emotionally. Value may be contained within the product offering – the actual fashion range or collection, the quality of the products, how they are designed and whether they are produced ethically, for example – but it can also relate to the overall service a company might provide and the total experience that consumers encounter at every stage of their interaction with a brand. The concept of value works both up and down the supply chain; whatever is delivered must not only be of value to consumers, but also create profit and value for the businesses involved.

Remarkable marketing

The company LittleMissMatched was founded in the USA way back in 2004 by three entrepreneurs who recognized a great marketing opportunity: how to solve the age-old problem of the disappearing sock. 'Why do we have to wear socks that match?' the entrepreneurial friends pondered. 'Why not start a company that sells socks that don't match? Why not sell them in odd numbers so even if the dryer eats one, it doesn't matter?'

LittleMissMatched only ever sells socks in odd numbers, three in a pair. Now that is remarkable. And if you get three odd socks that coordinate in fun and colourful ways, in essence you get three

Communicating value

THE BODEN OWNER'S CLUB MANUAL

Boden is a global fashion company, originally launched in the UK. It started as a mail-order business back in 1991, when catalogues for fashionable people were really not a 'thing'. The original idea was inspired by the high standards of US mail-order companies at the time. From its earliest days through to the present time, the heart of the brand is about making clothes worthy of staying in the customers' wardrobe for a long time. That means good quality and styles you will want to keep. The brand's website launched in 1999. Boden owed its initial success to the fact that it broke new ground by delivering directly to the customer's home. It is amazing to think that when the company started, online retailing was a novel idea. The company now sells online, via its catalogue and through stores in the UK, Europe and the USA.

The website and catalogue are used not only to sell products for women, men, children and babies, but also to communicate the Boden brand ethos. Online this is easier to accomplish; the challenge is how to include extra content in a printed catalogue. One tool that can be used to great effect is to insert a special-edition brand booklet. Each edition is unique, beautifully designed and jam-packed with information about the details and quality of garment design and the value of the Boden product.

→↙ The designers behind the Boden brand believe design details make a difference, so *The Boden Owner's Club Manual* highlights the hidden extras that make a Boden trench coat so special.

↓ The cost-per-wear principle is used to calculate and communicate the true value of a pair of Boden chinos. By dividing the retail price by the number of times the trousers have been worn over the years, it is possible to determine their value per wear. The message is that although the chinos might not be the cheapest on the market, they are good quality and will stand the test of time.

The
Boden
**Owner's
Club**
Manual

10½ EASY STEPS
to *ultimate* Boden
enjoyment

Step 4:

Appreciate the
hidden **extras**

We believe that when it comes to clothing, no detail is small enough to be overlooked.

We're never happier than when we're agonising over an unexpected feature others might find trifling – such as the contrast trim on the reverse of our Trench Coat belt. Some of the detail we've created in a whole host of our products is purely for an 'audience of one'. But *you'll know it's there* and that's reason enough for us.

8

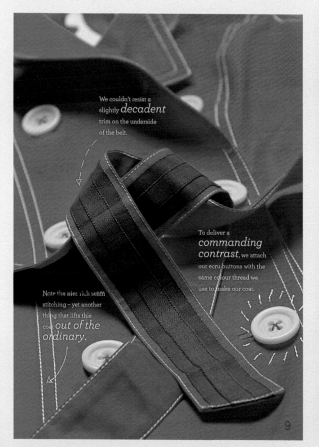

We couldn't resist a slightly *decadent* trim on the underside of the belt.

To deliver a *commanding contrast*, we attach our ecru buttons with the same colour thread we use to make our coat.

Note the nice rich seam stitching – yet another thing that lifts this coat *out of the ordinary*.

9

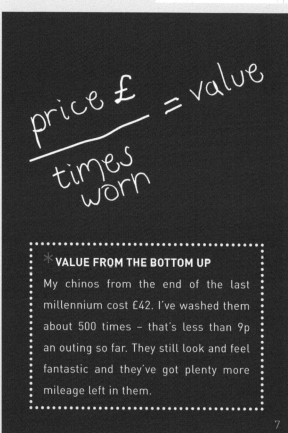

$$\frac{price\ £}{times\ worn} = value$$

* **VALUE FROM THE BOTTOM UP**

My chinos from the end of the last millennium cost £42. I've washed them about 500 times – that's less than 9p an outing so far. They still look and feel fantastic and they've got plenty more mileage left in them.

7

combinations per pair instead of just one. Revolutionary! Not just boring socks but a crazy way to express yourself and be creative. With a core philosophy of 'nothing matches but anything goes', the message is to inspire girls to 'be bold and to have fun while being true to themselves'. It all started with socks and the idea to disrupt the marketplace, but today LittleMissMatched is a lifestyle brand that spans many different product and entertainment categories, including colourful and mismatched gloves and hats, sleepwear, flip-flops, bedding, stationery, gifts and hair accessories.

Marketing as a social process

Fashion has a unique ability to be used as a vehicle for social connection and communication. Individuals often choose to dress in a specific and recognizable style so that they can express their ideas visually and signal membership to a like-minded group. Members of this style group may not actually know one another directly, but might share similar values and cultural attitudes, and by adopting a specific mode of dress, individuals can shape their identity and gain a sense of belonging to a larger community. In 2014 Nicola Formichetti at Diesel used this idea for the Spring/Summer WE ARE CONNECTED #DIESELREBOOT campaign shot by fashion photographers Inez & Vinoodh. The campaign featured artists, musicians, creatives, models and students, intriguing individuals – among them bikers, cyberpunks and Japanese teens – belonging to style gangs that represented the bravery and ingenuity of the Diesel brand. The concept was to show a global community united by the idea that if you belong and are connected, you are not alone.

We frequently make our fashion choices either consciously or subconsciously based on what peers, friends, colleagues or celebrities are wearing. When consumers promote products or pass on style ideas to one another it is known as word of mouth (WoM), word-of-mouth marketing (WoMM) or peer marketing. Sharing ideas and promoting via word of mouth can be very cost-effective for a fashion brand. Social media is an essential tool for spreading the word, so you may also hear the term 'word of mouse'.

Style groups: Exactitudes

'Exactitudes' (a contraction of 'exact' and 'attitudes') is a project by the Rotterdam-based photographer Ari Versluis and stylist Ellie Uyttenbroek. They work together to systematically document the conspicuous dress codes of numerous fashion style tribes around the globe. Selected individuals are photographed standing in an identical pose in a studio setting. The resulting photographs

→ 'Exactitudes' documents the dress of fashion tribes from around the world.

Top row: Geeks – London 2008
Skinny boys in V-necks and specs display their fashion geek credentials.

Second row: Charitas – Rotterdam 2007
Power ladies dressed to impress in suits or skirts and structured jackets; handbags at the ready, these women mean business.

Third row: Yupster boys – New York 2006
Yupster = yuppie + hipster. Grown-ups who don't grow up, this tribe of urban creative professional hipsters came of age during the first wave of indie rock and hip hop. Yupster uniform: T-shirt that communicates values or affiliations, zip-up hoodie and all-important cross-body bag.

Bottom row: Pin-ups – London 2008
Girls inspired by 1940s and 50s pin-up style. Pencil skirts and blouses with cinched-in waists accentuate the figure, and retro-styled hair is adorned with accessories or hats.

are placed in a grid framework that serves to amplify the striking similarities of each member of the style tribe.

The project illustrates clearly the subliminal influence and pull of belonging to a style group. The people photographed by Versluis and Uyttenbroek were spotted in the street and had no personal knowledge of the others photographed wearing such similar clothing styles. Although only 12 individuals appear in each style collective, responses to the work indicate that many people who viewed the photographs were able to identify themselves in one of the featured looks.

Exchanging products and value with others

Marketing is a process of exchange. Traditionally, the commodities for exchange are the goods and services sold by the brand, and the currency is of course money paid for those goods and services by the customer. However, there are other commodities of value to bear in mind. For a business, in addition to the financial gain received from customers, there is also data. This can provide the company with detailed information about their customers' preferences, social media usage and purchasing behaviour. Viewed creatively, the exchange process can be seen as a trade system with exciting potential to generate a diversity of assets for both consumers and businesses. Social media content generated by the brand and/or its audience is one of the most valuable assets. Content created and controlled by the brand is known as **owned media**, whereas content

MARKETING AS AN EXCHANGE PROCESS

Marketing can be viewed as an exchange process or system. The purpose is to generate a diversity of assets for both the company and its customers.

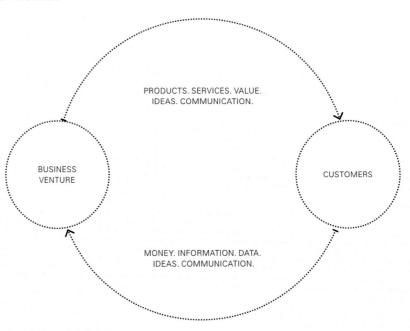

PRODUCTS. SERVICES. VALUE.
IDEAS. COMMUNICATION.

BUSINESS
VENTURE

CUSTOMERS

MONEY. INFORMATION. DATA.
IDEAS. COMMUNICATION.

created by users is termed **earned media**, since the brand did not pay to produce or share it. Free content, such as posts, photos, stories and reviews, that is shared by all users (the brand or the audience) on their social media feeds is known as **organic media**.

A managerial and business process

It is important not to lose sight of the purpose of marketing, and remember that it is designed to ensure a business can flourish and generate a profit. Marketing must therefore be managed as an integrated function of business. The ultimate aim is not only to satisfy customers, but also to ensure an advantageous result for the business. As the Chartered Institute of Marketing's definition states, 'Marketing is the management process responsible for identifying, anticipating and satisfying customer requirements profitably.'

The next section guides you through the key strategic tools available to the marketer. You will be introduced to a framework known as the marketing mix, and to the principles of market segmentation, targeting, positioning, differentiation and competitive advantage. These concepts are explained and illustrated with examples and case studies detailing how fashion designers determine a unique selling proposition and create a distinctive signature style for their brands.

"Buzzmarketing captures the attention of consumers and the media to the point where talking about your brand or company becomes entertaining, fascinating and newsworthy."

Mark Hughes

The marketing mix

The marketing mix provides a framework that can be used to manage marketing and incorporate it into a business context. The concept of the marketing mix is that several strategic ingredients must be considered and blended effectively to achieve the marketing and strategic goals of a company. The principles that underpin the marketing mix were first shaped in the USA during the 1940s and 50s. The term was coined in response to the idea that marketing managers were considered 'mixers of ingredients'. Neil H. Borden, professor of advertising at Harvard Business School, originally listed 12 marketing variables, but in the 1960s E. Jerome McCarthy rationalized these into four simpler variables – product, price, place and promotion – known as the 4Ps of marketing.

The marketing mix can be thought of in a similar way to a recipe where the four ingredients (product, price, place and promotion) can be blended in varying proportions, giving emphasis to whichever aspect is most appropriate to the company, brand or product. There is no correct formula; the mix that is employed will be unique to each company or situation. Fundamentally, it comes down to ensuring that the product is right for the specified market, that it

↑ Designers, buyers and product technicians generally work as a team to fit garments and approve specifications. Each aspect of the jacket being fitted, right down to the buttons, closures, pockets, zips and stitching, must be approved and accurately specified. Behind-the-scenes photos or even a video of a fitting have great promotional possibilities – showing the care and attention the company puts into considering the fit and detail of the garment.

is priced correctly, that the balance of merchandise is correct, that it is in the right place at the right time, and that customers are aware of the offer or service through appropriately targeted promotion. Whatever the market level, an effective marketing mix must weigh up a company's overall objectives while also taking into account any changes and challenges operating in the market at that time.

The drawback of the traditional 4P marketing mix is that it tends to focus on the internal needs of the company rather than the ever-changing requirements of customers. This more limiting version of the mix was developed primarily during the rise of mass consumerism to market the physical benefits of a product, the limelight falling on producing, pricing and promoting product. Newer thinking believes the consumer should be at the heart of the matter. An expanded 7P version of the marketing mix has been developed to address this change in emphasis; it includes three further criteria: physical evidence, process and people. It is a common mistake to consider fashion as a product-based industry, however; it should really be viewed as service- or people-based, which is why the extra criteria are so necessary. Each of the 7Ps is discussed in detail below.

Product

For apparel, 'product' relates to product design, style, fit, sizing, quality and fashion level, as well as performance and function. In the fashion and textile industry, product is rarely a singular item. Commonly it will be a complex range or integrated collection of products. Designers are generally required to construct well-balanced collections or wholesale or retail ranges that include a variety of product categories offered at appropriate price points for specific target markets. When taking a strategic marketing approach to product, some useful questions to consider are:

> » Are the products suitable for the specified market?

> » Do the products meet the tangible needs of consumers?

> » How will the products satisfy the intangible desires or aspirations of customers?

> » Does the total product offer or range address the variety of needs relating to the target customers?

> » Is the balance of the range or collection correct? Does it have enough choice and variety within it? Or does it offer too much choice; should it be pared down and streamlined?

Product attributes and benefits

Product attributes refer to the features, functions and uses of a product. Product benefits relate to how a product's attributes or features might benefit the consumer. At the most basic level, clothing has core attributes that offer protection and safeguard against exposure and nudity. At the next level there are the tangible attributes, integrated into the design, manufacture and function of the garment. These are intrinsic to the product itself and offer concrete and physical benefits to the consumer. So a raincoat made from a water-repellent fabric will have the intrinsic attribute of being waterproof and have the benefit of keeping the wearer dry. Such a garment may be presented in-store with accompanying marketing material informing consumers about the specific attributes and benefits of the design or waterproof material.

An item of clothing can also have what are known as intangible attributes. These are more abstract in nature and connect to the ideals, perceptions and desires of the consumer. These intangibles are extremely important for fashion, since consumers do not really buy a product but rather a set of expectations and interpretations, each person perceiving a product's combination of attributes and benefits according to their own particular needs and viewpoint.

The total product concept

The example of the waterproof coat illustrates what the economist Theodore Levitt called the augmented product or the total product concept. Levitt's model describes four different levels to a product:

> » The generic or core product

> » The actual or expected product

> » The total or augmented product

> » The potential product

If we consider a waterproof coat, such as a classic trench, at the most basic level the product is a coat. At the next level it is a waterproof coat with specific design features and styling details, offered at a particular quality and price. The next tier up is the total or augmented product. This represents everything the customer receives when they purchase the raincoat, including all elements that contribute to added value, intangible benefits, branding and emotional benefits. The total augmented product relates to everything that is currently being offered, but there is another highly significant layer to consider, and that is the potential product. This is

↑ The Regatta women's jacket (top) and men's jacket have several important functional attributes: made from Isotex 1000 XPT, an extreme performance fabric, the jackets are waterproof, breathable and windproof. They also incorporate technical and functional details, such as taped seams, a detachable hood, a centre front zip with storm flap, and a map pocket.

"Marketing is still an art, and the marketing manager, as head chef, must creatively marshal all [their] marketing activities to advance the short- and long-term interests of [their] firm."

Neil H. Borden

everything that could be offered or might be offered in the future. For fashion the future happens very fast, and designers spend most of their time working on potential product. They must innovate and update, moving product design forward each season with new design ideas, fabrics and technology. The concept of potential product is therefore of vital importance.

Levitt's model highlights another important point: 'Consumers don't buy products or product attributes. They purchase benefits and emotional meaning.' This means that potential product must also be about identifying innovative ways to deliver extra value and benefits to the customer.

Price

In this context price means manufacturing costs, wholesale and retail prices, discounted prices, and, of course, margin and profit. For marketing purposes it is possible to view pricing from two perspectives. The first is cost: what an item actually costs either to produce or for the buyer to purchase. It considers tangible expenditure so that a cost price can be calculated. The second, selling price, looks at the situation from the customer or end-consumer's perspective. It considers what might be a realistic selling price and factors in such issues as affordability and perceived value. Perceived value reflects the apparent worth of a product; this may not relate directly to the actual cost of production or the wholesale

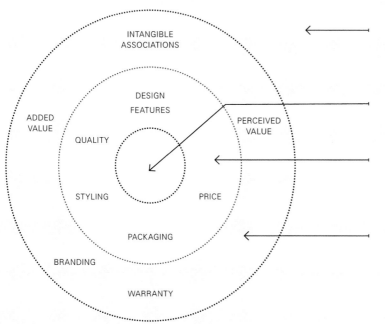

THE TOTAL PRODUCT CONCEPT

THE POTENTIAL PRODUCT
This represents the potential features not yet offered. It is also about innovation, and concerns what the product could be in the future.

THE GENERIC PRODUCT
This is the core product, such as a coat, jumper or dress.

THE ACTUAL OR EXPECTED PRODUCT
The real product is a combination of the generic product plus the tangible attributes. This represents the customer's basic minimum expectation or requirement.

THE TOTAL PRODUCT
This is what Theodore Levitt calls the augmented product. It represents everything the customer receives: generic product + tangible attributes + intangible attributes. The total product represents the added value, that is, all extras added to elevate the product and make it different from product offered by competitors.

THE MARKETING MIX

What is the correct price for the product?

What price will provide the right value to customers?

How will the customer perceive this price?

How does this price compare to that of competitors?

What is the total cost to customers – are there additional or hidden costs?

What might be the environmental cost?

Demand: Do customers want this product?

Where will the product be designed and produced?

Could this product solve a problem for consumers?

What would make this product desirable to customers?

How can technology best be used to design and manufacture the product?

What is the most sustainable and ethical way to make this product?

How will it be packaged?

Who is the target customer for this product?

How will the product be recycled, repaired, upcycled or disposed of at the end of its life?

PRICE   PRODUCT

PEOPLE

PLACE   PROMOTION

Distribution: Where will the product be available to customers?

What distribution channels will be used?

How much of the product will be available?

How accessible will it be for consumers to find and purchase?

How convenient will it be for customers to access and purchase?

Awareness: How will customers know about this product?

Will there be any special sales promotional activity?

Will there be a promotion or PR campaign to promote the product or service?

Communication: What do we want the customers to know? What messages do we want to communicate?

What promotional channels will be used?

purchase price. An understanding of customers' perceptions of value is therefore very important, as is knowledge of competitor pricing within the marketplace.

Research is an essential element in understanding pricing both from a customer or end-consumer perspective and in terms of what the competition is up to. And, of course, prices change frequently, so research brings insight into:

» How customers perceive price

» What customers consider good value

» How much customers are willing to pay for specific products

» What customers will pay more for

» How much competitors are charging

The fashion brand Telfar has an interesting take on pricing. There is a click-through on the website labelled, 'WARNING LIVE PRICE'. This takes the user to a page where it says 'WARNING: TELFAR LIVE IS A SALE IN REVERSE'. Below it is an explanation of how this

↑ This version of the marketing mix refers to 5Ps. It places Product, Price, Place and Promotion as a constellation around the central hub, People. This is a new derivation of the traditional 4P marketing mix, incorporating and highlighting the importance of people within the mix.

Synthesizing the practical with the emotional

A WATERPROOF COAT

A waterproof coat or jacket is a good example of a garment that can be designed with many practical features and tangible attributes. A coat made of a fully waterproof material has the obvious benefit of keeping the wearer dry in the rain. For someone who wanted a coat to protect them during outdoor or country pursuits, a loose-cut waxed jacket might provide the required benefits. If it also had a detachable lining, the benefits of flexibility and keeping warm could be added to the list. At an emotional level, a consumer might choose a waxed Barbour country jacket, not only because of the durability, warmth and protection it offered, but also because emotionally, the heritage and values of the Barbour brand resonated with the wearer. The wearer might feel 'earthy' or 'connected to the land' when they wore it. They might appreciate quality, tradition and practicality. A different consumer, on the other hand, who wanted to feel 'active and alive' or 'daring and adventurous', might purchase a lightweight waterproof with high-performance features, even if they wore it in an urban setting or to go to the shops. The wonderful benefits of a high-performance or practical country jacket are likely to be of no interest to someone who wanted to feel alluring, fashionable and chic while they kept dry. For this consumer the silhouette or shape of the coat may be of major importance, along with the fashion status of a brand name. They may desire a designer-label raincoat with a belt so that they can cinch in their waist and show off their figure to best advantage.

Each garment described provides the functional benefits necessary for specific uses or activities. But clothing provides more than mere functionality. The clue to understanding this is to view attributes from the consumer's perspective and try to determine what consumers might feel, desire or aspire to when they purchase fashion product. Each attribute will generate a set of emotional meanings that augment the tangible or physical benefits. This is why fashion in general and branding in particular can be so powerful: they have a unique ability to confer the intangible and create a shortcut straight to the emotional.

← The American actor Maggie Gyllenhaal looks sophisticated and urban in a belted trench coat.

↓ The French actor Fanny Ardant makes a simple, classic raincoat look alluring and desirable.

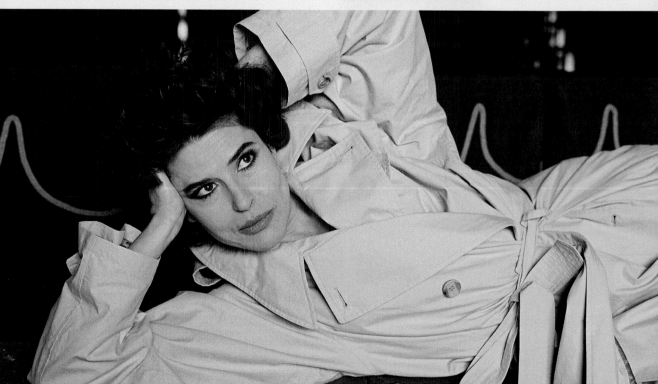

works. The collection drops at wholesale price, which is more than 50 per cent of the normal retail price. The price then goes up every second until it reaches full price. Whatever price the item sells out at becomes the price. So full price is determined by customers and demand, not by the brand. As Telfar says, 'YOU DECIDE THE PRICE: the more you want it – the lower the price.'

When planning pricing in a more traditional way, a brand will need to set the prices for individual items and additionally consider how the pricing would work across an entire collection. A well-balanced selection of product will need to be constructed and a coherent pricing strategy devised not just for each individual item but for the entire offering.

Price architecture

A pricing structure will have to be planned or built up from the lowest-cost items right up to the most expensive. This is known as the price architecture. Within the price architecture there should be products offered at:

> » Introductory or low price points
>
> » Medium prices
>
> » High price points

It is customary to create a price band for each of these tiers. For example, a high-street retailer might set its lowest price band at £15–49, the mid-price band at £50–99 and the top band at £100–200.

Each retail price band can then be subdivided with specific price points. The top price band might, for example, have only four price points: £115, £125, £150 and £200. The lowest pricing tier might have something in the region of 8–12 separate price points. Skilful setting of price points and consideration of the number of styles offered at each price within a price band are essential to the planning of a balanced range. It may not be possible to achieve the desired profit margin on every style, but judicious flexing of prices should help to increase margin on enough product so that a workable margin is achieved overall.

Place

In essence, place is about getting the right product to the right place at the right time and in the right amount. It concerns logistics and the various methods of transporting, storing and distributing merchandise, and the means by which a company's products reach their target customer; termed the 'route to market', this relates to distribution

↓ The fashion brand Rixo was launched in 2015 by university friends Henrietta Rix and Orlagh McCloskey, inspired by their love of vintage. The window display in the London flagship store features not only the products, but also the prices – indicated discreetly in gold.

PRICE ARCHITECTURE

Price architecture depends on the type of market, the market level and the product concerned. The proportion of styles and the stock volumes within each of the tiers are adjusted so that the business can satisfy the greatest number of customers and generate the highest potential sales margin and profit.

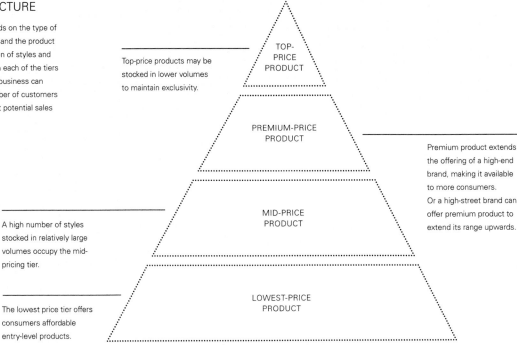

Top-price products may be stocked in lower volumes to maintain exclusivity.

Premium product extends the offering of a high-end brand, making it available to more consumers. Or a high-street brand can offer premium product to extend its range upwards.

A high number of styles stocked in relatively large volumes occupy the mid-pricing tier.

The lowest price tier offers consumers affordable entry-level products.

TOP-PRICE PRODUCT

PREMIUM-PRICE PRODUCT

MID-PRICE PRODUCT

LOWEST-PRICE PRODUCT

↑ Looking at the tag and checking the price on a product in store is one of the first things most customers do. Online, the price is generally prominent; in store, it can take a bit of searching to find the information.

and sales channels. From a customer's point of view, 'place' is about where they can purchase a product, whether this is in a bricks-and-mortar retail location or via e-commerce. From a manufacturer's or retailer's perspective it relates more to distribution and how the product gets from the producer to the end-consumer. The processes involved in distribution vary depending on the size of the business and the complexity of the number of businesses involved.

The distribution process

The most straightforward distribution process is from producer to customer, known as B2C, business-to-customer. This is when the individual producer or fashion business sells directly to the customer. This could happen in a number of ways: online via Instagram, Pinterest, Facebook or their own website; in their own store; in a pop-up shop; at an event, such as a trunk show or maker's fair; or via an e-commerce platform, such as Shopify, or online marketplace, such as Etsy, Depop or Tmall, Koala, Kakao Shopping in Korea, or Taobao or Redbook in China. When using an e-commerce platform, the producer pays commission; this might be a flat percentage fee per item, or it could involve a joining fee, annual subscription, monthly payment or additional listing fee. Once the sale has been made online, the product must be sent out to the customer. The individual producer may be responsible for posting the package to the consumer, or, depending on the size of the online selling operation, the producer might use an order fulfilment company to process the receipt, packing, delivery and return of orders.

The next distribution scenario is when the producer sells directly to a multi-brand retailer or online seller, which then sells the product to the customer. This interaction could be described as B2B and then B2C, meaning that the first stage is business-to-business and the second business-to-customer. This type of transaction is known as wholesale and applies to designer fashion sold in department stores, boutiques and online retailers, such as Net-A-Porter, Mr Porter, Farfetch and Shopbop. The producer (the fashion brand) sells the product at a wholesale price, also known by the retailer as the cost price (the price at which they buy the product). The retailer then determines their retail price (the price that they will sell the item in-store to the end customer). Another option is to sell via a concession. This is when a fashion brand rents space in a department store or other boutique and sets up its own mini-store within a store.

For individual producers or small businesses, getting products in front of the business buyers is not always easy. One option is to try to contact the buyer directly and set up an appointment for them to view your product or collection. If the buyers don't know you and if you have not yet built up a reputation, this can be hard to achieve. Another option is to go via a specialist agent, who will represent you and carry your collection in their showroom. The agent will charge you a fee, but they will have built up relationships with the relevant buyers and the press. They will organize a press day, make sure you get good PR, and set up the buyer appointments. Larger independent fashion brands might choose to pay for a stand at a trade fair, or show at fashion week. Such events usually draw large numbers of trade buyers and press visitors.

The distribution chain can be extended if a fashion wholesaler is involved. In this type of scenario the producer sells directly to a wholesaler who purchases a range of fashion products from a variety of manufacturers, often from several global locations. The wholesaler then sells on to a large number of mass-market and independent retailers. This distribution example is B2B, then B2B and finally B2C, when the retailers sell to the end-customers. This method is typically used for larger volumes and when the original producer does not want to handle the distribution, passing this responsibility on to the wholesaler. The distribution chains described above make use of several different sales channels:

>> Social media, e-commerce platforms and online marketplaces

» Direct to consumer via own retail store, pop-up shop, social media or e-commerce site

» Direct to consumer or B2B via a trunk show

» Wholesale via an agent's showroom

» Wholesale via an own-company showroom, either at head office or in key global locations

» Wholesale via a trade show

» Concession (renting space in another store)

» Direct from manufacturer or wholesaler

Distribution strategy

Another aspect of distribution is to consider which products should be procured or produced and in what quantity, as well as how many will be distributed to different locations. This is usually the role of fashion merchandisers and/or fashion buyers. Having determined what products to buy or manufacture, the next question is the volume. For a mass-market retailer, these quantities can be in the thousands, tens of thousands or even hundreds of thousands. For a small independent label or boutique it could be only one or two of each item, or perhaps tens or hundreds.

If the scenario relates to a retailer with several stores or trading in several global locations, buyers and merchandisers must consider if they will distribute the same number of items or styles to all locations. Generally, a flagship store, for example, would receive more options in terms of styles and colourways. There may also be a special selection of what are known as 'top-line', hero or standout pieces that would go only to a flagship store. A smaller store would receive less stock, perhaps fewer style options and fewer colourway options.

It is also customary to try to ensure that competing department stores in the same city don't stock the same pieces as one another of any particular brand. The agents or sellers of these brands work hard to distribute the collection differently between competing stores. This gives each store a better chance of remaining unique and catering to its specific customers.

Trunk shows

A trunk show is a special preview event where a designer shows off their latest collection to a select group of invited guests and customers. Usually the designer does a tour, packing their collection

↓ The seersucker suit, as seen below, was originated by Haspel, a company founded in New Orleans in 1909. As a brand, Haspel is strongly associated with the South, and its seersucker suit is an icon of American style. It has been worn by the nation's presidents, and Gregory Peck sported one in the film *To Kill a Mockingbird* (1962). The suit is still relevant, as indicated by an article by Joseph DeAcetis in *Forbes* magazine in 2021, 'Haspel, the New Face of Seersucker Cool'.

in trunks and taking the show on the road, visiting several locations nationally or internationally. Trunk shows are commonly held in a boutique or in the designer section of a department store, and are excellent for marketing since they allow the designer to reach an audience that would not normally attend catwalk shows. These events, co-hosted by the designer and retailer, provide customers with exclusive early access to the designer's collection, where they can purchase directly or pre-order. Designers typically do 8–12 trunk shows a year at which they preview their new collection before it hits the stores.

Trunk shows have several benefits for designers, retailers and customers. For the retailer, a trunk show offers the opportunity to strengthen the relationship with invited customers. The customers get to meet and talk to the designer face-to-face, and the designers obtain vital pre-season information on which styles are popular and therefore likely to be successful later, when the collection launches to the wider public. Designers and retailers have also noted that because attendees can try on the clothes before purchasing, there is a reduced number of returns compared to online sales. An article in *Vogue Business* published in 2021 suggested that as the COVID-19 restrictions began to ease, designers were re-embracing the trunk-show model as a way to connect with customers, and that this interaction was building loyalty.

↑ Stella McCartney talks to customers at a trunk show in the Chicago store of Barneys New York.

↓ Timberland's trade-show stand for its
Outdoor Performance range, designed by
the Michigan-based firm JGA. Graphics set
the mood in the central 'meet and greet'
space, where trade buyers are welcomed
by Timberland sales representatives
to view and order products. The stand
was created using repurposed industrial
objects and natural recycled materials,
reflecting Timberland's commitment to
environmental sustainability. An impressive
88 per cent of the stand was recyclable at
the end of its use.

↓↓ JGA also designed the stand for the
Timberland Pro series. The highly flexible
build was designed to accommodate
different trade-show footprints. Sales
rooms displayed the Pro Series products
and provided work-table seating for
8–10 people.

The presale format has also been adopted by the luxury e-commerce site Moda Operandi, which usually hosts about 150 virtual trunk shows a season. Not everything from a designer's collection makes it through to mainstream retail, so Moda's virtual trunk shows give clients the chance to shop the full collection before it is edited down. The clients enjoy the insider aspect of shopping the collection early, while the e-tailer gets an early read of consumers' buying preferences six months in advance of the main release.

Trade fairs and exhibitions

Industry trade fairs provide an important opportunity for companies to showcase their new product ranges and sell to retail buyers from around the globe. The advantage of a trade fair or exhibition is that buyers can view and compare a variety of brands all showing at the same event. Shows are sector-specific: for instance, Première Vision in Paris for fabric; Pitti Immagine Filati in Florence for yarn spinners; CPD in Düsseldorf for womenswear and accessories; and Kingpins in Amsterdam and New York for denim and sportswear fabrics. Exhibiting companies invest heavily in creating show stands that represent their brand and their products to best advantage.

Promotion

Promotion is about communicating with customers, and includes all the tools available for marketing, communicating and promoting a company and its products and services. The combination of promotional activities – among them advertising, sales promotion, public relations, personal selling and direct marketing – is known as the promotional mix. The idea behind this is similar to the marketing mix and relates to the mixture of tools that can be employed to achieve a company's promotion objectives. Some of the most recognized promotional vehicles for fashion are advertising in high-profile fashion magazines, such as *Vogue*, *Harper's Bazaar* and *Elle*; catwalk shows that attract extensive media and public interest; and the PR and razzmatazz that surround celebrities and their endorsement of designer fashion. However, many of these traditional approaches have come into question in the twenty-first century. Print advertising started to decline as digital formats took over; fashion shows were challenged on the grounds that they were unsustainable; and brands turned to micro- or nano-influencers for endorsement, rather than traditional megastars. There is a great deal more to say about promotion in terms of promotional theory, promotion in practice and how campaigns are conceived and delivered. This will all be discussed further in Chapter 6.

Physical evidence

Consumers increasingly demand more in terms of value, experience or extra service, and as the ability of fashion retailers to match one another's product offer rises, so the criterion of physical evidence plays an ever more important role in differentiating one retailer from another. Physical evidence encompasses packaging, brochures, business cards, carrier bags, staff uniforms, in-store décor, ambience, facilities, retail fixtures, store windows, signage and the use of interactive digital displays in store.

The fashion experience is about much more than just the clothes or accessories themselves. It's the little extras that make a difference: the label in the garment embroidered with the designer's name; the well-designed, beautifully crafted swing ticket; the carrier bag so special that it is treasured as a souvenir; the imaginative windows and store displays that make a shopping trip thrilling. Such extras are vitally important aspects of the marketing mix. They are persuasive factors that add value, enhance customer perception of a retailer or fashion brand, and elevate one company above another in the hearts and minds of consumers.

The art of unboxing

Unboxing has become a recognized trend on social media. This is an interesting phenomenon that highlights the importance of physical evidence – in other words, packaging – in a digital era. It may seem counter-intuitive, but for a fashion brand to increase its profile on social media, it may need to invest in its packaging and see this not as a commodity expense but as a marketing spend. There is definite evidence that product packaging can affect sales. Macfarlane Packaging released a report and survey into unboxing in 2022, stating that 52 per cent of online customers would continue purchasing from a company if they received their orders in premium packaging. The report points out that when a customer orders something and receives their package, it has a **100 per cent open rate**. This distinguishes it from all other forms of marketing media. In addition, if the customer then releases a favourable unboxing video on social media, the brand in question gains free positive promotion.

Several brands have designed their packaging with the unboxing video in mind. The fashion brand Balzac Paris ships its products in a brown cardboard box adorned with the slogan 'Toujours Plus Responsable', which translates as 'ever more responsible'. The box is sealed with a sticker made from a large printed picture of the brand's new collection. Inside, there is another printed image that acts as

↑↑↑ The Dutch fashion label Laundry Industry sold its promotional material in-store. This branded View-Master came in a presentation box with two reels, one showing images of a previous collection and the other with information on the history of the brand.

↑↑ Kate Spade purse and packaging, which comes in a range of joyful colours to complement the product.

↑ A Tracey Neuls shoebox is wrapped in a publicity poster and transformed into a bag with the addition of plastic handles.

a wrapper around the product, which often comes in a protective cream fabric drawstring bag printed with 'Balzac Paris 1830'. The brand shares its customers' unboxing videos, thus creating further engagement with its brand community.

Glossier, originally a direct-to-consumer beauty brand, has also gained a great deal of social media coverage via customer unboxing videos. Many spend time describing the packaging, as well as the little extras Glossier includes to delight customers. The delivery is sent in an outer cardboard box sealed with Glossier tape. Inside, there is a branded Glossier box. This has a pink interior printed with '#Glossier' and an uplifting message: 'Skin First, Makeup Second, Smile Always'. The beauty products themselves are sealed inside in a pink bubble zip-top pouch. Included as an extra is a sheet of colourful stickers as well as a product sample card.

Process

Process describes the customer's experience of the brand or service from the first point of contact onwards. It considers the experiences and procedures they may have to go through in order to make a purchase either in-store or online, and includes such issues as information flow, ordering, payment, delivery, service and return of products. In the modern marketing climate, with increased reliance on e-commerce and marketing via digital media, process is a potent tool, especially for businesses wishing to build customer loyalty and ensure customer retention. Whatever the exact nature of a business, it is always worth taking time to review the processes customers must go through and to consider each step of the journey from the customer's perspective, rather than just what might be efficient for the company.

A customer purchasing a wedding dress, for example, will go through a series of steps from first consideration to final purchase and ultimately wearing the dress on her wedding day. The first steps may include looking at wedding magazines, checking out relevant Instagram accounts, visiting wedding planning websites and doing other online research to find suitable ideas, designers or retailers. Next, there could be telephone or online conversations and emails to gather further information or book an appointment to view a collection; sessions to select fabric and develop a personal design; followed by several fittings, the final fitting, taking delivery of the dress and then the wedding itself. Each step in the process is a moment when the consumer and the company providing the service interact. Every interaction provides an opportunity for the business to differentiate itself from competitors, create value and ensure a positive experience for the customer. With social media at

↑↑ The subscription beauty brand Glossybox delivers in pink boxes as well as special limited-edition promotional packaging. The August 2023 box came in mauve and green with 'BEAUTIFUL' written in white. This image shows a Valentine box for the 'Galentine'-themed February edition in 2018.

↑ An Ipsy Glam Bag packed with make-up products including a face mask, mascara, illuminating cream and lipstick.

their fingertips, it is worth remembering that consumers have the power to broadcast their views and opinions of your brand, whether positive or negative.

Bear in mind that the criterion of process expands the marketing viewpoint beyond the product itself and recognizes the value of smooth interactions and good service. Process, in combination with great product, builds trust, loyalty and repeat custom. Hopefully, a wedding dress will be a one-off, once-in-a-lifetime purchase, so positive customer experience is less likely to result in a repeat purchase, but it will certainly contribute to an enhanced reputation for the brand, and customer recommendations. Conversely, customer irritation with any part of the process could lead to a lost sale, deterioration in trust and erosion of customer goodwill or loyalty. In the case of a wedding dress, there may be other people to please along the way: the bride's mother, for instance, or a best friend or bridesmaid. Process may appear to relate to systems and organization, but in reality it is all about people and their potential.

People

'People' in this instance does not just refer to consumers; it has much wider implications and opens up the scope to include all those who add value to the development and delivery of a product or service. People can therefore include employees, partners, investors and other stakeholders, collaborators, producers and suppliers. It can be a trap to consider fashion as only a product-based industry; it is just as important to view it as retail and a service experience. People add value along the entire length of the supply chain and are, of course, integral to the service provided by any company. People should therefore be considered a vital part of the marketing mix.

Within fashion, thinking of the product first might be a natural focus. However, there is a trend towards what is known as customer-centric marketing. This is an approach that puts the customer front and centre. The aim is to offer customers value at every point in their buying journey, based on their needs and interests. This relates to all aspects, such as online searches, in-store visits, delivery, returns, promotion and advertising. It calls for a business to consider how its customers connect with the business or brand. Is it via social media, the website, email or phone, for example? Does the business help the customer at every point in this journey, and what could be done to improve this experience along the way? To this end, what is known as the customer journey has become a very important consideration within marketing. It will be discussed in more detail in Chapter 4, when we look at understanding customers in more depth.

Valuing people and their traditional knowledge

CULTURAL SUSTAINABILITY

Monica Boṭa Moisin is an intellectual property lawyer and cultural sustainability advocate. In 2018 she launched the Cultural Intellectual Property Rights Initiative® (CIPRI), which is designed to be a 'worldwide movement supporting the recognition of cultural intellectual property rights for craftsmen and women who are the custodians and transmitters of traditional garments, traditional designs and traditional manufacturing techniques'. The aim of the initiative is to 'eliminate culturally appropriative behaviour in the fashion industry with a vision to create a system that nurtures, sustains and protects Traditional Knowledge (TK) and Traditional Cultural Expressions (TCEs)'. It is supported and endorsed by Fashion Revolution and the European Fashion Heritage Association, among many other organizations.

Current Intellectual Property (IP) law is not designed to protect the rights of a community, such as a village of handloom weavers in India, or the *beeralu* bobbin lacemakers in Galle, Sri Lanka. Making *beeralu* lace is a very intricate and lengthy process. It takes an experienced *beeralu* lacemaker about a week to create 1 m (3 ft) of lace that is only 5 cm (1 in) wide. CIPRI works to build bridges between the fashion industry and traditional creative communities, with the aim of valuing and protecting their traditional knowledge and skills and gaining recognition and acknowledgement for their specific cultural designs. Boṭa Moisin calls this 'weaving the threads of system change'. She supports communities with specific craft skills to achieve 'collective custodianship rights'.

CIPRI supports several ambassador companies around the world. These include: Cho'jac Items, which helps to preserve the ancient Indigenous Mayan technique of braiding net bags; Nata Y Limón, a premium ethical craft label and social business that collaborates with skilled Mayan weavers and seamstresses in Guatemala;

the Traditional Arts and Ethnology Centre, a social enterprise in Luang Prabang, Laos, dedicated to promoting the appreciation and transmission of Laos's ethnic cultural heritage and livelihoods based on traditional skills; the United Artisans of Kutch and the House of Amoda, both in Gujarat, India; and SICA, based in Brazil.

The United Artisans of Kutch was founded by Kuldip Gadhvi, who runs Kutch Adventures India, a company that has won Gold in the Responsible Tourism Awards for 'best in engaging with people and culture'. Kutch Adventures was created after a devastating earthquake in 2001, to help revive the fortunes of the local community. On his guided tours, Gadhvi took visitors to see some of the bigger textile and craft studios – but then he came to a realization: 'By doing this we were supporting a pyramid structure, where some people on the top benefit most and many at the bottom, the real makers, the real artisans, are working within limited financial and social circumstances.' He realized that he could also support these less visible local artisans, because without help they would either stop their traditional work forever or have no choice but to work for big businesses, shops or textile companies. Gadhvi's work now ensures that these artisans get a platform to represent their crafts as well as their stories. Many of these crafts, such as naturally dyed yarns, hand-weaving, hand-painting and block-printing, have been practised by local communities for hundreds of years and have evolved over that time.

The House of Amoda is a family business founded in 2015 by Meeta Solanki Jadeja in Ahmedabad, Gujarat, India. The foundation of the brand was seeded long before, in 1991, with the original aim to empower local craftspeople, to create a better balance between the work done by men and women, and to keep alive their traditional knowledge and inherited skills.

"It is not about owning, it is about caring for something, it is community interest at its core."

Monica Boṭa Moisin

← One of the United Artisans of Kutch, Gujarat, block-printing fabric.

The overall aim was to create financial security using a holistic approach to sustain the cultural essence and tradition of the textile-craft sector in the modern world.

The next generation have now joined the business. Meeta's son Yuddhavir Singh Jadeja is the creative director, and her daughter Aashka Jadeja is responsible for the cultural business development. Aashka is a heritage professional and holds a master's degree in heritage management; her focus is on conserving cultural heritage and reviving lost textile crafts. She refers to the business as 'From Farm to Fashion'. The cotton is farmed organically and locally. Local skilled craftspeople are employed in dyeing the yarn, weaving the fabric on handlooms and hand-printing it in various ways, before the final fabric is used for the creation of one of Amoda's garments, which Aashka describes as 'wearable heritage art pieces'. She explains that the craft sector is India's second-largest economic area after agriculture, and that the House of Amoda 'links traditional textile crafts to contemporary apparel – to achieve a culturally sustainable business'.

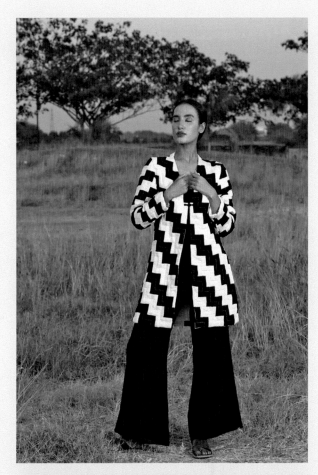

....

"Amoda is a cultural brand – every garment has a mindful story."

....

Aashka Jadeja

SICA Upcycling Design™ was founded in 2006 by Simone Simonato in Curitiba, Brazil. Simonato is a designer and entrepreneur, and further describes herself as a facilitator, activist and educator. Her desire to create fair solutions for society drove her to establish her upcycling design label using textile waste and preserving traditional crafts. SICA creates unique clothing, accessories and homewares from the vibrant textile waste of factories in southern Brazil. In 2013 the company expanded into Berlin, where it markets and sells its 'Proudly made in Bangladesh' products. For this SICA outsources textile clipping waste from Bangladesh's ready-made garment industry and brings them into the hands of skilled craftswomen in rural Rangpur, northern Bangladesh. This move to support workers in Bangladesh coincided with the tragic collapse of the Rana Plaza factory building in Dhaka in April 2013, with the loss of 1,134 lives. Simonato spends a lot of time in Bangladesh, nurturing the relationship with the makers and local organizations. She lives within these communities, helping the artisans to develop their skills, and providing fair employment and support.

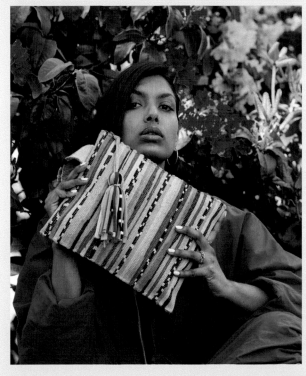

↗ One of House of Amoda's handcrafted pieces, a hand-stitched quilted cotton jacket.

→ A SICA pouch bag woven in Bangladesh from cotton jersey clippings.

Challenging the marketing mix

The marketing mix is the primary framework used by marketers, in either the 4P or the 7P version. However, there is debate as to whether this tool is still relevant and if it should be updated. Most of the people challenging the framework do so with the idea that the emphasis should shift away from the product as the primary focus, and on to the customer. The most up-to-date marketing theories, such as relationship marketing, recognize the importance of building relationships between a business and its customers or social media followers. The aim is to put the customer front and centre in order to develop brand loyalty and foster a sense of engagement. The next section will look at a selection of models that theorists and practitioners are proposing as an alternative to the traditional marketing mix. These are just some of the models, and are not necessarily being endorsed here, but presented for discussion and debate.

Changing the Ps to Cs

A model devised by Professor Robert F. Lauterborn in 1990 reframes the marketing mix by changing the Ps into Cs. Lauterborn shifted the emphasis away from product, price, place and promotion on to the customer, and this is why he chose the letter C to represent the concept, proposing the following: Customer needs and wants; Cost to the customer; Convenience; and Communication. The Lauterborn model may not have been created with fashion specifically in mind, but it is possible to consider its implications. What, for example, might it cost consumers in real terms to satisfy their fashion needs?

RELATIONSHIPS IN THE SUPPLY CHAIN

The framework of the marketing mix and the overall business and marketing processes can be applied to any business throughout the fashion and textile supply chain. Each interaction along the chain should be viewed as a business relationship; this is why it is important to include the criterion of 'people' within the marketing mix. This diagram represents a simplified version of the supply chain, but it could be expanded to take into account other businesses, such as agents and distributors.

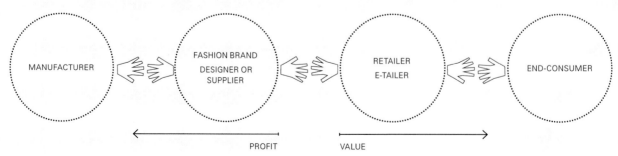

PEOPLE... PRODUCT... PRICE... PLACE... PHYSICAL EVIDENCE... PROMOTION

MANUFACTURER — FASHION BRAND DESIGNER OR SUPPLIER — RETAILER E-TAILER — END-CONSUMER

PROFIT   VALUE

Is their enthusiasm for fashion limited to product alone, or does it include pursuing a deeper level of satisfaction by engaging with fashion via digital and social media content? Factors such as time and convenience also have to be integrated into the framework of marketing, and this is a key element now for customers in terms of e-commerce, especially with delivery and returns of products. The luxury shopping sites Net-A-Porter and Mr Porter launched their 'You try – We wait' service for their top tier of customers, known as EIPs, or Extremely Important Persons. This is convenience at a luxury level, offering same-day delivery so that customers can try on potential purchases in the comfort of their own home, while a personal shopper or delivery person waits. The customer is billed for the items they decide to purchase, and those they reject are taken back immediately, for maximum convenience and no faff with returns. Lauterborn concluded his revamp with Communication as the replacement for Promotion. This may seem like a subtle shift, but he viewed promotion as manipulative – pushing messages from the company to the consumer. Communication, in his opinion, is more cooperative, a two-way conversation that has been facilitated with the growth of digital marketing, which allows dialogue between the brand and its consumers.

Consumer psychology and communication are the unifying principles that tie this new set of criteria together. There is a need to understand the psychological impulses behind consumer fashion choices and to recognize sensitivities to time, cost, value and convenience. By viewing marketing from the consumer's perspective, far more must now be achieved than just delivering the right products at the right price. The way consumers value fashion, style, self-expression and identity could also be viewed as part of the marketing equation.

A different 4Ps

Anne Lise Kjaer of Kjaer Global is a futurist. She sticks with 4Ps, but proposes a new business model comprising People, Planet, Purpose and Profit. The aim, according to Kjaer, is to balance profit with purpose in order that organizations take a more ethical stance and have a positive impact on people and planet. This model links more directly with what is known as the Triple Bottom Line, an ethical accounting system that measures a company's success in economic, social and environmental terms.

Converting the Ps to Ds

Olga Mitterfellner in her book *Fashion Marketing and Communication: Theory and Practice Across the Fashion Industry* (2020) converts Ps

↑ Virtual try-on technology provides potential customers with an opportunity to visualize a product as worn. This is a convenient way to decide if it is the right product for them, and, ideally for the brand, acts as an enticement to purchase.

to Ds, stating that the twenty-first century calls for a new approach. The starting point for this revision of the marketing mix is the idea of Diversity. This takes the premise that companies must think globally, that they will be trading in diverse regions and cultures, and that this therefore replaces Place as one of the variables of the mix. Digitalization replaces Promotion, with the idea that in modern marketing most promotion is digital in nature. Design replaces Product; this looks at the idea of new technology and how it can revolutionize the way products are designed. Circular design is an example, whereby consideration of the end of a product's life is built in at the design stage, ensuring that it can be recycled time and time again and does not become waste. The last substitution is Desire, which replaces Price. The argument here is that the creation of desire in the customer's mind is the driver to price acceptance.

Sticking with the traditional 4Ps

Mark Ritson is a brand consultant and former marketing professor who writes frequently for *Marketing Week*. A purist, he is very much against tinkering with the original 4P marketing mix, believing that the traditional 4Ps have endured for a reason and that the original model stands in its own right without adjustment. Writing in *Marketing Week* in March 2021, he stated that, 'Whenever a marketer sets out to improve, augment or adapt the four Ps, they reveal the absurdity of the exercise.' He makes a compelling case by pointing out that 'the four Ps summarize the tactical considerations of what a company wants to do.' He goes on to suggest that these tactical decisions are not the same as the steps in the marketing process, 'namely diagnosis and then strategy'. This is a highly salient point, which he illustrates by putting the proposed new P, Purpose, under the spotlight. Purpose, Ritson believes, is an element of brand positioning that is 'tackled during the strategic phase of marketing planning'. He makes a very solid case by differentiating clearly between strategy and tactics. We will look at marketing strategy and brand positioning in the next section of this chapter, and discuss the difference between strategy and tactics in more detail in Chapter 3 (page 132).

Newer versions of the marketing mix are perhaps valid if they serve a clearly defined function, but we need to question if they help us to interrogate the tactics of marketing, or whether they serve a function outside marketing and therefore should not be considered as a replacement to the traditional 4Ps.

STP marketing strategy

Now that we have looked at the marketing mix, it is time to look at another key strategic tool used by marketers: STP marketing strategy. The fundamental strategic principles underpinning this framework are **Segmentation**, **Targeting** and **Positioning**. It is an extremely tough challenge for a fashion manufacturer, supplier, designer brand or retailer to appeal equally to all customers or consumers. It makes sense, therefore, for a business to concentrate its resources and activities and focus on a specific area of the market, fine-tuning or 'positioning' the brand, product offer, service and digital content so that they appeal more directly to a specified and well-defined 'target' audience. This is the fundamental principle of STP.

Segmentation and targeting

Market segmentation is a key function of marketing; its purpose is to divide a market into smaller, more focused sectors. The fashion market can be segmented in several ways, such as by product type or market level. There is a market for couture, the luxury designer market, the accessory market and the branded sportswear and sneaker market, for example. The process of segmentation can also be used to cluster consumers into groups that share similar characteristics. This is termed customer segmentation.

Think OUTSIDE IN!

In other words, imagine being the customer. What kind of service do they require? How can you improve the processes they go through to purchase your products? How can you make the process smoother, more exciting, more engaging, more efficient and memorable for the right reasons? If we view marketing from the consumer's perspective, far more must be achieved than just delivering the right products at the right price. The way consumers value fashion, style, self-expression and identity could also be viewed as part of the marketing equation.

Now think INSIDE OUT.

Have you made internal processes smooth and efficient? Will those processes support customer experience? Even if employees don't deal directly with customers, internal or interdepartmental processes may cause glitches that indirectly affect results.

VERSIONS OF THE MARKETING MIX

Please take the time to debate this in class or within your business. Are you for or against these revisions? Most importantly, consider the implications for the fashion industry. What should fashion brands of the future focus on when designing, producing, marketing, promoting, selling and disposing of their products? The challenge is to navigate our way to a sustainable and healthy future, and any framework that helps to achieve this is worthy of our consideration.

MARKETING MIX 4Ps	LAUTERBORN: Cs	KJAER: Ps	MITTERFELLNER: Ds
PRODUCT	CUSTOMER NEEDS AND WANTS	PEOPLE	DESIGN
PRICE	COST TO THE CUSTOMER	PLANET	DESIRE
PLACE	CONVENIENCE	PURPOSE	DIVERSITY
PROMOTION	COMMUNICATION	PROFIT	DIGITALIZATION

Creating an inviting retail space

ALICE + OLIVIA

Fashion brands must offer beautiful and inviting physical environments in which to sell their products. The New York-based brand Alice + Olivia by Stacey Bendet opened its first stand-alone store in the International Finance Centre mall in the Central district of Hong Kong. The 74-sq-m (800-sq-ft) boutique, nicknamed 'the jewel box', has a vibrant colour scheme. The black-and-white chequerboard floor stretches out of the store and into the mall, connecting the store to its environment and drawing customers in. The fun, fresh and eclectic style of the Alice + Olivia brand is reflected in the décor. The Hong Kong store, the first to open as part of an expansion programme in a partnership venture with ImagineX, a leading distribution and brand-management company in Asia, allowed the Alice + Olivia brand to extend its global reach far beyond the US.

←↓ The Alice + Olivia Hong Kong store, nicknamed the 'jewel box'.

Customer segmentation is the research and analysis technique used to define these groups. It categorizes consumers in terms of their age, attitudes, behaviours, the type of product and service they might need, or the way they interact with and use social media. (This is described in greater depth in Chapter 4.) Segmentation is a means to an end; the tool that facilitates the next step in the process is targeting. This is the practice of developing products, services, branded content and promotional messages that are aimed specifically to appeal to a particular customer segment. Companies that offer petite ranges, for example, are targeting smaller customers. A fashion brand targeting older female customers might design and cut garments to flatter the figure of the older woman. A brand that creates content for TikTok will target users of that specific platform, particularly those likely to share the content with followers and friends.

Positioning

Having segmented the market and selected which sector and consumers to target, a company must now position its brand within the market so that it will appeal directly to the target market.

Positioning is a slightly complicated issue because it is really a matter of perception. It is about the position a brand occupies in the mind of a consumer or potential consumer. Furthermore, this position is relative. Positioning is about where a brand or product is perceived to be within the marketplace relative to the other brands or products operating within the same sector. For example, consumers may feel that Balenciaga ugly trainers are inherently more desirable than trainers sold by another brand, which they might perceive to be more traditional or less on trend. Or they might consider the garments made by one sports brand to be of a higher quality than those of another, when in reality both use the same factory to manufacture their apparel.

In order to position itself, its brands or its products effectively, a business must develop a positioning strategy. The strategy will depend on where competitors position themselves and how the business wants its brands or products to compete. Taking the Balenciaga example, the brand positions itself to be more cutting-edge than its competitors in the trainer market. So a competitor brand that wished to compete head-to-head could decide to position itself strategically close to Balenciaga in the trainer market – and beat them by developing a shoe that is seen as more desirable in the eyes of the consumer. It is, of course, risky and costly to compete aggressively with a market leader, and there may be no real advantage for consumers in having two virtually identical brands.

Another option would be to position the brand within the same market but to offer something distinctly different, or provide extra benefits.

When working on a positioning strategy it is helpful to create a **positioning map**. This can be used to pinpoint the desired position for a brand and give a visual overview of this position relative to that of competitor brands within a market. Given that positioning is actually dependent on the perception of consumers, the company must also obtain knowledge of how consumers perceive their brand within the market. Once research has been carried out, a **perceptual map** can be produced. This is very similar to a positioning map, but is based solely on consumers' perceptions of the brand, rather than on where the company wishes to position it. The map will indicate the consumer perceptions of the brand's current position and identify where shifts are required to align them with the company's desired position. This pursuit of alignment is called repositioning, the process of redefining the identity of an existing brand or product in order to shift the position it holds in consumers' minds relative to that of competitors.

To summarize, the steps of the positioning process are:

» Define the market in which the brand or product will compete

» Decide where to position within this market in relation to brands or products that are already out there

» Determine whether to compete directly against a competitor or to differentiate and compete by being different

» Understand how consumers perceive the current position of your brand, or how they might perceive it if you are a new brand just entering the market

» Determine if repositioning is necessary, if you are an existing brand

Once a clear position for the brand or product has been established, the next step is to ensure that it is communicated to consumers. All facets of the brand – its image, products, packaging, retail environment, promotion, advertising, website and social media strategy – should convey this position, so it is vital that every aspect is congruent and supports the strategy. Positioning and repositioning are costly exercises; moving a brand's position is not a tactic to be carried out repeatedly. The aim is to establish a strong and recognizable position that is consistent over time and to make sure products and brands are clearly different from those offered by competitors. This is the principle of differentiation. Closely allied to positioning, it is the next strategic tool to be discussed.

Differentiation

Differentiation is the concept of developing and marketing products or services so that they are different and clearly distinguishable from those offered by competitors within the same marketplace. It is a fundamental strategic approach that ensures products and services stand out from the crowd.

The aim of differentiation is to achieve what is known as a competitive advantage. A company achieves an advantage if it is able to provide products or services that are of greater value to consumers than those offered by competitors. As mentioned earlier in this chapter, value is not just a question of price. Customers might value premium service, luxury quality or the high status of a particular fashion label, and they may indeed be willing to pay more for it. Alternatively, it might be street credibility that gives a brand a competitive edge, or the fact that a world-famous celebrity endorses the brand. It could be as simple as one brand's trainers being more comfortable than those of other brands, or the sizing and fit of a particular fashion label being more suitable for the customer's particular body shape. It is such aspects that can augment the basic product, add value and help to achieve competitive advantage.

POSITIONING OR PERCEPTUAL MAP

A positioning or perceptual map plots the relative positions of brands or products. Two key criteria are chosen, one for each axis, and the polarities of each criterion are positioned at the ends of the axis. This example shows pricing ranging from prestige to more affordable levels.

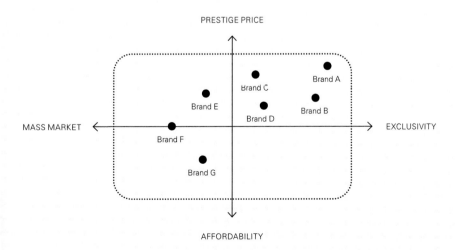

→ This table is designed as a tool to help identify potential areas by which a company can differentiate itself and its products and services. The marketing mix should be used as a framework. Some initial ideas for differentiation have been given here as an example. Once relevant areas for potential differentiation have been identified, specific objectives can be set and tactics devised to achieve each particular aspect of differentiation.

Opportunity to differentiate exists at every stage of the marketing process. Differentiation and competitive advantage can be achieved through design and technological innovation, by strategic management of the supply chain, or in the way a brand or product is retailed, distributed or promoted. Differentiation can be achieved by thinking through the process a customer goes through, from first awareness of the brand or product to purchasing. This can include how the brand is promoted, content that is posted on social media, and interactive experiences offered by the brand along that purchasing journey; there are many creative ways to differentiate across the steps involved in the customers' interaction and experience when engaging with your brand. The Potential for Differentiation table shown opposite uses the 7P marketing mix as a framework for exploring possible areas for differentiation and competitive advantage. Once relevant areas for differentiation have been identified, practical steps can be planned and strategic actions put into place so as to achieve the desired outcome. The chosen tactics must also contribute to creating a competitive advantage for the company and, of course, offer clear value and benefit for the consumer.

Competitive advantage

The Potential for Differentiation table opposite highlights some of the ways a business might differentiate itself and achieve an advantage over its competitors. One tactic used by high-street brands in particular to compete in a marketplace is to be the cheapest and gain a cost advantage. In this case, the design or quality of products might be comparable but the competitor that offers them at the lowest price might gain the advantage. However, this is likely to be a short-lived victory. The problem with this approach is that it soon becomes unsustainable. Competitors usually reduce prices to match, and a vicious cycle of cost reductions eventually leads to erosion of profits for all concerned. Cost alone does not always provide a strong enough advantage; it must be aligned with other beneficial factors, such as speed and what is known in the trade as fashionability. In other words, companies that manage to get reasonably priced catwalk-inspired styles or the right trends into the market faster than their rivals achieve not only a cost advantage but also a speed advantage and what could be termed a fashion advantage; this, of course, is the operating principle behind the concept of fast fashion. Zara, one of the brands owned by the Spanish Inditex Group, has consistently been able to offer reasonably priced, stylish interpretations of catwalk trends at exceptional speed. A tightly controlled production system allows

POTENTIAL FOR DIFFERENTIATION TABLE

MARKETING MIX VARIABLES	POTENTIAL AREAS FOR DIFFERENTIATION	TACTICS TO ACHIEVE DIFFERENTIATION	COMPETITIVE ADVANTAGE	VALUE FOR CONSUMERS
PRODUCT	» Design and construction of products » Quality of products, fabrics and components » Range of products on offer » Fashion level of merchandise » Sustainability and end of life of product			
PRICE	» Prices in comparison to competitors » Pricing structure/price architecture of a range » Price discounts or offers			
PLACE	» Routes to market » Locations of stores » E-commerce platforms			
PROMOTION	» Designer collaboration » Advertising » Celebrity endorsement » Sales promotions » Limited editions			
PHYSICAL EVIDENCE	» In-store environment: signage, seating, changing rooms, etc. » Website and content, such as blog, social media, newsletter » Marketing extras – swing ticket and labelling, carrier bag, brochure, in-store magazine, desirable packaging			
PROCESS	» In-store and customer service » Website and e-commerce design and ease of use » Aftercare, return of products			
PEOPLE	» Structure of company » Opportunities for staff » Ethics of garment production » Collaboration and co-creation with consumers and social-media followers » Stakeholders and business partners			

Zara to move swiftly from a design drawing to a finished garment delivered to store in a period of between two and three weeks. The international retailer achieves its speed advantage because Inditex possesses its own manufacturing and distribution capabilities and operates what is termed a vertical supply chain. The company is well known for perfecting its highly integrated production and distribution model. It is Zara's legendary lead time (the time between placing an order and the stock arriving in-store) that gives it its competitive advantage.

ASOS illustrates the next developmental stage in the competitive platform. The company that started life as 'As Seen On Screen' was established in June 2000. The e-tailer entered the market and stole the advantage by bringing must-have fashion ideas direct to the consumer. ASOS gained a competitive advantage by adding new dimensions to the cost, speed and fashionability dynamic, namely convenience, interactivity and connectivity. Suddenly, Zara's vertically integrated production model and speed to market became old news; ASOS extended the parameters of fashion beyond retail into a new realm of interactive consumer engagement.

The Zara and ASOS examples illustrate what have now become standard criteria for competitiveness within a fast-fashion market:

> » Cost
>
> » Speed
>
> » Fashionability
>
> » Convenience
>
> » Interactivity
>
> » Connectivity

ASOS recognized the need to play at an emotive level and tap into the desires of a new breed of consumer. Capitalizing on emerging technology and a growing consumer appetite for engaging directly with brands, it published an online fashion magazine, generated its own content, integrated social media into its strategic arsenal and harnessed the potential of e-commerce technology with such features as Scan to Shop, mobile-phone apps and shoppable videos. These features – which seemed so advanced at the time – are of course now commonly used. It is no longer just the product that counts, but also service, delivery and returns, social media content and interactive engagement between brand and consumers.

When a fashion brand competing in a specific market achieves these fundamental measures of competitiveness, it raises the bar for others to match or surpass, and eventually new platforms for differentiation and advantage emerge. Consumers are becoming increasingly aware of the climate crisis, sustainability and the ethics of fashion manufacturing. This is helping to establish new areas for competitive advantage, such as sustainability, accountability and authenticity. It could be said that these highly important factors are imperative areas for all fashion brands to consider and act on if they are to earn their place in the market. Increasingly, consumers – particularly Gen Z – are calling brands to account on these matters, wanting more transparency about where and how garments and fashion products are produced.

Newer areas for competitive advantage include:

» Authenticity

» Sustainable practices

» Accountability, transparency and traceability

» Warranty or aftercare services for repair and increasing product longevity

» Customization and personalization

Collaborate beats compete

Fashion companies now recognize that competition may not always be the best strategy. It has become increasingly apparent that collaborating can be a better option. The Hacker Project, launched in 2021, was a notable collaboration (collab) between Gucci and Balenciaga. The concept released by Gucci to celebrate its centenary was a hack of the Balenciaga iconography, infusing Gucci's offering with the hallmarks of the Balenciaga brand, merged with Gucci's own notable brand motifs. In the same year Tommy Hilfiger released a 17-piece capsule collection in collaboration with Timberland; and the Californian skate-shoe brand Vans entered into a collab with the Italian outdoor apparel brand Napapijri. These examples are just the tip of the iceberg. The collab concept was conceived in 2004, when the high-street retailer H&M collaborated with Karl Lagerfeld to produce a capsule collection that launched in about 500 H&M stores and sold out within hours, and since then there has been an ever-growing number of collaborations between an array of brands. There have also been collabs between fashion brands and artists, musicians, architects and other creatives.

There are many benefits to collaborating in this way, and it has become a favoured tactic for strategic branded product development and promotion. There is more to discuss on this, and the subject will be picked up again in Chapter 6, with further examples and details of the benefits, as well as consideration of any risk that might be involved.

↑ A look from the Gucci 'Aria' collection shown in Rome in April 2021. Dubbed the 'Hacker Project', it merged the iconic codes and silhouettes of the Gucci and Balenciaga brands in what Gucci's creative director Alessandro Michele called a 'hack' of Demna Gvasalia's signature Balenciaga details.

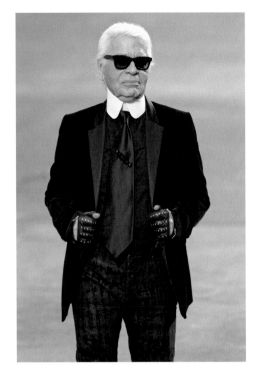

↑↑ Karl Lagerfeld takes a bow at a Chanel show in 2013, wearing his trademark black leather gloves, high collar and sunglasses.

↑ Net-A-Porter released an exclusive limited-edition Karl Lagerfeld x Tokidoki doll, made available only at the Berlin, Paris and Amsterdam Karl Lagerfeld concept stores in 2013.

Unique selling proposition

When ASOS arrived on the scene it set itself apart, not only because it was one of the first companies in the UK to make the internet a viable fashion retail destination, but also because it provided a unique 'As Seen On Screen' ideology. That is what gave this internet brand its distinctive emotional pull and provided its unique selling proposition or unique selling point (USP). A USP represents the fundamental distinguishing proposition being offered to the customer. It is the synthesis of a brand's positioning and differentiation, and should encapsulate its overall competitive advantage. The USP is a marketing tool that can be used to emphasize and articulate specific points of difference that make a particular product, service or brand unique and therefore distinctive in the marketplace.

Signature style

For many designers or fashion brands, it is their unique signature style that helps to define their USP. A signature style is a look that is so clear and distinctive that it can easily be attributed to the designer or brand in question. It is also possible for an individual to have a signature style. Karl Lagerfeld, for example, had an instantly recognizable and clearly defined personal style, as did Coco Chanel, the originator of the renowned luxury brand that bears her name.

Directors of style

For a fashion designer or creative director, developing an individual signature style or being able to interpret or update the style of an existing fashion house brand is an advantageous and important skill. This can be quite a challenge, and a delicate balancing act. When Tom Ford was promoted to creative director at Gucci in 1994, he transformed the failing brand. Between 1995 and 1996 Gucci increased its sales by 90 per cent. The 1996 Autumn/Winter collection was and remains iconic, featuring sheath-style dresses with flesh-revealing cut-outs augmented with metal hardware, silky shirts unbuttoned to the navel, and suiting in sumptuous velvet. It is not exactly clear when, but a white silk-jersey plunge cut-out dress from the Gucci 2004 collection by Ford later sold on a rare vintage fashion site for US$5,000.

Three designers were appointed on Ford's departure. John Ray took on the role of creative director for menswear; Alessandra Facchinetti became creative director for womenswear; and Frida Giannini, previously head of accessories, became the overall creative director in 2006, launching such 'neo-classics' as the New Bamboo and New

Jackie handbags. The key look for Gucci during this era reflected the sexy approach from the Ford era – but it was considered to be time for a rethink. So when Marco Bizzarri became CEO in 2014, he appointed Alessandro Michele, who took on the role of creative director in 2015.

Michele transformed the house of Gucci, taking what he described as a brand for the jet set into a more inclusive, floral-powered, printed, sequinned and fun-loving realm, open to all, across gender, race, body size and age. This approach trickled down the fashion market and became a defining look for nearly a decade. However, by 2022 Gucci's sales were beginning to dip, and Michele's departure was announced at the end of that year. His replacement, Sabato De Sarno, was announced at the beginning of 2023. Kering, the parent company, stated that the new direction was to be a 'balance between a recognized fashion positioning and products linked to its [Gucci's] history and heritage'.

All of the above highlights the challenge for any incoming creative director: how to modernize, reflect your design handwriting, and also pay homage to the brand's historical signature style. It is also crucial to achieve sales targets and gain the right type of publicity for the look and the brand.

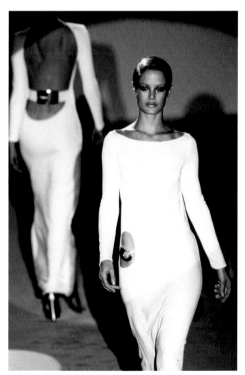

↑ Iconic Gucci over the decades. (Top left) Maximalist, quirky, geeky Gucci: the quintessential look under Alessandro Michele, Milan Fashion Week Spring/ Summer 2016. (Top right) Historic Gucci: the bamboo bag, Museo Gucci, Florence. (Above) Showstopper: the iconic cut-out dress designed by Tom Ford and modelled by Carolyn Murphy, Autumn 1996.

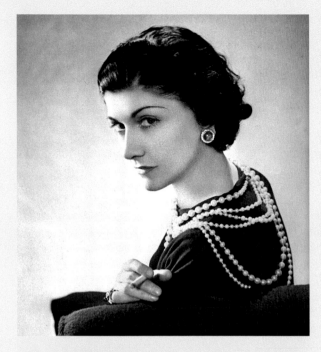

A timeless signature style

COCO CHANEL

Gabrielle 'Coco' Chanel was renowned for her signature personal style, often challenging the dress conventions of her day; she wore black, for example, a colour more traditionally associated with mourning. Accessorizing her quintessential look with copious oversized strings of pearls, she created a stir with her dramatic costume-style jewellery in an era when the wearing of 'fake' jewels was a novelty. The custom at the time was to embellish outfits with precious or heirloom jewellery so as to indicate wealth and status. Key elements of her signature style are the little black dress, the classic Chanel suit with gilt buttons, costume jewellery and the quilted handbag. These emblems have become the established signifiers of the brand that bears her name. They are so powerful that they were reinterpreted and used season after season, not only for the clothes, but also on the sets of Chanel ready-to-wear catwalk shows in Paris. Virginie Viard, who was appointed creative director in 2019 after Karl Lagerfeld's death, once again referred to the house's long-time classic style in her Spring/Summer 2021 collection. Alexander Fury, writing for *AnOther Magazine* in October of that year, pointed out that she was able to remix 'the formula for younger generations hankering after instantly recognizable Chanel-isms'.

↑ Chanel wearing her signature pearls, photographed by Boris Lipnitzki in 1936.

↖← A colossal Chanel quilted bag adorns the carousel-style catwalk at the Autumn/Winter 2008/9 Ready-to-Wear show in Paris, and models stand on the carousel with giant versions of other Chanel signature emblems.

2

The Fashion Market

"We all have to participate in the fashion industry,

because we all have to wear clothes."

Sinéad Burke

Fashion is a global industry with a complex structure that operates on many different levels to reach everyone, from fashionistas to those who just purchase clothing as a necessity of everyday life. The scope of fashion is immense, encompassing garments ranging from an ornate haute-couture gown made by hand in a Paris atelier to a simple mass-produced T-shirt manufactured in China.

This chapter explains the basic **structure of the industry**, outlining the different **market sectors**, such as womenswear and menswear, and highlighting the varying **levels of fashion**, from couture to high street, and **product categories**, such as denim and streetwear. There is a section on the **fashion system** and **seasonal fashion cycle**, looking at the original model of two seasons a year as well as newer approaches, including the pre-season collection, See Now Buy Now and Direct-to-Consumer. The chapter also describes the **traditional centres of fashion** – Paris, London, Milan and New York – and considers the wider **global fashion market**, which includes other parts of Europe, and Asia, the Middle East, Africa and South America.

Fashion market sectors

The fashion market can be subdivided in a number of ways depending on what aspect of the market or industry is being analysed – for example, by product sector, such as clothing and apparel or accessories; by geographic market, such as Europe, USA, Asia or South America; by market level, haute couture or ready-to-wear; or by function, such as sportswear, performance wear, formal wear and so on. Information is broken down in this way so that

→ Work carried out by Allied Market Research valued the athleisure or active-wear market at US$425.5 billion in 2022, projected to reach US$771.8 billion by 2032.

FASHION MARKET SECTORS

CLOTHING AND APPAREL				ACCESSORIES & FOOTWEAR	FRAGRANCE & BEAUTY	LIFESTYLE & HOMEWARE
WOMENSWEAR	**MENSWEAR**	**GENDER-NEUTRAL CLOTHING**	**CHILDRENSWEAR**			
Evening and occasion wear	Bespoke tailoring	Tailoring	Baby	Shoes		
Bridal wear	Evening and occasion wear	Contemporary	Toddler	Bags		
Formal work and office	Formal work and office	Casual	Girls	Sunglasses		
Contemporary fashion	Contemporary fashion	Streetwear	Boys	Gloves and scarves		
Denim	Denim	Sportswear	Gender-neutral	Wallets and purses		
Streetwear	Streetwear			Hats		
Casual wear	Casual wear			Men's ties		
Resort or cruise wear	Resort or cruise wear			Luggage		
Slouch or lounge wear	Sportswear					
Sportswear						
Lingerie						

This diagram indicates some of the key market and product sectors within fashion. As new market areas develop, so the chart can be adapted. For example, jewellery or fine jewellery is an area that several fashion brands now include in their product ranges.

↑ A young Emirati couple shopping for sunglasses in Dubai.

↗ Matthew Zorpas, seen here wearing a suit by Hardy Amies, is a London-based fashion consultant who blogs at www.thegentlemanblogger.com. There is growing demand for designer and trend-led men's fashion, and Zorpas has become an authority on men's style.

companies are better able to analyse market data and monitor their business results. Market statistics can be compiled and analysed by one or more of these criteria. The list below and the diagram opposite outline some of the criteria that can be used.

Market or product category

» Apparel, accessories, eyewear, perfume, homeware

» The apparel market can be subdivided into womenswear, menswear and childrenswear

Product type, end use of product or fashion style

» Streetwear, denim, lingerie, active sportswear, leisure wear, loungewear, formal wear, evening wear, bridal wear

Market level

» Haute couture, couture, luxury, premium, mid-market, mass market, value market

Location of market

» Global, international, national, regional, local

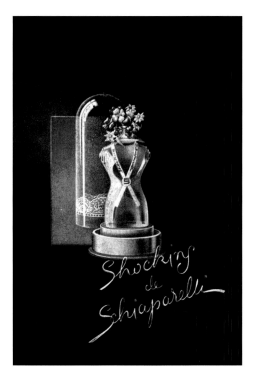

The fashion system

Traditionally, the fashion calendar consisted of two seasons: Spring/Summer and Autumn/Winter. This later expanded to include additional pre-season collections for both womenswear and menswear. The sustainability and ethics of the system have been under scrutiny for a while, with many calling for change, and this was exacerbated when the COVID-19 pandemic hit in 2020. Many brands realized that it was time for a radical rethink. This section looks at the fashion system, reviewing how it evolved and the traditional cycle of fashion seasons that was established for haute couture and ready-to-wear. It will then discuss some of the newer approaches that are being adopted, such as producing fewer collections a year, reducing the number of fashion shows by combining men's and women's presentations, designing genderless fashion collections, and experimenting with seasonless fashion collections. Other innovations include See Now Buy Now (SNBN) and direct-to-consumer (D2C) business models.

The origins of the traditional fashion cycle can be traced back to the nineteenth century and the Englishman Charles Frederick Worth, who was born in Lincolnshire in 1825. He is important because he was the first true fashion designer or haute couturier, the first to become the eponymous head of a fashion house, and also the first to use a live model, having his wife, Marie, act as mannequin to showcase his new designs. He created seasonal collections, showing for the Spring/Summer and Autumn/Winter seasons, which at the time was a totally new concept. He was also the first designer to hold 'fashion parades', which became what we know as the modern fashion show. The presentation of two seasonal shows a year became the established system for **haute couture** and also for **ready-to-wear**, which was first established in the early twentieth century. These two sectors have traditionally acted as the foundation for the system.

Haute couture

'Haute couture' translates literally as 'high sewing' or 'fine sewing', and is fashion at its highest level. Haute couture operates at a quality and standard far above that of luxury designer ready-to-wear. Prices are extremely high (an haute couture dress can sell for a six-figure sum), so there is an unwritten rule of limiting sales of any garment over £100,000 to one per continent to ensure the exclusivity that clients expect. For lesser-priced garments, sales are usually confined to three per continent. Haute couture clients view themselves as art patrons and consider these clothes to be a collectable form of

← An advert for Shocking, the fragrance launched by Elsa Schiaparelli in 1937. The curvaceous bottle, shaped like a woman's torso, was modelled on the physique of the screen siren Mae West and designed by the surrealist artist Leonor Fini.

↙ The Jean Paul Gaultier signature fragrance takes inspiration for the bottle design from the Schiaparelli original.

→ Lady Gaga launched her unisex perfume, Fame, in 2012. The photographer Nick Knight designed the bottle, and Steven Klein shot the advertising campaign. The perfume itself is a black liquid that becomes invisible when it touches the skin.

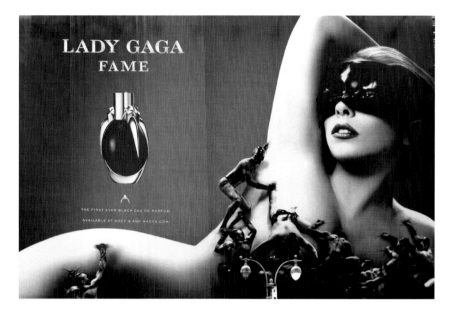

art and an investment. The term 'haute couture' is protected by law and governed by very strict rules set by the Fédération de la Haute Couture et de la Mode in Paris. To be classified as a bona fide haute couturier, a fashion house must create made-to-order garments for private clients. It must also produce two collections a year, in January and July, employ a minimum of 20 full-time staff, run an atelier in Paris, and show a set minimum of runway looks ('exits', as they are known) of evening and daywear. In the 1980s and 90s the Italian designer Valentino showed over 180 exits for his haute couture show; now the house produces only 40. Very few design houses are approved as haute-couture establishments. There is a small number of designated French couture establishments, including Chanel, Dior, Givenchy, Schiaparelli, Alexis Mabille, Alexandre Vauthier, Julien Fournié, Giambattista Valli, Stéphane Rolland and Franck Sorbier. The Fédération also grants correspondent membership to houses based outside Paris, such as Azzedine Alaïa, Elie Saab, Fendi, Giorgio Armani, Valentino, Versace and Viktor & Rolf. In addition, there are special guest members, among them Iris van Herpen and Guo Pei.

Haute couture relies on the expertise of many highly skilled artisans and craftspeople who labour behind the scenes to produce all the luxurious embroideries, trimmings and accessories required by the haute couturiers. Traditionally, Paris has been home to a large number of studios or ateliers specializing in millinery, shoemaking, embroidery, beading, creating decorative flowers, buttons and costume jewellery. In 1900 Paris had over 300 plumassiers or feather specialists; today the Lemarié atelier is virtually the only one still in existence. Chanel bought the business along with five other specialist craft ateliers: Michel, specializing in millinery; the

↓ The ability to work as a team is another vital skill in fashion. Designers rely on a team of skilled technicians to help them realize their creative ideas.

→ A fantastical look from Guo Pei's 'Alternative Universe' collection for Autumn/Winter 2019/20, shown at l'École des Beaux-Arts as part of Paris Haute Couture.

→→ Balenciaga's Spring/ Summer 2020 Ready-to-Wear collection was a 'genderless' presentation featuring both men and women wearing Demna Gvasalia's signature boxy silhouette with outsize shoulders and a nipped-in waist.

BASIC HIERARCHY OF FASHION

Haute couture sits at the pinnacle of fashion. Although it is only a small sector of the overall market, its influence on designer and high-street fashion is of great importance. Designers distil ideas from their own couture collections and use them in a more commercial format for their ready-to-wear collections. In turn, the designer and luxury brand ready-to-wear collections set the trends that are followed by mass-market fashion retailers. When trends work their way down from the top of the market to the bottom, it is known as a trickle-down effect.

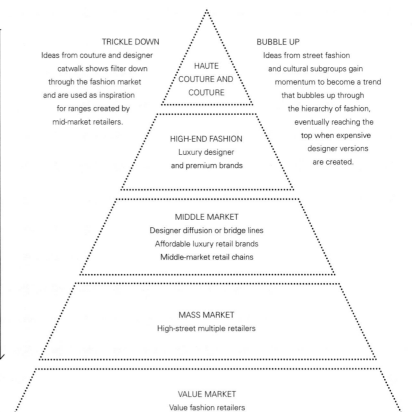

TRICKLE DOWN
Ideas from couture and designer catwalk shows filter down through the fashion market and are used as inspiration for ranges created by mid-market retailers.

BUBBLE UP
Ideas from street fashion and cultural subgroups gain momentum to become a trend that bubbles up through the hierarchy of fashion, eventually reaching the top when expensive designer versions are created.

HAUTE COUTURE AND COUTURE

HIGH-END FASHION
Luxury designer and premium brands

MIDDLE MARKET
Designer diffusion or bridge lines
Affordable luxury retail brands
Middle-market retail chains

MASS MARKET
High-street multiple retailers

VALUE MARKET
Value fashion retailers
Discount retailers

shoemakers Massaro; the embroidery house Lesage; the button and costume jewellery maker Desrues; and the gold- and silversmith Goossens. While many argue that something as arcane and extravagant as haute couture cannot or should not survive, it seems that demand has not diminished, but rather has shifted to a new set of younger, more fashion-conscious clientele from emerging rich nations, such as China, Russia and countries in the Middle East.

Haute couture is a relatively small business in terms of the overall fashion market; the real value is its power as a marketing tool. Haute couture houses receive valuable press coverage, raising the status and desirability of their brand and keeping it in the public eye.

Fashion designers who are not recognized by the Fédération can still produce exclusive custom-made clothing, but this must be marketed as couture rather than haute couture. Prices for couture can still be high. The price of a Vera Wang wedding dress can be in the region of US$25,000, although in an attempt to keep customers happy during the recession, Wang introduced what she calls **demi-couture**, with a lower price tag.

Ready-to-wear

Fashion collections that are not custom-made for an individual client are known as ready-to-wear or off-the-peg clothing. Ready-to-wear garments are premade, come in predetermined sizes and are usually mass-produced and industrially manufactured. Ready-to-wear fashion is available at all levels of the market, including:

» High-end fashion

» Middle market

» High street

» Value fashion

Middle-market fashion is designed and priced to cater for customers wishing to purchase at a level between luxury and mass market. A designer or fashion brand that has established itself within the high-end market may decide to introduce a secondary **diffusion line** or **bridge line**, as it is known in the United States, so that it can extend its brand and appeal to a wider range of customers. There was a time when this was the preferred strategy for many designer brands, but more recently there has been a reversal, with companies axing sub-brands and cutting back operations post-pandemic. Examples of diffusion lines are Emporio Armani, Miu Miu (a sister brand to Prada), See by Chloé, Isabel Marant Étoile and Rick Owens DRKSHDW. Other designer diffusion lines are the affordable collections created for such stores as Target, The Outnet, Payless

A fashion brand is constructed to make money from merchandise designed for different levels of the market. At the top of the range, the most expensive and luxurious product may be exclusive and available only in limited quantities. These couture and ultra-premium ranges may operate as a loss-leader but act as a promotional tool to secure the brand's status. To make money, brand companies must extend their offering to a wider range of customers.

For example, the brand architecture of Armani is as follows (see images opposite):

Armani Privé Couture and ultra-premium, top-of-the-range product with very high price points. Targets customers in the 35–60 age bracket.
Armani Collezioni Priced approximately 20 per cent lower than the main line, and aimed at the discerning customer who cannot afford the signature price points.
Emporio Armani Diffusion line providing contemporary Armani designs, targeted at the young professional aged 25–35.
Armani Jeans and **A/X Armani Exchange** Both aimed at a younger age bracket of 18–30. A more casual and relaxed style, making the Armani brand accessible to more consumers.

BRAND PYRAMID MODEL

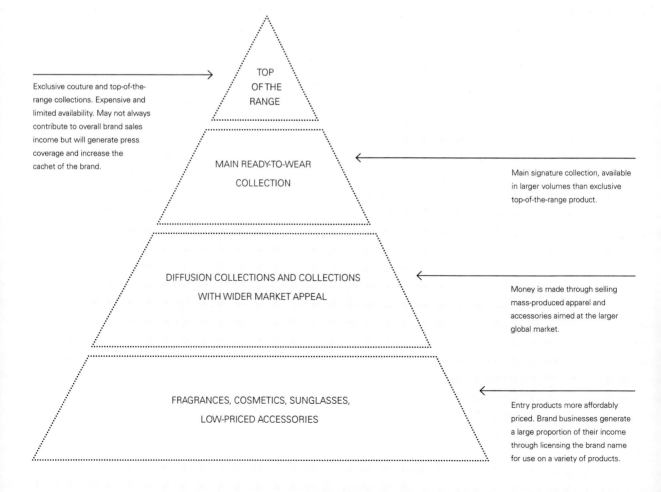

Exclusive couture and top-of-the-range collections. Expensive and limited availability. May not always contribute to overall brand sales income but will generate press coverage and increase the cachet of the brand.

TOP OF THE RANGE

MAIN READY-TO-WEAR COLLECTION

Main signature collection, available in larger volumes than exclusive top-of-the-range product.

DIFFUSION COLLECTIONS AND COLLECTIONS WITH WIDER MARKET APPEAL

Money is made through selling mass-produced apparel and accessories aimed at the larger global market.

FRAGRANCES, COSMETICS, SUNGLASSES, LOW-PRICED ACCESSORIES

Entry products more affordably priced. Brand businesses generate a large proportion of their income through licensing the brand name for use on a variety of products.

and J.Crew in the USA. Retailers such as Banana Republic, Cos, The Frankie Shop, Reformation, Maje and Sandro can also be considered mid-market. The term 'middle market' is not particularly inspiring and is not always perceived by brands as a position they wish to aspire to. Some combat this by re-stating their market level, claiming they offer affordable luxury or premium fashion. This is seen as an important market opportunity now that so many fashion consumers view luxury as something that should be available to all, even those with limited budgets. The biggest area of growth for mid-market fashion is online. Without the burden and cost of owning stores, there has been a proliferation of affordable and stylish online brands.

Mass-market fashion refers to high-street multiples or fashion retail chains such as Gap, H&M, Zara and Forever 21, available on high streets in most major cities and towns, and internationally. This also can include online retailers, such as Shein (which is described as an international business-to-consumer [B2C] fashion e-commerce platform) and Boohoo.com.

The demarcation between the various levels of the fashion market is becoming ever more complicated and hard to pin down with clarity. An increasing number of fashion companies are implementing strategies to extend their businesses or brands into the lower price ranges in an attempt to appeal to a wider range of customers. Alternatively, they can reposition upwards by offering luxury and premium products aimed to attract a more discerning customer willing to pay a higher price.

↑ (Left to right) Armani Privé; Armani Collezioni; Emporio Armani; A/X Armani Exchange.

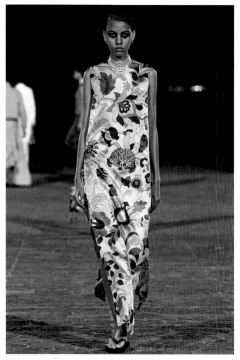

↑ The pre-season collection has risen in prominence, and a significant number of the major fashion houses now hold pre-season runway presentations. Pictured here are Erdem's Pre-Fall 2023 show (top) and Dior's Pre-Fall 2023 show in Mumbai.

The fashion cycle and seasons

Traditionally, there are two fashion seasons: Spring/Summer and Autumn (Fall)/Winter. Fashion houses presented their collections twice a year, originally for couture, and later including ready-to-wear. For haute couture, the Spring/Summer collections are presented in January. This allows the customers to select the styles they would like to purchase, allowing time for the garments to be custom-made to their specifications and measurements, ready to be worn during the spring and summer seasons. The Autumn/Winter shows take place in July, again so that the clientele can order their wardrobe pieces, have fittings and receive their clothes ready for the autumn and winter.

For women's ready-to-wear, the Spring/Summer collections are shown in September and the Autumn/Winter collections in February or early March. It is important to understand that ready-to-wear works on a wholesale system and functions mainly business-to-business or B2B. Originally, ready-to-wear shows were for the press and retail buyers only, and the latter would purchase pieces from the collection to sell in their boutiques and department stores. Fashion shows are now major events, packed with celebrities and influencers, and viewable by the public on the brand website or via live-streaming. There is also a cycle of shows for menswear that operates on a similar system, with the shows kicking off slightly earlier than those for womenswear.

The challenge for fashion brands producing only two ready-to-wear collections a year and selling through a department store, boutique or retailer was that they received income only twice a year, when they delivered their orders. This made the cash-flow situation very difficult. On top of that, consumers had to wait six months before the new season's collections became available. To counter this, a new season was created. Known as the Resort or Cruise collection, its origins go back to the 1920s, when overseas travel became more common, particularly taking a winter cruise. It was designed for those who travelled to warmer climes in the winter and would therefore need a spring- or summer-style wardrobe ahead of the main season. Such collections can also be termed 'pre-season'. The concept of the pre-season has grown in recent years, driven mainly by retailers wanting to sell a higher proportion of merchandise at full price. It is now common practice for fashion designers to release four seasons a year: the original Spring/Summer and Autumn or Fall/Winter collections, along with Pre-Spring and Pre-Fall collections.

The benefits of pre-season

The pre-season offers several business benefits for brands and retailers. It provides stores with new full-price merchandise while the main season products are marked down. It is transitional and trans-seasonal in nature and forms a bridge between the previous season and the next main season. Pre-season products are often simple and functional, and can be readily mixed and matched with other elements of a seasonal wardrobe. Most importantly, pre-season merchandise limits risk for the retailer and can be available in stores selling at full price for up to six months, since the cohesive nature of the pre-season and main season merchandise means that unsold pre-season stock can carry over into the main season and be sold at full price. Pre-season allows the designer to test ideas that are then developed further for the main season, when product details, embellishments and fabrications can be more complicated, richer and more experimental.

The challenges of pre-season

There can, however, be a downside to all this. With a more strenuous roster of shows, there is much more pressure on designers to design, plan and execute many more concepts, produce more and more products, and put on ever more extravagant fashion shows. The concept of the pre-season has rolled over into menswear as well, adding to the overall workload for design teams and expanding the schedule of fashion shows and presentations that take place globally each year.

↓ The main season show: Zegna's Spring/ Summer 2024 Ready-to-Wear show as part of Milan Men's Fashion Week.

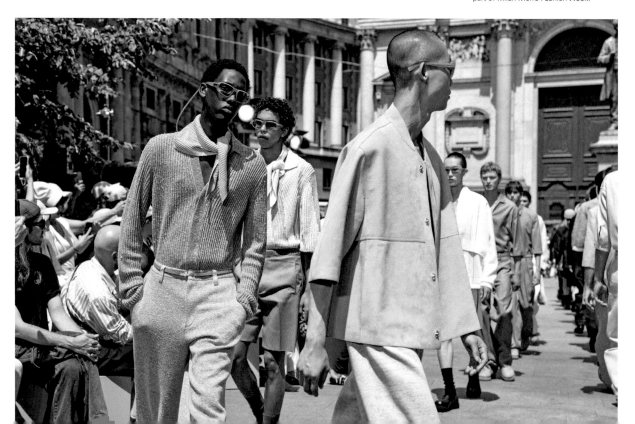

CALENDAR OF MAIN FASHION WEEKS

CITY	COLLECTION	SEASON	TIMING
LONDON	Menswear	Autumn/Winter	January–early February
MILAN			
PARIS			
PARIS	Haute Couture, Women	Spring/Summer	
NEW YORK	Menswear	Autumn/Winter	
NEW YORK	Women's Ready-to-Wear	Autumn/Winter	February–early March
LONDON			
MILAN			
PARIS			
NEW YORK			
LONDON			
MILAN	Menswear	Spring/Summer	Throughout June
PARIS			
PARIS	Haute Couture, Women	Autumn/Winter	End June/early July
NEW YORK	Women's Ready-to-Wear	Spring/Summer	September–early October
LONDON			
MILAN			
PARIS			

This table illustrates just how packed the fashion-week schedule is and how much travel is involved for those who attend all the shows.

New approaches

Concern has been growing about the sustainability of the fashion system, with calls for a more ethical and less environmentally damaging model for the industry. Even before COVID-19, the industry was entering a phase of self-reflection and looking for ways to disrupt the system. These included combining menswear and womenswear presentations (thereby cutting down on the number of shows); creating trans-seasonal collections in an attempt to uncouple from the fashion seasons and make fashions more wearable across the globe; and developing gender-neutral collections. In many cases the new gender-neutral garments constituted not the full collection, but a selection of items in the show, or a capsule additional collection. For Autumn/Winter 2020, for instance, Stella McCartney launched 'Shared', a gender-inclusive capsule collection. The concept was about the 'shared wardrobe', inspired by her parents, who shared clothes. Tommy Hilfiger teamed up with the non-binary actor and activist Indya Moore to produce a pre-fall collection for 2021. The pair raided the Tommy archive to reimagine classic pieces for a gender-neutral collection. For the Louis Vuitton Spring/Summer 2021 collection, Nicolas Ghesquière presented his vision for a gender-neutral future, stating that he wanted to 'abolish the last [gender] frontiers'.

The market for gender-fluid clothing is on the rise. This is highlighted in the article 'The Rise of Gender-Neutral Segment in Fashion' by Srishti Kapoor in *Apparel Resources* (June 2023). The article talks about the rise of this sector within India, where the demand is mainly in the most metropolitan cities, those in which there is a more 'progressive and inclusive mindset'. It mentions several Indian fashion designers who are creating gender-neutral collections, among them Parul Gupta (the designer behind the brand Yuga); the label One Less by Hansika Chhabria; and Mriga Kapadiya and Amrit Kumar, co-founders of NorBlack NorWhite.

Market research has shown that the gender-neutral fashion market could grow by 6.5 per cent year on year. In December 2022 the *Business of Fashion* (BoF) posted an article entitled 'The Year Ahead: Gender-Fluid Fashion Hits the High Street'. Research by the BoF team and McKinsey & Company stated that the interest in gender-fluid/gender-neutral or androgynous* fashion is driven mainly by Gen Z customers, and that 'around half of Gen Z globally have purchased fashion outside of their gender identity.' It went on to say that 'online searches for "genderless" and "gender neutral" fashion are increasing year on year.'

Genderless or gender-inclusive fashion brands are situated across the market, from the top-end designer level to more affordable mid- and mass-market labels. Most notable are Telfar, by Telfar Clemens, and Aimé Leon Dore, founded by Teddy Santis. Neither brand markets to either gender specifically, and both their websites show products categorized by type and not by gender. Other androgynous or gender-fluid brands include Big Bud Press from Los Angeles; Bode New York by Emily Bode; JACQ by LGBTQI+ designer Jackie Yang, who was raised in Singapore; Barragán, founded by the Mexican-born Victor Barragán; and Junya Watanabe, the avant-garde Japanese designer whose collections blur the line between fashion, sculpture, menswear and womenswear. In the United Kingdom there is the British designer Charles Jeffrey Loverboy and the British-American designer Harris Reed, both of whom are known for their political stance when it comes to fashion and inclusion. Stella McCartney's website has a unisex section that features sweatshirts, shirts, trackpants, bucket hats and baseball caps, shoes and bags. In 2023 Dior featured the Chinese pop star Liu Yuxin as the new

↑ The New York-based Dominican-American designer Raul Lopez is the creative force behind the fashion label Luar. The brand's Spring/Summer 2022 presentation, featuring Lopez's androgynous designs, took place in an underground car park in Brooklyn during New York Fashion Week.

*The terms gender-fluid, gender-neutral, androgynous and gender-inclusive have been used interchangeably in this section to indicate the growing market within fashion. Other terms, such as 'unisex' and 'gender-free', are also being used to describe fashion collections. The appropriate use of these terms must be considered carefully to communicate effectively to target audiences.

face of its campaign for the new genderless, inclusive fragrance Gris Dior. According to an article by Umesh Bhagchandani in the *South China Morning Post* in May that year, she was chosen for her 'distinctive androgynous style … and gender neutral approach to self-expression'.

See Now Buy Now

See Now Buy Now (SNBN) surfaced around 2015 and was adopted by Burberry in 2017. Burberry called its collection and presentation 'The February Show', and it featured seasonless collections for both men and women, thus uncoupling Burberry from the seasonal merry-go-round described earlier in this chapter. The idea of this marketing tactic is for customers and fashion followers to be able to purchase pieces from the collection either during the show or directly afterwards. Immediacy is the name of the game, and this newer business model reduces the time it takes for products to get to market after the collection is shown. This creates a sense of urgency to 'buy now' that is completely at odds with the traditional

↓ The Burberry February Show in 2017 featured the label's fashion alongside sculptures and drawings by the artist Henry Moore. The aim was to present a seasonless show of both womenswear and menswear, rather than adhering to the traditional seasonal fashion calendar.

system of 'see now and wait', where the process takes six months. An article in *The National* newsletter in May 2019 commented that 'by cutting that time lag … SNBN offers a direct connection to a new, more demanding consumer.'

However, the process of converting from the traditional cycle to the SNBN timing is not easy, nor is it cheap. To do this, a brand must forgo an entire season, missing the normal scheduled shows, which can mean a whole season of lost sales. Imagine the fashion system is like a carousel; a brand must jump off this ever-revolving cycle and pause while it adjusts all its timings in order to climb aboard a new carousel, one that is spinning out of sync with the original. Before the pandemic, this shift proved to be too disruptive for several of the brands that trialled the new approach, Thakoon and Tom Ford among them, and after a couple of seasons they switched back to the familiarity of the old system. Producing a collection that can be purchased as soon as it is shown can be achieved more easily by a new start-up business that integrates this business model from the get-go.

The SNBN model resurfaced again for Autumn 2021, when the French designer brand Jacquemus announced that its 'La Montagne' collection would be available straight after the runway show. The collection could be purchased on the Jacquemus website, as well as on Net-A-Porter, Matches and Selfridges. Jacquemus stated that the aim was to 'maintain the momentum between the presentation and product availability'. It is also interesting to note that this system works on-season, so an SNBN presentation taking place in September will be for the current Autumn/Winter season, rather than – as would traditionally have been the case – for the following Spring/Summer.

Direct-to-consumer

Direct-to-consumer, usually abbreviated to D2C or DTC, has been made possible mainly by the rise in e-commerce and m-commerce (mobile), and for many start-ups this is the preferred way to operate. D2C is when the company manufactures and ships its products directly to the customer, rather than relying on selling to a traditional store. This way of operating offers a range of benefits. It is a more agile method of doing business than the slower and often more risky wholesale model. Brands can control their own distribution and production time frames, respond to customer demand and react much more easily to market trends. The use of social media for promotion and marketing can help them to reach new customers and build deeper relationships with existing purchasers and brand engagers.

↑ The actor and singer Victoria Justice takes part in Rebecca Minkoff's 'See Now, Buy Now' fashion show at The Grove, Los Angeles, in 2017.

The D2C model has been highly successful for US e-commerce businesses such as the shoe brand Allbirds, Everlane (which focuses on modern basics), the eyewear brand Warby Parker, and the denim brand AYR (All Year Round). The British Fashion Council (BFC) released a report in 2019 backing its belief that the D2C model has significant potential to 'power a new wave of growth' for the British fashion industry. In the report, the BFC identifies several key factors relevant to the D2C model. The first is the importance of the product proposition. At Everlane, for example, this means timeless classics that customers can wear for years; the Allbirds product proposition is to produce a comfortable shoe in natural materials; and for AYR it is to 'design seasonless essentials for everyday life', and to create 'confidence through clothing'. AYR, founded in 2014, is 'not about the label or logo. It's about the woman who wears it.' This links well with the second key factor identified by the BFC: a 'collaborative dynamic' between brand and end-consumer. In the D2C model, customer insight and feedback are integral to the concept, and the brand seeks actively to learn from its customers. With so many brands out there for customers to choose from, and because many D2C fashion brands offer seasonless classics, it is important for the brand to find a way to stand apart – to be distinctive and have a particular point of view that will resonate with customers.

Nothing stays still in fashion, and although D2C was the initial mode of business, many of the pioneer D2C brands are now investing in physical stores. The beauty brand Glossier has several stores in the United States and one in London, and in 2022 the eyewear retailer Warby Parker opened 40 stores, with plans for further expansion.

HANDCRAFTED AND MADE TO ORDER

GORAL SHOES

GORAL is a family-owned business in Sheffield, UK. It has been handcrafting shoes for more than 80 years. Every pair is made to order in the GORAL workshop and shipped directly to the customer. This reduces overproduction and waste, and keeps the price as low as possible by cutting out any wholesalers or retailers that would add a mark-up. All of the production takes place at the GORAL workshop by master craftspeople, so that GORAL can proudly claim the high standard expected of 'Made in England' high-quality products.

The shoes are made using the same traditional methods that Franciszek Goral first used when he set up the business in 1936. Each shoe goes through over 200 separate stages from start to completion. Most of the shoe components are sourced locally, with leather coming from a local tannery, or from tanneries in Europe.

With many D2C companies that operate online, it is not really possible to see behind the scenes, and the brand may not reveal much about the production or where clothes or products are manufactured. But with GORAL, everything is shown clearly on the website. There are films showing the production processes and photographs of the craftspeople, and customers can even arrange to visit the factory personally, to see their shoes being made. What is more, GORAL wants its customers to be able to keep and treasure their shoes for a lifetime. It therefore offers a lifetime repair guarantee and a resoling service called REBUILD+, which offers resoling and refurbishing of the shoes.

↑ The Goral Skelton waxed-cotton low-top trainers.

← A diagram on the Goral website compares the company's made-to-order approach with the more traditional mass-production model.

↙ An image of the shoe split into its constituent parts, detailing the components of a hand-crafted Goral shoe.

TRADITIONAL MODEL

MASS PRODUCTION

x50+

50 PAIRS PER COLOURWAY (MINIMUM)
outsourced

WEB   RETAIL

CUSTOMER   LANDFILL

OUR MODEL

MADE TO ORDER PRODUCTION

x1

ONE PAIR
in-house

DIRECT DELIVERY, NO THIRD PARTY

CUSTOMER

→ Adele Dejak is a Nigerian jewellery
designer based in Nairobi, Kenya.
Here, a model backstage wears
Dejak's dramatic oversize earrings
at AFI Cape Town Fashion Week in
South Africa in 2018.

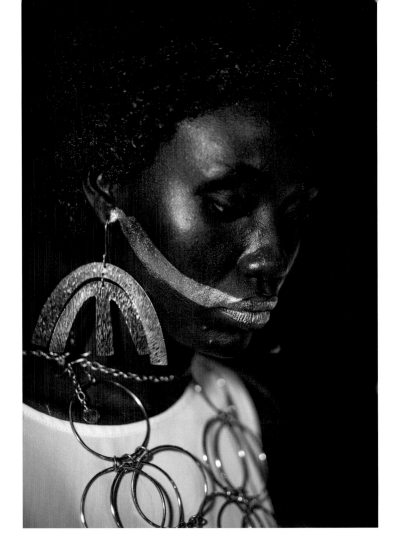

Global regions

For the purposes of business and marketing, continents or countries
may be clustered into regions. You might see in someone's business
title that they are vice president of marketing EMEA, for example.
EMEA stands for Europe, Middle East and Africa. APAC – Asia Pacific
– is another common acronym, encompassing East Asia, South Asia,
Southeast Asia and Oceania (Australia, New Zealand and Pacific
islands, including Fiji, Papua New Guinea, French Polynesia and the
Maldives). AMER refers to North, Central and South America. MENA
is used for the Middle East and North Africa, and BRIC signifies
Brazil, Russia, India and China.

Global fashion weeks and trade fairs

Traditionally the main centres for fashion were Paris, London, Milan
and New York, with each hosting biannual Fashion Week events
to showcase the women's collections. Menswear collections are
shown twice a year in Paris, London and Milan, and there is growing
pressure to mount a New York showcase for menswear.

Perhaps less well known is the range of other cities that host Fashion Week shows and events: Amsterdam, Beijing, Berlin, Brisbane, Cape Town, Colombo, Dakar, Istanbul, Johannesburg, Kyiv, Lagos, Los Angeles, Miami, Moscow, Mumbai, Stockholm, Sydney, Tokyo, Toronto and Zurich. There is also a Digital Fashion Week in New York, and Metaverse Fashion Week launched in 2022.

Added to this is an enormous number of trade fairs. There is Première Vision fabric fair in Paris; Pitti Immagine Filati, a yarn fair in Florence; and Modefabriek in Amsterdam, with brand presentations, fashion shows, expos, talks and masterclasses. Spain, which is well known for the manufacture of footwear and leather goods, holds an international leather goods trade fair, MOMAD Metropolis, incorporating Modacalzado + Iberpiel in Madrid and Futurmoda in Alicante. This is only a minute selection of what is on offer; there are also international bridal shows, swimwear collections, lingerie shows, denim and sportswear trade events, dance fashion and full-figured fashion collections.

The emergence of global fashion in so many locations is especially beneficial to new designers in markets around the world, giving them a platform to show to local and regional press and buyers, as well as to the increasing number of international fashion professionals who attend. However, the sway of the big four fashion nations – France, the UK, Italy and the USA – and their fashion capitals should not be underestimated.

↙ The South Korean fashion designer Minju Kim has become known for her style, which combines youthful playfulness and avant-garde haute couture. Her imaginative collections present bold silhouettes with feminine characteristics and an overarching joyfulness. Pictured below is Kim's show at the Fashion in Motion event staged at the Victoria and Albert Museum, London, in April 2023.

↓ Models backstage during the Lino Villaventura fashion show, São Paulo Fashion Week, May 2023.

← Emmy Kasbit, the fashion label designed by Emmanuel Okoro, shows at Lagos Fashion Week in October 2022. This annual Fashion Week provides a platform for African designers to present their collections to buyers, media and fashion enthusiasts in Nigeria's commercial capital.

Paris

Paris is the spiritual home of fashion and the epicentre of haute couture. Paris Fashion Week is considered a particularly prestigious place to show, and designers from all over the world choose to present their seasonal ready-to-wear collections in the city – and also haute couture, if they have been accepted by the Fédération. France's historic fashion houses, such as Louis Vuitton, Dior, Chanel, Hermès and Saint Laurent, show there, along with a raft of internationally known designer brands: among them Rick Owens, Off-White, The Row and Thom Browne from the United States, Valentino from Italy, Issey Miyake, Comme des Garçons and Sacai from Japan, Ann Demeulemeester and Dries Van Noten from Belgium, Acne Studios from Sweden, and Akris and Ottolinger from Switzerland.

The list of designers who show in Paris is not always the same. Designers often choose to change their location. For example, Victoria Beckham moved her presentation from London to Paris, debuting there for her Spring/Summer 2023 collection.

As well as Paris Fashion Week, there is Prêt à Porter Paris® at the Porte de Versailles, a trade show where over a thousand exhibitors from a variety of fashion markets exhibit their product. There is also Première Classe, a fashion accessory show, and Première Vision, or PV, which is held twice a year. This is the largest European textile trade show and a major date in the calendar for international designers and buyers. The fair is an important trade opportunity for textile suppliers from all over the world, but fashion designers and

buyers visit because of its focus on colour and trend prediction. Paris also hosts Le Cuir à Paris, showing the latest trends in leather.

London

Ever since the Swinging Sixties and Mary Quant, London has been famous for its street style and avant-garde fashion, and this remains one of the city's biggest claims to fashion fame. During the 1990s and up to 2011, it was the designers themselves who became London's greatest fashion export. John Galliano, Alexander McQueen and Stella McCartney worked in fashion houses in Paris, and many other hard-working British or London-trained designers continue to find employment in New York, Milan, China, India and Japan. London is a magnet for fashion students from around the globe. After graduation some stay on, start their own labels and make London their base.

London Fashion Week is a major event on the fashion circuit. British designers and brands, such as Burberry, Christopher Kane, JW Anderson, Erdem, Simone Rocha, Richard Quinn, Eudon Choi, Molly Goddard and Margaret Howell, all show in London, as do some overseas labels and international designers who have made the city their home.

↑ In February 2018 Queen Elizabeth II attended the Richard Quinn runway show at London Fashion Week. The Queen is seated between Anna Wintour, editor-in-chief of US *Vogue* and chief content officer for Condé Nast (third from left), and Caroline Rush, chief executive of the British Fashion Council.

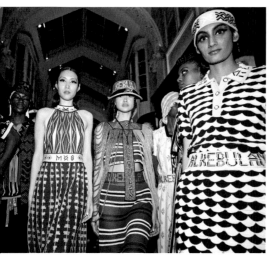

↑ Maxhosa is a South African brand
founded by Laduma Ngxokolo in 2010.
The collections celebrate traditional
Xhosa patterns, colours and beadwork,
realized through knitwear stitches and
printed textiles.

London also hosts India Fashion Week and Africa Fashion Week. Founded by Ronke Ademiluyi, the latter is the largest annual catwalk showing of African fashion in Europe. According to the event website, the work of more than 800 emerging designers and exhibitors from Africa, Europe and America is presented to almost 70,000 visitors. In 2022 the designers included London-based Toomey & Koko, Ade Bakare from Nigeria, Mumini Fashion from Sierra Leone, Soboye (the label of London-based Samson Soboye), Maxhosa (see left) from South Africa, and Kaffy Kreate from Abuja in Nigeria.

For wholesale brands, there are trade shows such as Pure London, which gives a platform to over 800 brands. Although not traditional fashion trade fairs, the spring and autumn fairs at the NEC (National Exhibition Centre) in Birmingham and Top Drawer and Pulse in London showcase companies selling gifts and fashion accessories, such as bags, scarves, hats and jewellery.

Milan

Italian couture, or alta moda (literally 'high fashion'), can be traced back to 1951, when the Marquis Giovanni Battista Giorgini held the first haute couture fashion show in Florence for a select few designers and clients. Rome took over as the centre for high fashion in Italy during the 1960s but lost ground during the 1970s and 80s to Milan, which became the commercial capital for Italian ready-to-wear.

Today, Italy is an important country for the design and manufacture of luxury and mid-market fashion, with particular expertise in leather goods, footwear, knitwear and high-quality ready-to-wear for both men and women. Milan is a major trade centre, where most of the design houses have their headquarters and where the majority of Italian fashion shows take place. It is also an important location for Italian fashion magazine publishing, so satellite industries, such as styling, photography and modelling, also gravitate to the city.

In addition, Italy is well known for its textile industry; Florence and Prato are important centres for the manufacture of yarn and knitwear, Como produces silk fabrics and the Piedmont area manufactures wool textiles. Key industry trade fairs and catwalk shows are held in Milan, Florence and Rome. Milan hosts Milano Moda Donna for women's ready-to-wear, and Milano Moda Uomo for menswear. AltaRomaAltaModa in Rome shows Italian couture and high-level ready-to-wear, and Florence is the location for the Pitti Immagine Filati knitwear and yarn fair, the Pitti Immagine Uomo menswear fair and Pitti Immagine Bimbo childrenswear fair.

The Fashion Market   69

←↑ The London Edge trade fair caters for the alternative clubwear market. Within this market there are several niche categories, such as gothic, punk, cyber, techno, glam rock, heavy metal, rockabilly, industrial, underground, festival, ethnic and biker. London Central trade fair, meanwhile, focuses on urban streetwear, showcasing brands covering the skate, hip hop, surf and hippy end of the youth market.

New York

New York is the heart of the US fashion and apparel industry, and some of the world's most recognizable brands, among them Donna Karan, Ralph Lauren, Tommy Hilfiger and Kenneth Cole have their offices and design studios in the city. American fashion is renowned for its relaxed, fluid, casual and chic style, epitomized by such designers as Lauren and Karan, as well as Michael Kors and Calvin Klein. Retailers like Gap and Banana Republic also have strong global appeal for their accessible and desirable fashion.

Historically, apparel and textiles constituted one of the USA's largest manufacturing sectors. In recent years it has suffered a decline owing to competition from other manufacturing countries, such as China, and there is a drive to support a renaissance for American apparel manufacturing. A growing number of fashion brands manufacture onshore in the USA, among them Haspel, AMVi, Grown & Sewn, New Balance and Reformation.

Before the pandemic, Fashion Week in New York attracted 100,000 trade and press visitors and brought huge economic benefits to the city, generating US$850 million in visitor spending each year. After the pandemic, the show still featured over 100 brands showing over five and a half days, and included runway shows, appointment-only viewings and immersive experiences. In 2022 the roster of designers and brands included the Italian houses Fendi and Marni, along with US brands Carolina Herrera, Christian Siriano, Anna Sui, Gabriela Hearst, Prabal Gurung and LaQuan Smith, to name just a few.

Several key trade and fabric shows are held in the USA. There is the New York Fabric Show and Texworld New York City. Kingpins is a denim and sportswear fabric fair with events in New York City, as well as Amsterdam and China. LA Textile is held in the California Market Center in Los Angeles. Portland, Oregon, is an important centre for fashion and active sportswear companies. Nike, Adidas, Columbia Sportswear, Jantzen swimwear and Keen footwear all have headquarters there.

↓ The Princess of Wales wears a bright green dress by Solace, London. This dress was rented from the UK rental platform HURR for the Earthshot Prize in December 2022 in Boston, Massachusetts, a ceremony for which guests were requested not to buy new.

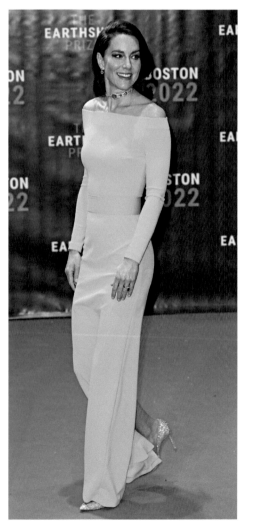

Other fashion markets

In addition to the basic fashion sectors described so far, there are other markets, such as vintage or thrift fashion, sustainable fashion, luxury resale and rental fashion. The growth of these sectors has been fuelled by a raft of online social platforms catering to all levels, from luxury resale to thrift and upcycling.

The resale market

This market is made up of charity shops and specialist vintage or thrift fashion shops, as well as a growing number of online resale platforms. Examples of the last category include ThredUP, an online consignment and thrift store; Vinted, an online marketplace with a community of 75 million users who can buy, sell or swap new or second-hand clothes and accessories; and Depop, a peer-to-peer social app that allows users to buy and sell second-hand, upcycled and handmade fashion items. Over 30 million people signed up to Depop, mainly 18–26-year-olds in the UK and USA, with 3.3 million active buyers and 1.8 million active sellers in 2023 according to the *Business of Apps*. The resale sector also has more upmarket options. Vestiaire Collective is a global online marketplace where it is possible to buy and sell authenticated pre-owned luxury fashion. The online fashion platform Farfetch launched its Second Life service, allowing customers to resell designer bags to gain store credits, and its competitor Net-A-Porter teamed with Reflaunt to offer a pre-loved luxury resale option – again in return for store credits.

The resale market is growing fast. According to Statista, the global market value of second-hand and resale fashion was US$96 billion in 2021, and a global report conducted by ThredUP in conjunction with the market-research company GlobalData suggests that the second-hand fashion market will be twice the size of traditional retail and fast fashion by 2030. An article by Amy de Klerk in *Harper's Bazaar* in June 2021 explains that the research also showed that Millennial and Gen Z customers are reticent about purchasing new sustainable clothing in comparison to second-hand, owing to the higher price of sustainable fashion and concerns about what is termed **greenwashing**. This is when the sustainable credentials of a product or company are promoted, when the total picture is perhaps not as positive as the marketing material claims it to be. This relates particularly to the use of such terminology as 'eco-friendly' or 'sustainable', which are vague and not easily verifiable. An example was highlighted in a report by the Changing Markets Foundation, which found that H&M was using labels stating that clothing was "Conscious" or a "Conscious Choice" without any explanation as to the actual sustainable benefits of the products.

Rental fashion

The rental market is also growing. According to experts cited in an article by Fashion United in November 2021, the global online fashion-rental market is set to reach a value of just over US$2 billion by 2025, almost double the figure from 2019. The article also highlights that there will be significant growth in the rental market throughout the Asia Pacific region. The luxury rental market is driven by consumers' desire to wear designer labels without owning the items. This way it is possible to keep up to date with fashion but with a more responsible and sustainable approach, by renting, reusing and sharing rather than direct purchasing.

By Rotation, founded by Eshita Kabra-Davies in the UK in 2019, is a peer-to-peer rental app. According to the website, users – or 'Rotators', as they are termed – can rent and lend their designer fashion directly among themselves, thereby creating a community of sharers. In the USA there is Rent the Runway, which follows a membership model and is one of fashion's biggest rental sites. Other fashion rental sites include HURR, My Wardrobe HQ, Janet Mandell and Fashion to Figure Closet (the last of which offers larger sizes, 12–24 and XL–3XL).

The vintage market

Vintage or thrift fashion refers to collectable second-hand garments, shoes or accessories from the past, sold in specialist vintage stores or charity shops and on websites. An increasing number of consumers choose vintage or thrift as a way to make a fashion statement, stand out from the crowd, save money, and/or be more sustainable and consume less. The scope of the

Vintage paradise

BEACON'S CLOSET

The three Beacon's Closet stores are well-known destinations for those seeking original vintage finds in New York. The Manhattan store, near Parsons School for Design and New York University, is a favourite spot for emerging designers to find inspiration for their work, and has featured in *Vanity Fair*, Italian *Vogue* and French *Vogue*. The website has a fresh, contemporary vibe, and the Beacon's Blog is kept up to date with posts on essential fashion information and trends. Key seasonal looks are promoted on the homepage with styled photo shoots worthy of a top fashion magazine.

← The stylist Bunny Lampert created this New Year's Eve themed look to promote the holiday season on the Beacon's Closet website. The models are all staff members, including one of the co-owners, Cindy Wheeler. The photograph was taken by Carly Rabalais, who runs the online store.

market varies from second-hand merchandise in a thrift or charity store to rare designer dresses. Buying luxury vintage fashion has become an interesting way of investing, and many people now view vintage items as tradable assets. Stores such as Liberty in London and Bergdorf Goodman in New York recognize the potential of vintage, and both now house curated selections of vintage fashion. The online world of vintage has also had a makeover. Sites such as It's Vintage Darling and Juno Says Hello offer luxury vintage fashion online.

There is, however, a troubling side to the second-hand or thrift clothing market. Many of the garments donated end up not in a store, but in landfill. The donor of the items may do so in good faith, but thrift stores and charity shops in the USA and UK can't always cope with the volume of items they receive. The excess is shipped overseas, often to Africa (15 million garments are shipped to Ghana every week, for example), where they are sold cheaply in street markets or dumped in landfill.

It is worth thinking carefully about whether donating to a charity shop is the right step, particularly when it comes to fast fashion. Organizing a clothing swap or using a resale app could be better alternatives. Mending, altering, upcycling or deconstructing clothing to make other items are other possibilities to consider.

Sustainable fashion

The sustainable fashion or conscious consumption market is another that is set to grow. A Research and Markets report published in 2022 estimated that ethical fashion reached a value of US$5.84 billion in 2021 and is expected to reach US$8.3 billion by 2025.

The ethics of fashion production, the sustainability of the products and processes, and the impact of over-consumption on the climate are of great concern within the fashion industry, and also for many consumers. The fashion industry is reported to account for 5–10 per cent of global greenhouse-gas emissions. Issues of sustainability and ethics affect every aspect of the fashion supply chain, from production of raw materials, clothing manufacture, distribution and marketing through to retail. Determining what is or is not sustainable is extremely complicated, and this is not helped by the fact that 'sustainable fashion', or 'eco-fashion', is used as an umbrella term to describe a range of practices that include:

» Use of certified organic fibres, such as cotton or linen

» Use of renewable fibres, such as bamboo and maize

» Recycling of fibres, fabrics and garments

» Upcycling, mending and repair

» Use of natural dyes or low-impact dyes

» Breaking the cycle of consumption by creating a long-lasting product

» Fair-trade raw materials and fibres

» Ethical labour and ethical farming practices

» Reduction in energy consumption

» Minimal, reduced and/or biodegradable packaging

» Adopting circular economic principles

A growing number of designers, fashion retailers, industry bodies, governments and legislators are working to clarify the issues, set clear standards and introduce regulation in an attempt to improve the situation. An article in the *New York Times* by Elizabeth Paton in

↑ Parmis Beyzaei is a designer and pattern-maker with a commitment to upcycling and a keen focus on sustainability. She breathes new life into discarded materials, crafting a limited series of unique items that resonate with conscious consumers. She started by upcycling old pairs of unused trainers during the COVID-19 pandemic and sold them through the luxury concept store WEDLT117 in Toronto. She then started a TikTok, @not parmis_, which she uses to sell her pieces, experiment and increase her audience.

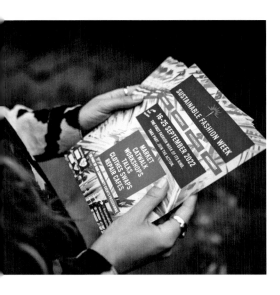

↑ Flyers for Sustainable Fashion Week, London, 2022.

October 2022 catalogued some of the proposals. France, for example, announced that from 1 January 2024 every item of clothing would 'require a label detailing its precise climate impact'. The rule states that manufacturers will have to list the amount of water required in making the item, the use of chemicals, risks from microplastics and information on any recycled textiles used. At the end of 2023 France also brought in a new repair bonus scheme. This offers a discount worth between €6 and €25 per repair, for example €7 for a new heel and €10–25 for a new lining in a jacket. The cost to the French government for the duration of this five-year scheme is estimated at €154 million. The aim is to support the repair sector and create new jobs.

In 2021 the Garment Worker Protection Act was passed by the state of California. This requires manufacturers to pay hourly wages for garment workers and to prohibit payment by piecework (when workers are paid per garment). The act aims to ensure that manufacturers and fashion brands are penalized for illegal pay practices. The New York Fashion Sustainability and Social Accountability Act, known as the Fashion Act (Bill number S7428/A8352), is a proposed state bill that, if passed, would hold fashion brands selling in New York State that generate revenue of more than US$100 million to be accountable for their environmental and social impact in terms of labour practices, greenhouse gas emissions and chemical use. Other legislative steps are being taken in Europe, also designed to work towards a more sustainable future (see Chapter 3).

Opportunities to sell and promote wholesale collections of sustainable fashion are improving, with London Fashion Week, Prêt à Porter Paris®, Berlin Fashion Week, New York Fashion Week and Portland Fashion Week all incorporating sustainable fashion within their remit. There is also an increasing number of dedicated eco-fashion weeks, among them Brasil Eco Fashion Week, which has been taking place since 2017 in São Paulo; and an Eco-Fashion Week in Vancouver. Globally, there is an increasing number of conferences and related trade initiatives designed to educate and support the growth of this sector.

Sustainable fashion is a difficult subject because there is a lack of clarity on what exactly constitutes 'sustainable', and most fashion initiatives tackle one element but not all at once. There are several different types of accreditation, but no single universal system. One type of accreditation that is gaining traction is B Corp.

B Corps

B Corps are companies that have been verified by the non-profit organization B Lab as meeting high standards of verified performance, accountability and transparency on factors from employee benefits and charitable giving to supply-chain practices and input material. B Labs was launched in 2006, and the B stands for Benefit for all. Since its inception, more than 150,000 businesses have signed up to be assessed, but only a small percentage gain the valued B Corp accreditation. According to the B Corp website, in order to achieve certification, a company must:

» Demonstrate high social and environmental performance by achieving a B Impact Assessment score of 80 or above and passing the B Labs risk review

» Make a legal commitment to ensure that its corporate governance structure is accountable to all stakeholders, not just shareholders

» Show transparency by allowing information about its performance measured against B Lab's standards to be made publicly available on its profile on B Lab's website

The B Corp Declaration of Interdependence highlights a vision where business is used as a force for good, with an emerging economy driven by B Corporations who believe:

» That they will be the change they seek in the world

» That all business ought to be conducted as if people and place mattered

» That, through their products, practices and profits, businesses should aspire to do no harm and to benefit all

» That we are each dependent upon one another and thus responsible for each other and future generations

At the time of writing 233 fashion businesses and brands were listed on the B Corp site as certified. These include Wakami, a social business that designs, develops and exports fashion accessories, clothing and decoration products made in rural communities in Guatemala; the American casual and outerwear brand Patagonia; the French fashion house Chloé; the fair-trade trainer brand Veja; the US company Unspun, which runs a design studio and micro-factory in California. Mud Jeans (see page 78) was one of the first to gain B Corp status. It pioneered a leasing model, whereby customers can lease jeans and return them after use, putting circular economy principles into practice.

The circular economy

The world's economy is run on a linear model, whereby natural resources are used to make products that may then be discarded after use and end up in landfill. This can be described by the shorthand: Take–Make–Waste. A circular approach, on the other hand, operates on a Reduce–Reuse–Recycle principle. The aim is to increase a product's lifespan and the amount it is used, then recycle it or its materials back into the economy. Another option is to ensure that it is biodegradable and can be used in some way to regenerate nature. The aim of a circular economy is for waste to be fed back into the system and reused over and over again for as long as possible. In this way, the waste becomes the new raw material and the cycle becomes truly circular.

The Ellen MacArthur Foundation is a charity committed to creating a circular economy, which it sees as an economic system designed to deliver better outcomes for people and the environment. The Foundation is one of the most prominent authorities that researches the concept and practice of circular design and economy. Its website states that the circular economy is 'a systems solution framework that tackles global challenges like climate change, biodiversity loss, waste, and pollution. It is based on three principles, driven by design: eliminate waste and pollution, circulate products and materials (at their highest value), and regenerate nature.'

FROM A LINEAR TO A CIRCULAR ECONOMY

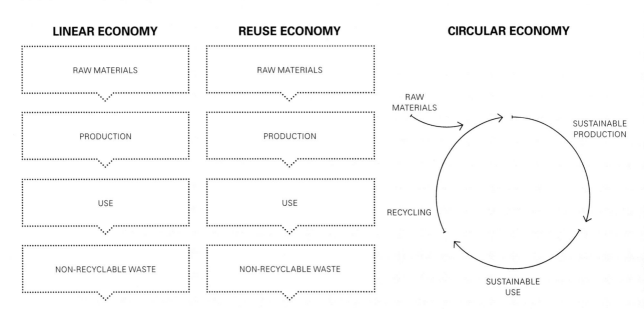

This diagram (adapted from one at www.government.nl) shows the transition from a linear economy that goes from raw materials to waste, with no recycling or reuse, to a reuse economy where there is some recycling, but that still ends up with non-recyclable waste. The aim is to establish a circular economy, where the raw materials are used continuously and only recyclable waste produced.

The Foundation believes that we need to develop 'innovative fashion production systems, materials and business models that allow clothes to have less impact on the environment, be worn [for] longer and turned into new clothes when no longer needed'. Its website and the reports it produces offer a wealth of information on the circular economy. There are several case studies relating to fashion, including the use of dissolvable thread, developed by the start-up Resortecs, which helps with the recycling of clothes. It is normally a lengthy process to unpick stitching when disassembling clothes for recycling, but this new type of thread can be melted in a commercial oven.

Another way of addressing over-consumption is for consumers to buy less and buy better, taking the trouble to understand the provenance of their garments and the materials from which they are made. This is similar to the idea of knowing where food is grown and sourced. There is a movement called slow fashion that has sprung up in the wake of the 'slow food' movement.

Slow fashion

Slow fashion advocates for a conscious approach to environmental and social justice in the fashion industry. The aim is to tackle over-consumption and overproduction, the idea being to buy fewer items of higher quality, and to choose brands that produce trendless or seasonless designs that are made to last longer than the throwaway approach of fast fashion. The philosophy aims for a shift from quantity to quality in both production and consumption. It's not hell-bent on constant growth or the idea that customers should accumulate more. The aims for slow fashion are:

» Quality not quantity

» Producing collections in small batches

» Using low-impact materials

» Working on a pre-order basis to avoid unsold stock

» Local production where possible

» Using deadstock (fabric that has not been used up from previous collections)

» Paying workers a fair wage and ensuring ethical working conditions

Good on You is an app founded in Australia in 2015 by Gordon Renouf and Sandra Capponi. It has rated more than 3,000 fashion brands, analysing their impact on people, planet and animals. A long list of criteria determines the Good on You rating, including:

Creating a world without waste

MUD JEANS

Bert van Son founded MUD Jeans in 2012. From the very beginning, he wanted to do things differently. Jeans are one of the most polluting items in fashion. According to the United States Geological Survey, it takes 6,800 litres (1,800 gallons) of water to grow enough cotton to make just one pair. From the outset, MUD Jeans put circular principles into practice with its 'Lease a Pair of Jeans' business model, and it was one of the first companies to be awarded B Corp status. Its jeans are made with a mixture of organic and recycled cotton, and each pair requires only 373 litres (98 gallons) of water to make.

The brand operates a take-back scheme, collecting jeans of any brand as long as they are at least 96 per cent cotton. In collaboration with denim experts at Recover and Tejidos Royo in Valencia, Spain, the fabrics are shredded and blended with virgin cotton, thus producing a 'new' denim yarn for the next pair of MUD Jeans, containing up to 40 per cent post-consumer recycled cotton. The design of the jeans is thought about very carefully to ensure they can operate in a circular system; for example, the labels on MUD Jeans are printed, not leather. This means that the worn-out jeans can be recycled more easily.

Van Son and his team admit that it can be difficult for brands to adopt the circular approach: 'In order to make the circular economy an attractive proposition in fashion, recycled cotton would have to be cheaper than newly produced cotton, and not the other way around.' Sadly, this is not the case yet. Even so, MUD Jeans has chosen to be a pioneer, showing the world that it can create a circular denim brand. This at least is proof of concept, and it is to be hoped that other brands will follow.

↙ Campaign images from the MUD Jeans press kit 2023.

↓ A diagram on the MUD Jeans website explains how the brand's circular system works. Customers can either lease or buy a pair of Mud jeans, which can be sent back after use to be upcycled as vintage jeans or recycled into new jeans.

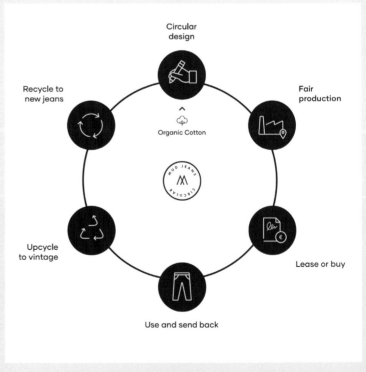

Circular design

Recycle to new jeans

Organic Cotton

Fair production

Upcycle to vintage

Lease or buy

Use and send back

» Environment and resource management

» Workers' rights and gender equality

» Worker empowerment

» Supply chain and supply-chain relationships

» Animal welfare

» Animal materials and products used

» Traceability of animal materials

The aim is to help fashion customers to make informed choices. According to Good on You's guide to its rating system, brands and products are rated as Great, Good, It's a Start, Not Good Enough, or We Avoid. The organization believes it is making a difference, and states that such big brands as Nike and H&M are contacting it to find out how they might improve their Good on You score. It also has a list of fashion brands that it considers to be the best at slow fashion. The ones it rates as Good include D2C brand Asket; Unrecorded from the Netherlands, selling non-seasonal unisex clothing; the German brand Lanius, a member of the Fair Wear Foundation that uses Global Organic Textile Standard-certified organic cotton; and Dressarte Paris, which sources luxurious surplus fabrics to produce custom-made fashion for its global clientele.

Mend and repair

Closely aligned to the concept of slow fashion is the idea of making clothes last, looking after them well, and mending or repairing them to ensure they can be used in the long term. A growing number of repair services are emerging to cater to this rising customer need. In 2023 the Spanish brand Loewe opened Loewe ReCraft, a dedicated repair shop, within the luxury department store Hankyu Umeda in Osaka, Japan. Boasting an in-house artisan, it offers repairs, restoration and maintenance for Loewe leather products. In a statement, the brand explained, 'Loewe ReCraft is about the joy of craft beyond the new. It's a commitment to breathing fresh life into long-cherished possessions.'

SOJO is a UK repair app started by Josephine Philips in 2021. With the aim of making it easier for younger generations to get their clothes mended or altered, instead of buying new, the app connects its customers with local sewers and sewing shops. The company acquired the zero-emissions courier Spedal in 2023 to strengthen its operations. Couriers on bikes collect items for mending; the clothes are then worked on before being delivered back to the customer.

↑ The clothing repair company SOJO uses bike couriers to collect items that need repair or alteration and to return them to their owners once the process is complete.

In the USA there is Coblrshop, a start-up founded by tech veterans Leslie Bateman and Emily Watts. The number of craftspeople with the skills to mend shoes and leather goods declined during the twentieth century. According to the *Sourcing Journal*, in the 1920s there were 100,000 cobblers in the USA; there are now fewer than 4,000. This makes it hard for people to find someone to mend their shoes and handbags – hence the need for such a service. Customers submit a repair order online, then receive a mailer bag and pre-paid shipping label so that they can send their item in for repair. Once mended, the shoes or bag are returned in a fresh new box and shoebag. Coblrshop uses recyclable and compostable packaging materials to reduce the impact of shipping and delivery.

As you can see from the small selection of sustainable initiatives outlined here, several of them have shared principles, and each is trying to tackle the situation in its own way. In terms of services that customers require or expect, embedding repair and alteration services, recycling schemes or circular systems might offer competitive advantage for a brand. When customers are choosing between one brand and another, it may be these approaches and extra services that make the difference, not only for the customer's decision but also for the planet. In 2023 *The Sustainable Fashion Communication Playbook* was published. This was developed by the United Nations Environment Programme (UNEP) and the United Nations Framework Convention on Climate Change's Fashion Industry Charter for Climate Action. It states that 'Communicators must eradicate messages of overconsumption and instead point consumers towards lower-impact and circular solutions.' The author, Rachel Arthur of UNEP, writes that to achieve this, 'storytellers, imagemakers and role models need to help portray alternative models of status and success.'

Inclusive design and adaptive fashion

According to the British Standards Institute, inclusive design is the design of mainstream products and services that are accessible to, and usable by, as many people as reasonably possible, without the need for special adaption or specialized design. The aim of inclusive design is to benefit everyone: to ensure that places and experiences (including fashion) are open to all, regardless of age, disability or background.

Adaptive fashion refers to clothing and accessories that are designed specifically to be suitable for individuals with physical or sensory disabilities, who have difficulty dressing or experience severe discomfort and inconvenience wearing standard clothing. According to Coherent Market Insights, the adaptive fashion market

When the unwanted becomes wanted

MATERIAL EXCHANGE – DEADSTOCK DEPOT

The term **deadstock** refers to fabrics or garments that are left over after production. This could be fabrics that a brand didn't use during garment production, that had a minor fault and did not pass quality control, or that were overproduced by a textile mill and not sold. It has traditionally been incinerated, sent to landfill, or left on warehouse shelves. According to Earth.org, 92 million tonnes of fabric are disposed of each year.

Enter Material Exchange and its Deadstock Depot initiative, which is designed to get these materials back into circulation. The Deadstock Depot was launched in April 2023 at the denim trade fair Kingpins in Amsterdam. The aim is to reduce the quantity of materials that go to waste each year, and to contribute to making fashion more circular. Material Exchange achieves this through its state-of-the-art digital sourcing platform, which allows fabric suppliers to showcase their materials more effectively to fashion brands, and fashion brands to find the materials they need more easily. Boxes of sample swatches are also available for Deadstock Depot clients. These are branded with 'Your deadstock samples' and a special logo, UNWANTED, highlighting that the unwanted is now a coveted resource. The fabric samples come with a QR code that links to a high-quality digital image of the specific sample, along with detailed information on the fabric's attributes, its sustainability profile, where it was produced and by whom, and any relevant fabric test reports.

It is a big win for suppliers, who can purchase fabric at lower cost, get garments to market faster, and return to circulation materials that were gathering dust in a warehouse.

The Material Exchange and its Deadstock Depot is right on point. Also in 2023, Angelina Jolie announced the launch of her fashion venture, Jolie Atelier, which will use deadstock and vintage fabrics. According to an article published online by the *South China Morning Post*, this will help 'customers to participate in the making of their own creations with master tailors, patternmakers and artisans around the world while keeping discarded fabric out of landfills'.

The Deadstock Depot initiative has already gained traction with big high-street retailers and smaller brands and designers who are keen to launch more eco-conscious ranges. It seems the industry is beginning to take action so that these excess materials are brought back into circulation for the benefit of the mills, the brand, the consumers and, most importantly, the planet.

"Sourcing deadstock fabrics isn't just procurement; it's a commitment to sustainable innovation."

Darren Glenister, CEO, Material Exchange

↓ The Deadstock Depot website shows the UNWANTED branding and some of the deadstock fabric types available.

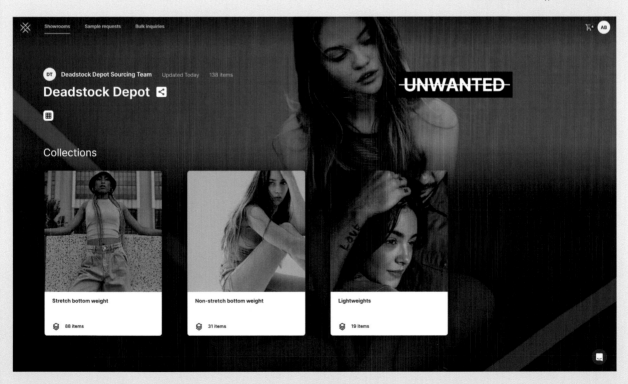

Your wardrobe reimagined

RESTYLE

Franceska Luther King is a fashion-industry insider. She worked as a designer and creative director for 25 years, travelling the globe pulling together trends and directions for some of the world's best-known fashion brands in the UK and USA. As a result she has an extensive knowledge of fabrics, vintage textiles, pattern-cutting and garment-making, but also, having seen at first hand the impact of fashion and clothing on the planet, she has become increasingly passionate about sustainability. This is why she launched Restyle. Quoting the designer and activist Orsola de Castro, Luther King believes that circular fashion is the best way forward for this industry, and that 'the most sustainable garment you have is the one already in your wardrobe.'

"I combat the cycle of fast fashion by applying my expertise to lend a new lease of life to everything from lingerie and lace to tailoring and leather."

Franceska Luther King

Restyle offers a range of services, including the specialist repair of intricate luxury fabrics, especially delicate silk, lace, organza, wool and leather; and customizing garments that are already in your wardrobe but that might need updating, adapting or altering. Having been properly trained as a fashion designer, Luther King understands some of the older techniques and skills used in couture, and has several VIP customers for whom she alters designer or couture pieces.

'Every job is different,' Luther King says. 'Each specific item presents a new challenge. I have to think carefully about the right techniques and approaches to use to ensure a really professional and tailored result.' She understands how clothes should fit and how to adjust ready-to-wear garments, tailoring them for a specific client. She has had clients who have been known to buy a garment in the wrong size, just so that they can have it. Then she gets to work, offering a couture-level service, believing that there is nothing more flattering than a garment made to fit properly.

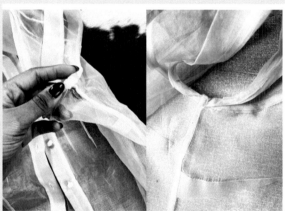

← An Instagram post by Luther King's company @restyle.uk showcases an example of invisible mending. The delicate organza is hard to handle. The garment was made with what are known as French seams, with which all raw edges are deftly encased in a special double seam, so as not to show in the finished garment. This adds an extra layer of complexity to the invisible repair.

← Another post shows how a client's designer dress was altered to fit. The job may look simple, but it involved taking the dress apart and removing the lining, to reshape the shoulder. Altering one element can affect another area, in this case the armhole and positioning of a dart or seam over the bust. All this must be factored in carefully and adjusted to ensure balance and fit. There is always more going on under the surface in the construction of a garment than meets the eye.

is estimated to exceed US$400 billion in 2027. The United Nations has a fact sheet on people with disabilities. This quotes data from the World Health Organization stating that 'around 15 per cent of the world's population, an estimated 1 billion people, live with disabilities. They are the world's largest minority.' Also, it is worth considering that many people experience some level of disability at different points in their lives – after an accident or surgery, for example, or as they age.

There are several fashion brands that cater for the adaptive fashion market. The best-known are Tommy Adaptive by Tommy Hilfiger and the Nike Go FlyEase, designed for all, but specifically for those who can't put on shoes independently. Other fashion brands in the inclusive/adaptive space include the Belgian brand So Yes; IZ Adaptive, started by Izzy Camilleri; the US brand Billy Footwear, started by Darin Donaldson and Billy Price; Unhidden, launched by Victoria Jenkins; Differently Enabled, launched by Craig Crawford; Megami, a post-mastectomy lingerie brand; and the inclusive design brand Social Surge, started in the USA by Meredith Wells along with three other founders. All these brands agree that personal style and a fashion identity are just as important for a disabled consumer as for anyone else.

This chapter has outlined the fundamentals of the fashion industry, the fashion system, seasonal cycles and the market sectors. The next chapter looks more deeply at research and planning. The topic of marketing research will be explained, with information on the processes of analysis, planning and developing a marketing strategy.

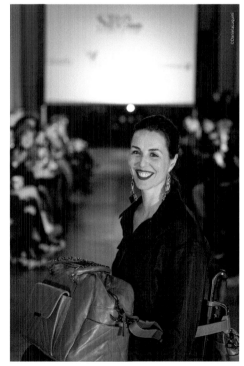

↑↑ Tommy Hilfiger 'Adaptive' collection fashion show during the 29th Annual Race to Erase MS in Los Angeles, 2022.

↑ Samanta Bullock at the London Represents fashion show, modelling a bag from her own accessible 'SB' collection. Bullock, an actor, model and disability activist, is a former number-one wheelchair tennis player in Brazil.

Treasure from trash

MICHELLE LOWE-HOLDER

The Canadian designer Michelle Lowe-Holder is driven by
the desire to produce beautiful, dramatic accessories using
sustainable and ethical practices. A philosophy of zero waste
and ethical production underpins her manufacturing methods.
Lowe-Holder's upcycled collars and cuffs are made using
ends of lines and 'cabbage' (scraps from previous collections),
biodegradable paper and vegan leather. Varying techniques,
such as flocking, are used to velvetize, revive and recolour
thrift-shop bangles, necklaces and rings. Collaboration with the
Self-Employed Women's Association, an initiative that gives
women homeworkers living in the city slums of India regular
work and fair rates for their skills, has enabled Lowe-Holder to
add beading to the repertoire of intricate artisanal techniques
– among them smocking, pleating, folding and foiling – that
are used to create her hand-made contemporary pieces. The
collection is exhibited in Paris at Première Classe and stocked
in boutiques worldwide.

↖ Striped tassel choker by Michelle Lowe-
Holder, made with woven cork offcuts
and nitrous-oxide canisters picked up from
the streets of east London. Modelled by
Mariam Taiwo, @mariamtaiwo (top), and
Sam (centre).

← A Michelle Lowe-Holder basket-
weave choker made with leather offcuts
and tassels with crystallized nitrous-
oxide canisters. Modelled by Adam,
@abfaurschou.

3

Research & Planning

"If you knew everything about tomorrow, what would you do differently today?"

Faith Popcorn

To be effective, marketing must be planned consciously, managed strategically, researched continuously and reviewed consistently. This ongoing cycle of endeavour is vital in such a competitive, fast-paced industry as fashion. This chapter highlights the importance of marketing research, explaining what it entails, what to research and how to do this. It also includes information on collating, analysing and using research material. Fundamental research and analytical tools, including **PESTEL** and **SWOT analysis**, **Porter's five forces analysis** and **Ansoff's Matrix**, are explained to show how key marketing and strategic tools are used in the planning process. The value of both **primary and secondary research** is highlighted, and helpful tips offered on carrying out simple but effective primary research and observation of the marketplace. The chapter concludes with information on how to use this research to write a **marketing plan**.

↑ An Indian worker processes raw cotton at the Cotton Corporation of India in Warangal District, 150 km (90 miles) from Hyderabad.

Competition exists at all levels of the supply chain. India, for example, is the world's second-largest cotton producer, after China. According to Better Cotton India, approximately 5.8 million farmers in this large country make a living from growing cotton. India competes with the other cotton-producing countries to sell its raw material, and, according to the Cotton Association of India, the amount of cotton sewn and the yield for 2023–4 were estimated to be the lowest in 15 years. This was because of bad weather caused by El Niño. Scarcity can affect the price of the raw material, forcing cotton buyers – who research the market to determine the best source in terms of quality, price and delivery – to go elsewhere.

Marketing research

Marketing research is a vital component of both business and marketing. For a fashion company to be able to determine its future business direction and marketing strategy, it must continuously gather, analyse and integrate information from a diverse range of business, fashion and market sources. You can see that the criteria of the 7P marketing mix – product, price, place, promotion, physical evidence, process and people – are all valid topics for marketing research. Philip Kotler defines marketing research as 'Systematic problem analysis, model-building and fact-finding for the purpose of improved decision-making and control in the marketing of goods and services.'

Marketing research may take place in order to analyse and resolve a specific problem, but it can also take place in order to keep up to date, assess the state of the market, stay proactive in a declining market, anticipate future trends, pursue opportunity or develop a business. This could be in terms of increased customer engagement, or to increase profitability via a more targeted approach, rather than just pushing to sell more 'stuff'.

Research is essential because it can help to eradicate false assumptions, expose risks and ensure that decisions are underpinned by relevant and current data. Research must be systematic and carefully planned, but it can be a creative and insightful exercise. Getting to know one's subject in depth and investigating a broad spectrum of relevant topics can be a stimulating experience that provides useful insight. The aim of research is not only to find reliable, unbiased answers to questions about the market, substantiate plans, determine production sources, reveal risk factors and decide strategy, but also to seek ideas and direction, draw inspiration and foster innovation.

It is important to define the difference between marketing research and **market research**. Market research forms a subset of marketing research and refers specifically to investigations of the market itself, comprising the marketplace, competitors and consumers. Marketing research relates to a much wider-ranging set of concerns, which include business, politics, economics, cultural and social trends, fashion trends, developing technology, logistics, promotion and product research.

The macro marketing environment

The macro marketing environment refers to the wider situation impacting on all businesses. This is a very important area to research, and often the starting point for the process. The macro environment is outside a company's direct control and comprises a complex set of variables that can be simplified into six key areas: **P**olitical factors; **E**conomic factors; **S**ocial and cultural factors;

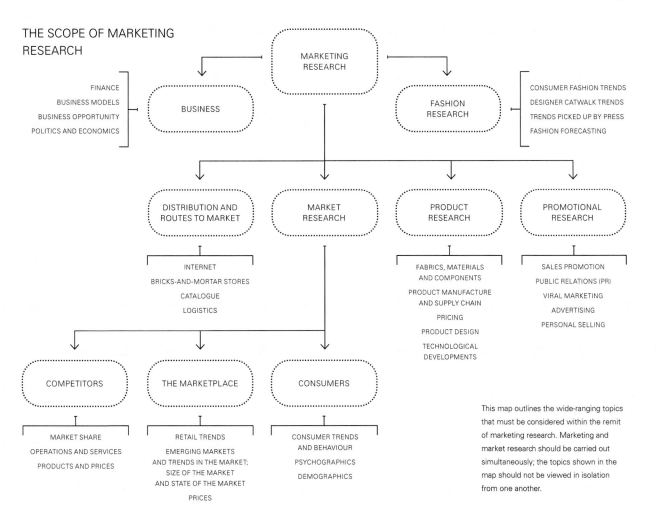

THE SCOPE OF MARKETING RESEARCH

This map outlines the wide-ranging topics that must be considered within the remit of marketing research. Marketing and market research should be carried out simultaneously; the topics shown in the map should not be viewed in isolation from one another.

Technological factors; Environmental factors; and Legal factors. Research and analysis of these factors is known as a **PESTEL analysis**, an essential element of marketing research. PESTEL analysis ensures an organization is responsive to the political, legal, economic, social, cultural and technological situation at any given time.

PESTEL analysis

Political and legal factors Although in the PESTEL model, political and legal factors are separated, it can be easier to consider them together since they are often interlinked and it is not always easy to determine which is which. The political situation and current or impending legislation can play a significant role in the direction and regulation of business. Anyone running a company must be conscious of the prevailing political and economic situation at home and abroad (if trading overseas) and keep up to date with relevant legislation, taxation and trade tariffs. They must understand the implications of interest rates, rates of inflation, employment levels,

THE MARKETING ENVIRONMENT

Marketing research takes place within the marketing environment, which these days is heavily influenced by an increasing array of factors within what is now a global marketplace. To be fully effective, a business must understand and recognize the impact of these factors at a local, national and possibly multinational market level. The marketing environment is subdivided into three perspectives: the internal marketing environment, micro-marketing environment and macro-marketing environment. Each must be explored in turn.

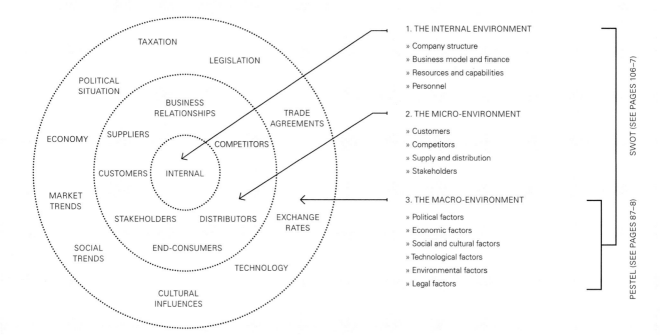

1. THE INTERNAL ENVIRONMENT
» Company structure
» Business model and finance
» Resources and capabilities
» Personnel

2. THE MICRO-ENVIRONMENT
» Customers
» Competitors
» Supply and distribution
» Stakeholders

3. THE MACRO-ENVIRONMENT
» Political factors
» Economic factors
» Social and cultural factors
» Technological factors
» Environmental factors
» Legal factors

SWOT (SEE PAGES 106–7)

PESTEL (SEE PAGES 87–8)

currency exchange rates and fluctuations in prices of raw materials, goods and services.

Although the examples that follow happened a considerable time ago, they illustrate how trade tariffs can affect the supply chain. In 1999 the cashmere industry was threatened by a tit-for-tat trade dispute between the USA and Europe over banana imports. The USA, angered by the EU imposing high tariffs on bananas produced by Latin-American growers, announced that it would fight back and levy 100 per cent import tariffs on certain European imported goods, including cashmere. The knock-on effects of the 'Banana Wars' were potentially disastrous; the livelihoods of Mongolian goatherds were threatened and thousands of jobs in the Scottish and Italian cashmere garment-manufacturing industry were put in jeopardy. Luckily, in an eleventh-hour reprieve, cashmere was spared and the

US government agreed not to carry out its threat. In 2013 the EU increased its import tariff on American-made premium jeans, which accounted for 75 per cent of the world's designer jeans market at that time. The top five US premium denim brands exporting to Western Europe were 7 For All Mankind, J Brand, Levi's, True Religion and Lee. These businesses had to decide whether to absorb the cost of the extra tax or move manufacturing out of the USA, to Mexico or Asia, for example. However, moving production offshore would impact the value of the brand and the desirability of their products, if they could not be marketed as 'made in USA' or 'made in LA' premium denim. The EU revoked the tariff increase in May 2014.

Economic factors The economic climate has significant influence on markets and affects consumer confidence and spending power. The cost-of-living crisis triggered by the COVID-19 pandemic, the war in Ukraine and the significant price rises for oil and raw materials meant that consumers cut back on discretionary spending, saving their money to combat rising fuel and food costs. Inflation acts to undercut consumer demand, driving consumers to curtail fashion spending or trade down for less pricey products. Economic factors, such as exchange rates, can also have an effect. For example, the weakness of sterling or other currencies against the dollar may affect retailers and wholesalers, since raw material and manufacturing purchase prices are usually quoted in US dollars.

Social and cultural factors As demonstrated above, it is not only economics that makes an impact, but also social and cultural trends. Changes in consumer attitudes and purchasing behaviour in response to political or economic events must be considered, but film, television, music and art can have a significant impact

← Young cinema-goers dressed up to attend a screening of *Minions: The Rise of Gru* (2022).

too. The HBO series and movies *Sex and the City* (SATC; 1998–), for example, were influential in bringing high fashion and designer brands to the attention of a new generation of young women, who fell in love with the SATC girls' fashion style. AMC's *Mad Men* (2007–15) had a major effect on fashion, particularly the trend of younger men wearing a classic slim-cut suit, white shirt and narrow tie. However, the wearing of suits and ties caused a bit of a problem when the #GentleMinions TikTok trend took hold. There were more than 61 million views on the platform and young male moviegoers filmed themselves as they dressed up in suits and sunglasses to attend screenings of *Minions: The Rise of Gru* (2022), the latest film in the *Despicable Me* series. In itself the trend was harmless, but as large groups of young men in suits gathered, there were reports of rowdy behaviour, so some cinemas banned their attendance.

Changes in social and cultural attitudes, and pressure from activist groups and consumers, have had some positive effects on the way fashion is viewed and promoted. For example, instances of cultural appropriation have been called out; fashion is becoming more inclusive in its representation of diversity in terms of model sizes, ethnicity and disability; and there is a rise in consumer sustainability initiatives, such as upcycling and fashion rental (see Chapter 2).

Other social and cultural factors to research include shifts in the demographic of the population, developing lifestyle trends and leisure activities, as well as changes in consumer attitudes and purchasing behaviour. These will be discussed in Chapter 4.

Technological factors Technology is of tremendous importance to the fashion and retail industry. Issues to consider are wide-ranging, including electronic data interchange (EDI) and just-in-time product-replenishment technology for stock management. Computer-aided

→ Perspex and 3D-printed jewellery by Sarah Angold Studio. Angold set up her eponymous London design studio in 2010, after graduating from the Royal College of Art with an MA in Constructed Textiles. Her passion for sleek avant-garde styling coupled with her desire to make visible the intricate structural engineering behind her pieces has informed the signature aesthetic for which she's now globally renowned. In her collections, hyper-modern industrial processes, such as 3D printing, routinely collide with a meticulous hand assembly more commonly associated with artisanal craft.

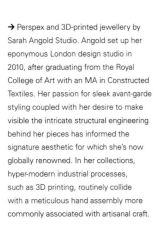

design (CAD) offers designers the opportunity to develop an entire fashion product range digitally, without having to make physical samples. Sophisticated computer software, such as CLO3D, allows greater flexibility for experimentation without having to cut the cloth or waste money sampling products in the early stages of development. 3D digital versions of garments and accessories can be used instead of making costly selling samples for wholesale in B2B settings, or for e-commerce product visualizations for selling direct to customers, on a website, app or social media. Augmented-reality (AR) technology can be used for virtual try-on, and artificial intelligence (AI) programmes, such as Midjourney, are being used to create fashion designs, illustrations and media content.

Physical 3D printing can be used to create fashion garments. The most notable and commonly known designer to be using this technology is Iris van Herpen, who was the first to enter this field. Printing only what is required to create a garment without wastage is one of the key advantages of this technology, and several other designers are working with 3D printing as a way to push boundaries and improve sustainability. Julia Daviy is a digital printing fashion pioneer, creating figure garments from 3D-printed fabrics; and Zer Era, an innovation lab and design studio, uses biodegradable filaments for 3D-printed garments, as well as body-scanners and a laser-cutting machine to help reduce wastage.

↑ A digital fashion collection created using CLO3D software by Diane Wallinger for her final Masters project in Fashion Futures. A Swiss designer, Wallinger is the leading force behind her eponymous studio, DNWLLNGR. For this project she delved into the intersection of well-being and sustainability, producing a collection that seamlessly blended physical and digital garments. CLO3D can be used for digital sampling, rendering true-to-life digital 3D versions of garments that mirror the properties of fabric in terms of drape and density. It can also be used for more creative and speculative projects, as can be seen here in Wallinger's work

Fashion metamorphosis: light-transforming technology

ANREALAGE

ANREALAGE is the brainchild of the Japanese designer Kunihiko Morinaga. The brand name is formed from a combination of 'real', 'unreal' and 'age'. For his Autumn/Winter 2023–4 show, Morinaga used photochromic technology on fabric to make it change colour when exposed to UV rays. The collection was inspired by the German concept of *Umwelt*, which means 'environment' and relates specifically to an organism's unique sensory world. A bee, for example, perceives a flower very differently from the way a human does. For the collection, Morinaga integrated photochromic technology into faux fur, velvet, lace, jacquard weaves and knits, among other fabrics, which were all shown in a neutral creamy-white colour. However, when a UV light bar was moved across the garments, the magic and true theatre of the show were revealed and the clothes metamorphosed into garments suffused in colour and pattern.

For the show, this took place under controlled conditions using the UV light tube. However, Morinaga's garments are also sensitive to the UV in sunlight and would also transform outdoors in the sun. The reaction would be specific to the particular weather conditions at the time.

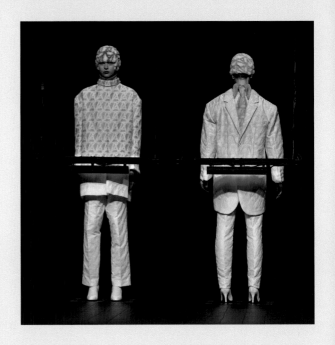

↑ The Anrealage Autumn/Winter 2023 fashion show during Paris Fashion Week. Hidden patterns and colours are revealed when a UV light bar passes over what appears to be plain white fabric.

↑ The Adidas 4DFWD trainer features an advanced digital-printed midsole using 4D technology.

The next step forward is 4D printing. This newer version of 3D printing enables more dynamic structures that can change their shape. 4D printing has been adopted quite significantly within the sneaker or trainer industry for developing the technical midsole element of shoes. The Adidas 4DFWD trainer (left) combines 4D lattice midsole technology with Carbon Digital Light Synthesis™. According to Carbon, the proprietor of this technology, it is a 'breakthrough resin-based 3D printing process that uses digital light projection and oxygen-permeable optics'. This enables the midsoles to be fine-tuned to specific patterns of movement for a precise running experience.

The implications of technological innovation can be dramatic. Take, for example, the invention of nylon in 1935 and the subsequent development of Lycra® by DuPont in 1958. These two innovations were used in the first tights, or 'pantyhose' as they were known when they were created by Allen Gant Sr. This ground-breaking hosiery development paved the way for the miniskirt revolution of the 1960s, a fashion trend that would never have taken off without the benefit of tights.

Gaming tech and fashion manufacture

NAK3D

How does a design studio in Manchester speak to a factory in Shanghai? Usually it is via email or on a video conference, or the designers have to travel to China. Kelly Vero, who has a background in design for video games, wanted to use her skills to solve this problem: 'I wanted to make the entire process a little more like games. Video games are a visual communication tool, really, so it was important that my starting point for the fashion projects I have created was to solve this communication problem.'

Vero started by using Unity and Unreal Engine technology, originally used for video games, and computer tomography (CT) technology – a novel and unique approach at the time – to develop scans of fashion accessories, such as shoes and bags. CT technology allows the deep vision or magnification of fibres, so Vero was able to make a highly detailed digital twin of a shoe or bag, configured in such a way that clients could see all the layers of the product: the leather texture, the canvas, the stitching and even the glue. The study she developed allowed companies to see exactly how much material was needed for every part of a shoe and every part of the process, cutting out an inordinate amount of time and wastage.

Vero's novel use of existing technology enabled her to look at everything in just one click, without the need to pull samples or designs apart. Many fashion houses like to keep detailed information on their couture, and to do that they must pull precious eighteenth-, nineteenth- and twentieth-century pieces apart at the seams. Using CT technology, Vero was able to help these notable houses and heritage collections preserve their work without breaking a single stitch. Applying the technology to her own Louis Vuitton Speedy bag, to show its constituent parts, she was able to measure everything from the provenance of the cotton of the painted canvas, to the patination and the zip technology.

Vero is now CEO of her own company, NAK3D, which uses digital items to explore the future of e-commerce. An R&D project using Alexander McQueen's fabulous men's trench coat from Spring/Summer 2023 shows how a garment can be digitized with 'active data layers', meaning that the information on a clothing label can now be found in the digital object itself. Vero is looking at how we can purchase clothing through video games and trace all our user data through the product life cycle management tool she has created from the data in the digital garment.

← This is not a normal 3D rendering of a Louis Vuitton bag. The image was created by Kelly Vero using computer tomography (CT) technology, which can be converted into something more visual and less data-heavy. Vero developed this process so that fashion and accessory product scans could be configured with leather textures, canvas and even glue. The study she developed allowed companies to see exactly how much glue they needed for a shoe, for example, thus cutting down on waste.

↑ People scavenge for reuseable clothing on a huge mound of discarded clothes at a rubbish dump in the Old Fadama area of Accra in 2021. This is where much of the second-hand clothing imported from Europe and the United States, but too poor-quality to be sold in the Kantamanto second-hand clothing market, is dumped.

↗ Yayra Agbofah (left), a creative social entrepreneur, and Kwamena Boison, a fashion enthusiast, are co-founders of The Revival, an up-cycling outfit in Accra. The Revival repurposes discarded, poor-quality second-hand clothing to produce functional designs and artworks.

Environmental factors There are two main foci for environmental factors. There are those that affect the fashion supply chain, such as flooding and rising sea levels in Bangladesh (the world's second-largest apparel exporter), or the drought in Texas, USA, which affected the cotton crop for the 2022/3 growing season, reducing the yield by 1 million tonnes. Then there are the environmental effects of the fashion industry itself. In 2022 eco-experts ranked fashion the sixth most polluting industry, stating that it produced 2.1 billion tonnes of greenhouse gas emissions per year. According to Earth.org in 2022, it is estimated that 11.3 million tonnes of textile waste end up in landfill every year in the USA alone. The same source states that dyeing and the finishing processes used to apply colour to fabrics are responsible for 3 per cent of global carbon-dioxide emissions, and more than 20 per cent of global water pollution. These factors cannot be ignored, and the way fashion businesses and brands deal with them is vital for the future.

Legal factors Legislation is an ever more important area to consider, and the call for legislation to curb fashion's impact on the environment is growing. We have already discussed some of the new legislation in the USA and France in Chapter 2 (see pages 73–4). In addition, in 2022 the European Commission announced a raft of proposed eco-design rules. These would, when enshrined in law, require large companies to disclose how much unsold fashion stock is sent to landfill, and verify how and why textiles and garments are 'eco' or environmentally friendly – rather than just marketing them as such without proof. Frans Timmermans, executive vice president of the European Commission for the European Green Deal at the time, said, 'The clothes we wear should last longer than three washes and should also be recyclable.' As we saw in Chapter 2, the Fashion Act, a bill proposed in New York State, will require brands of a certain

Fashion and disruptive technology

CAP_ABLE MANIFESTO COLLECTION

Cap_able Design was founded in 2019 by Rachele Didero and Federica Busani. The start-up evolved from a discussion on contemporary society, technology and human rights, a conversation that provoked the creation of the 'Manifesto' collection, a selection of knitted garments launched on the crowdfunding platform Kickstarter at the end of 2022. By early 2023 the concept and its underlying message had piqued the interest of the press, with articles featured in *Dezeen*, *PLAIN Magazine*, *Trend Hunter* and *Apparel Resources*.

Technology is central to the concept, both in the creation of the garments and in their purpose. Concerned about the misuse of biometric facial-recognition technology, the duo used AI technology to create patterns, known as 'adversarial patches', that could be used to deceive facial-recognition software. The collection fooled YOLO (You Only Look Once), the object-detection algorithm, into classifying people wearing the knitwear as dogs, giraffes or zebras. Didero and Busani have concerns that an individual's biometric data is not safeguarded by any law. In creating the 'Manifesto' collection, they aim to bring this to public attention. They have also used the law to their advantage. With the support and sponsorship of the Polytechnic University of Milan, they have secured a patent for their unique fabric.

↓ Cap_able Design's 'Manifesto' knitwear collection uses AI to create patterns that can fool facial-recognition technology.

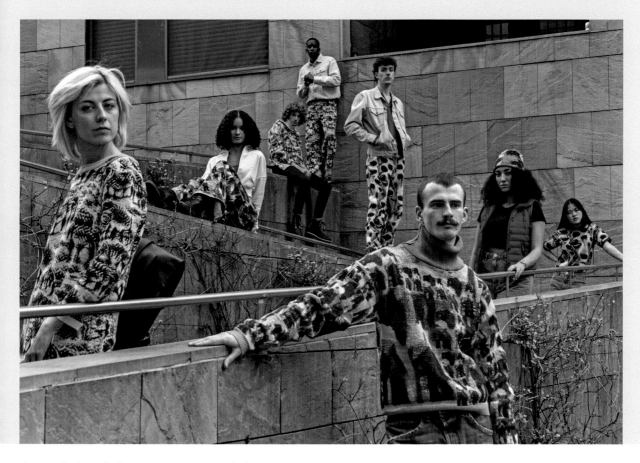

size to disclose their greenhouse gas emissions, energy, water and material use, and plastics and chemical management systems. These and many other legal factors must be taken into account by fashion businesses, and the impact of legislation considered carefully, to ensure not only that the business can be accountable to these laws, but also how they may affect the business's operations and profitability.

AI and fashion design

Artificial intelligence (AI) has many possible applications in fashion. It can analyse large amounts of data, which can help with supply-chain management, identifying trends, analysing past sales performance and predicting customer preferences. AI can also be used for personalization, suggesting products and promotions for individual customers based on the analysis of data relating to their personal preferences and past purchasing behaviour.

AI can also be used creatively by designers, for visualizing ideas for their collections and for virtual prototyping with less waste. The number of creatives using it to produce digital fashion designs and creative content is growing, and the conversation around its use is getting louder. One area of concern is the application of copyright law to AI-generated images. At the time of writing, in 2023, AI-generated artwork cannot be copyrighted. There are other ethical concerns about the use of AI, with fears that people could lose their jobs and that it will create a more narrow, homogenized result based on data rather than human creativity.

But there is a growing community of creatives who believe that AI can enhance human creativity, rather than replace it. Not everyone is good at sketching ideas, but with the right prompts, AI programmes can help a designer to explore new ideas and possibilities.

↓↘ AI fashion-design images created by @paiope_london using MidJourney.

From screen to catwalk

DOWNTON ABBEY, GATSBY AND BRIDGERTON

The television series *Downton Abbey*, which aired in more than 100 countries over the years 2010–15, inspired a rash of designer fashion collections, a phenomenon known as the 'Downton effect'. Prada, Louis Vuitton, Burberry and Ralph Lauren all looked to *Downton* for inspiration for Autumn/Winter 2012. Cloche hats, tweed caps, plus fours, Fair Isle knits and jackets with bellows pockets all made an appearance on the catwalk. Men fell under the turn-of-the-century spell too, and double-breasted suits and waistcoats featured in the menswear shows. Two-button and three-button jackets were included in collections by Rag & Bone and Burberry, while Thom Browne, Paul Smith and J.Crew showed round-collar shirts. Traditional men's outfitters and tailors on Savile Row in London reported a boom in trade fuelled mainly by interest from American clients. As the television story rolled into the 1920s, the fashion world kept pace, and dropped-waist dresses and 1920s-style evening gowns emerged as the next wave of the *Downton* trend. The 1920s theme gained further momentum with the launch of *The Great Gatsby* film in 2013.

More recently, the Netflix series *Bridgerton* (2020–) has also had an effect on fashion. The British Fashion Council worked with up-and-coming designers Aurélie Fontan, Edward Mendoza and Shanti Bell to develop contemporary pieces inspired by the show. The partnership was repeated for the launch of the second series in March 2022, this time featuring the designers Ifeanyi Okwuadi, Latifa Neyazi and Jeongmin Ji, whose Regency-inspired designs were modelled by the show's cast.

Bridgerton launched a 'Regencycore' trend. According to the Lyst Insights Data Drop for 1 June 2021, online searches for corsets went up by 123 per cent, for feather headbands by 49 per cent and for empire line dresses by 23 per cent. The most viewed items on the Lyst site were headpieces by Simone Rocha and Magnetic Midnight, corsets by Rasario and Dion Lee, and dresses by Brock Collection and Erdem.

"The Downton effect for us is a global appreciation of fine English tailoring, with British milled cloth as the gold standard of understated elegance."

Douglas Cordeaux
Managing director, Fox Brothers

↓ For the opening night of *Bridgerton* series 2 at Tate Modern, London, in March 2022, cast members modelled outfits designed by Ifeanyi Okwuadi, Latifa Neyazi and Jeongmin Ji. The collection was a partnership between Netflix, *Bridgerton* and the British Fashion Council.

The micro marketing environment

The micro marketing environment refers to factors that impact more directly on an organization and affect its ability to operate within its specific market. Factors to consider are:

» Customers

» Competitors

» Suppliers and supply-chain logistics

» Distributors and distribution channels

» Stakeholder and partner relationships

Unlike the macro marketing environment, which affects a wide range of businesses whatever their nature, the micro marketing environment is determined by the market sector in question and is unique to each company. The main thrust of the marketing environment is one of impact; the rationale is to investigate and understand factors that might have a significant effect on a business or organization, particularly those that influence the relationships a company has with customers, suppliers, distributors, partners and stakeholders. The factors within the micro marketing environment align with those indicated earlier as market research, and within this, researching customers is paramount. Understanding their requirements, purchasing behaviour and psychology constitutes an essential aspect of marketing and market research – so much so that the whole of Chapter 4 is dedicated to this topic.

Identifying competitors

It is important for a business to monitor its competitors, keep an eye on what they are up to and scrutinize the products and services they offer. The first step is to identify competitors and determine which to research. This is not always straightforward. A twenty-year-old Japanese fashion consumer may choose to purchase in Uniqlo and Louis Vuitton. A forty-five-year-old woman with an artistic sensibility and creative sense of style may purchase such designer labels as Crea Concept, Shirin Guild, Eileen Fisher or Oska, but may also shop in high-street stores, such as Zara, Uniqlo, Arket and Muji. Within the manufacturing market, an apparel manufacturer in China might find that they are in competition not only with other Chinese manufacturers but also with those in countries in the Asia region, such as Vietnam, that have lower labour costs, or with global producers in Turkey or Eastern Europe that are geographically closer to the European fashion markets.

The most basic way of categorizing competitors is to define those that offer and supply similar types of products and services at the same level of the market. One could say that Gucci and Prada, for example, or Nike and Adidas, are brands that are in direct competition. But this is a very simplistic way to view the competitive landscape, especially for fashion. Competition is not so much an issue of brand against brand; it is more a case of:

» Product type and usage

» Consumer psychology

» Product and brand positioning

» Shopping location (stores and online)

Let's take a man who wants to buy a well-made classic but *contemporary* suit from an upmarket designer brand. He wants to purchase a respected label because he feels that a designer suit will last, be well tailored and of *good quality*. This shopper lives out of town but plans a trip into the city to look for the suit. Before the visit, he goes online to gather information, compare prices and check store locations. He specifically wants to go into the shops so he can try suits on and feel the fabric and fit. He starts with a visit to Brioni. He likes the brand's quiet *luxury* and knows it has a great reputation for men's tailoring. On the basis of *classic simplicity*, Armani might be considered a direct competitor, so our potential customer heads for a department store to continue his search. Once there, he notices a suit by Paul Smith and is intrigued by the fusion of *classic style* with quirky designer details; the suit most certainly is contemporary. So now this brand also enters his consideration.

↑ Luxury fashion brands place products featuring their logo or brand iconography prominently in the store windows. This helps to promote the brand and differentiate its product from that of other luxury brands on the same street or in the same mall.

This short scenario should illustrate how competition is dependent upon the interplay of several factors: the type of product, the positioning of brands under consideration, the requirements, needs and psychology of the consumer, and the options available to the potential purchaser at the time of his shopping expedition. Of course, the man in question may check items online on his mobile phone while in the store, or return home and do further searches to purchase the same items at a better price via a competitor online seller. This is more convenient, and cost-effective. Net-A-Porter/Mr Porter have picked up on this, developing a premium delivery service called 'You Try, We Wait', aimed at their select EIPs (Extremely Important People). This same-day delivery service offers customers the possibility to try on in the comfort of their home or office, while a personal shopper waits before taking the returns away immediately, making the process smooth and convenient for customers. Such services also help to gain customer loyalty and, it is to be hoped, avoid the losses that might be incurred if customers ordered from competitors online.

Throughout this description certain words have been emphasized in italics, to indicate the qualities the man expects. He wants a suit that is luxurious but not flashy, classic yet contemporary, simple yet stylish, good quality and at the best price. Also important is that it should be a designer brand and that the process should be convenient. However, he may not adhere to these particular criteria for other products. Imagine he also wishes to purchase two or three basic white T-shirts to wear with the suit. He might not consider Armani or Paul Smith for these, but head straight to Cos, Uniqlo or Arket to buy what he considers a commodity product at a more reasonable price.

Pushing the idea further, if a consumer goes to a shopping centre with the aim of purchasing, any one of the shops in the mall or brands in a department store within the mall has the potential to be in competition for the shopper's custom on that particular shopping trip. The same applies to shopping online, where this customer could go to a marketplace site, such as Mr Porter, Farfetch, SSense, YOOX, 24S (a member of the Louis Vuitton Moët Hennessy, LVMH, group), or a department store online, such as Lane Crawford, Barneys, Bloomingdale's or Selfridges. This leads us to the concept of indirect competition. The best way to view this is to think of it as everything that might compete for a consumer's discretionary expenditure. Someone who wants to splash out and treat themselves may decide to spend their money on make-up, beauty or well-being products rather than fashion, or they might purchase a new tablet or smartphone rather than an item of clothing or fashion accessory. The trick in determining who competitors could be is to consider the topic from the customer's perspective. That is why understanding customers is so important.

Competitor analysis

Once competitors have been identified, the next step is to analyse their business. The aim is to evaluate how they are performing and investigate their operation in terms of size, **market share**, capabilities and resources, product offer, services, routes to market and number of retail outlets, if this is applicable. The purpose is to assess their strengths and weaknesses and determine how best to compete. Analysing a competitor is the first step towards creating a competitive advantage. Monitoring competitors also allows a company to react quickly to economic or strategic changes made by those competitors. Background research using published industry and trade data should reveal the competitor's overall financial situation, share of the market and operational activities. Market share is expressed as a percentage. It can be calculated by dividing the total market value by the sales revenue of each business operating in the market, or by dividing the total volume of units sold in the overall market by the number of units sold by each market participant. It is possible for a market leader to maintain a steady market share over a long period, but their share will not necessarily remain stable, so it is important to monitor the market and market share over time. Market share is used to indicate the composition of the market and highlight the value of key competitors relative to one another, thus helping to gauge their importance and power. This links to Porter's five forces, since powerful companies may have a stronger negotiating position with suppliers (see page 103).

Suppliers and supply-chain logistics

Monitoring existing or new supplier partnerships is a very important element of a fashion business. This could relate to manufacturers and factories if a fashion brand designs and produces its own merchandise, or to wholesalers and design houses/fashion labels if the business is a retailer or online marketplace. Determining who to work with is not always easy; supply chains can be long and complicated, and keeping track of all parties and processes involved can be a challenge. Supply-chain management and compliance is a hot topic. In June 2023 European lawmakers proposed the Corporate Sustainability Due Diligence Directive (CSDDD), requiring companies to monitor their supply chains for violations of human and environmental rights. This applies to large EU and non-EU businesses with significant net turnover in the EU. In essence, the businesses must ensure greater traceability and transparency in their supply chains, or risk being held accountable for non-compliance. According to the law firm Pinsent Masons, the law would encompass all established business relationships in a qualifying company's value chains, those 'that perform activities related to the production of goods or the provision of services both upstream and downstream in the supply chain'.

Such legislation is likely to have a significant impact on a number of large fashion corporations and businesses, not least on the negotiations and business agreements made between suppliers and buyers. This aspect is covered in more detail in the section on Porter's five forces analysis (see page 103).

Distributors and distribution channels

This topic is covered in Chapter 1, in the sections on distribution process and distribution strategy as part of the marketing mix (see pages 22–4). In terms of the micro marketing environment, the choice of distribution channels and/or distributors to work with should be researched in order to determine the best approach for the fashion business concerned. Also consider investigating and understanding what types of distribution business model are being used by competitors and market leaders in the relevant sector.

Stakeholder and partner relationships

It is very important to understand the various groups who have an interest in a particular fashion business. They could be investors, or other businesses that act in partnership to mutual benefit. Such relationships can form part of the business or operating model for a brand, so it can be vital to research options and work out the best course of action. As part of this, it may be necessary to investigate what competitors are doing, since this may affect which suppliers, partners and stakeholders you can work with; if they work with a competitor already, for example, that could cause a conflict of interest.

The right partnerships can increase sales and enhance brand recognition for those concerned. The cost of marketing could be shared, for example, especially if the manufacturer produces a recognized protected fabric, such as Harris Tweed.

Vivienne Westwood created her 'Harris Tweed' collection for Autumn/Winter 1987/8, reviving the material as a fashion fabric and leading to other designers using the cloth for their collections. It was the start of a long-lasting relationship between the Westwood and Harris Tweed brands, and gave a much-needed boost to the local Harris Tweed industry. Vivienne Westwood's website explains the uniqueness and importance of Harris Tweed:

> It is the only fabric in the world that is protected by its own Act of Parliament, meaning that by law, the cloth must be made from pure virgin wool which has been dyed and spun on the islands of the Outer Hebrides and handwoven without the aid of automation or electricity at the home of the weaver.

The brands are also linked through their logos. Harris Tweed is represented by a royal orb, and Westwood adapted this for her 'Harris Tweed' collection with the addition of a Saturn-like ring around the orb. The journalist Brian Wilson picked up the story in 2023, shortly after Westwood's death, in an article in the *Stornoway Gazette*. Wilson explains that lawyers did get involved at the time, but that there were just enough points of difference to distinguish the two logos. In the end it was agreed that the similarity and mutual identification did more good than harm for both parties.

Some fashion brands highlight their stakeholders on their websites. Adidas, for example, states that its stakeholders are 'those people or organizations who affect – or are affected by – our operations'. Among the stakeholders listed are:

» Adidas employees

» Business partners, suppliers, licensees, service providers

» Trade associations, shareholders and the executive board

» Customers, professional athletes, distributors, retailers, consumers

Porter's five forces analysis

This tool can be used to assess pressures in a competitive business environment. Porter's model identifies five forces that impact the competitive power and profitability of a business:

1. The bargaining power of suppliers

2. The bargaining power of buyers

3. Rivalry between competitors in the market

4. Threat of new entrants to the market

5. Threat of substitute products or services

The bargaining power of suppliers A supplier or manufacturer will have a strong bargaining position if it provides a unique product or necessary service. If a particular fashion trend takes off, perhaps one featuring lace or hand embroidery, then a manufacturer in India or China with capability to produce delicate handwork may find that they have a stronger bargaining position on price. Suppliers that have built up a strong relationship with their customers will also be in a stronger position, since it can be costly for customers to switch to a new

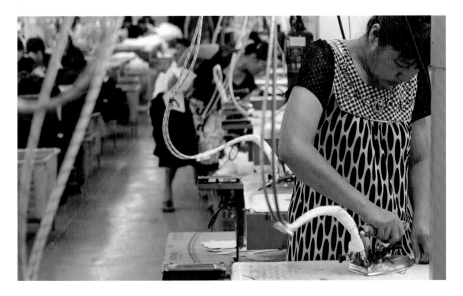

← Manufacturers and apparel suppliers have to achieve a difficult balance. The cost of raw materials, labour or export duties affects their pricing and the ultimate profitability of their business. They may be forced to put prices up in response to rising costs or changes to taxation or duties. There is, however, always pressure from customers to keep prices down, and the risk is that those customers will take their business elsewhere and buy from a cheaper source.

↑ Garment workers in a factory in the city
of Gazipur, Bangladesh.

PORTER'S FIVE FORCES

Porter's five forces model highlights key areas of investigation
that must be carried out in order to understand the specific
nature of the pressures affecting a business.

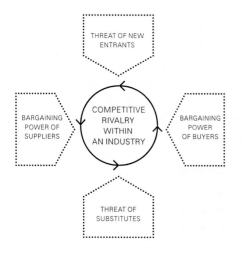

supplier or manufacturer, especially if considerable money, time and
energy have gone into product development, creating samples and
working on product fittings and specifications. Each season, suppliers
and manufacturers put pressure on their business customers by
attempting to put their prices up; if customers have driven a hard
bargain the previous season, a supplier is likely to try to claw back lost
revenue. If a supplier understands that a particular style is on-trend
and that there is great demand from end-consumers, the balance
will be tipped in their favour, particularly if they can offer a fast lead
time and deliver quickly. In this case the supplier will have stronger
bargaining power and may be able to demand a higher price, knowing
that the buyer needs the stock urgently.

The process of Western brands manufacturing overseas is called
offshoring. It has been standard practice for many years, while
costs in Asia particularly were low. However, recently the cost of
manufacture and shipping has risen dramatically, and there has
been a drive for shorter, more manageable supply chains with more
transparent sustainability, traceability and ethics. This has precipitated
a move to undertake reshoring or onshoring. Reshoring is when a
company moves its manufacture from far overseas to somewhere
closer, and onshoring is when a company brings its manufacturing
within its own national boundaries. In 2020 the US retailer Nordstrom
moved its manufacturing from Asia to Guatemala, when there was
a drive to move production to the Balkan countries and Latin America.
The Spanish retailer Mango moved production from Vietnam and
China to Turkey, Morocco and Portugal. In America there is growing
consumer sentiment to purchase 'made in America' labels, with
the idea that this is patriotic and that quality will be better. Brooks
Brothers moved 70 per cent of its offshore suit manufacture back to
the USA, and there is a rise in sales of clothing brands marketed as 'all
American', such as the All American Clothing Co. and Buck Mason.

The bargaining power of buyers On the other side of the equation,
buyers will naturally want to purchase products or services at the
best possible price, as well as negotiating profitable trading terms
and agreements, so that they can ensure they are competitive in
the marketplace. Suppliers need to keep their order books filled, so
they will be under pressure to meet buyers' demands, particularly
in difficult economic times, or if the market is strong and there
are lots of companies competing for the same business. Buyers
from the large retail chains will not only bargain for low prices
but also demand favourable discount terms and usually require
suppliers to contribute to mark-down costs on stock that does
not sell at full price. Fashion designers and retailers that produce
their own collections will gain the upper hand in negotiations with
manufacturers if they place large orders.

Rivalry between competitors in the market Competitive rivalry has been touched on earlier (see pages 39–43). Apparel retailing is awash with myriad brands and fashion labels, all competing for the end-consumer's custom. Retailers will compete with one another to have exclusivity on certain brands. It is standard practice for a boutique to refuse to carry a particular brand or label if it is stocked by a rival shop in the locality; and suppliers will be competing to ensure they are stocked in the most prestigious stores. Rivalry between competitors not only relates to retail, but also is an issue further back in the supply chain. Textile suppliers will compete to gain fabric orders, while manufacturers within a particular country or region are in competition with one another to gain an order from foreign buyers, and will compete on price, quality, lead time or extra services, such as design capability, warehousing and other logistics.

Threat of new entrants to the market New entrants to a market can threaten companies already operating within it. In fashion, it is costly and time-consuming to design, develop, produce and sell a collection or product range, so new start-ups may not pose an enormous threat in the first instance. However, an established brand diversifying into a new market could constitute a severe threat. A brand with loyal customers and a solid business might capitalize on its existing resources to extend its operation into a new sector of the fashion market; a successful womenswear retailer deciding to develop a range for men, for example. For retailers there is a constant risk that competitors or new companies will establish their stores just across the road. While this poses a threat, it can also increase footfall, raising the number of customers visiting the area and encouraging healthy competition.

Threat of substitute products or services If customers can find an alternative product or service, they may switch their custom, thus weakening the power of a business to succeed. The threat of substitution applies equally to the end-consumer, who may choose from several retailers offering similar fashion styles at comparable prices, and to business customers, who could decide to purchase from a competitor if they offer a replacement product or service that could reasonably substitute for the original.

The internal environment

The internal or organizational environment refers to factors inside a company that affect the way it carries out its business and marketing function. These include:

» Company and departmental structure

» Personnel

» Finance

» Resources

» Internal systems

» Technological capabilities

The internal structure and culture of a business organization will impact the way it operates. In Chapter 1 Seth Godin was quoted as having said that marketing is not a 'last-minute add-on'. To be really effective, marketing should be integrated throughout a business. If this is so, it follows that marketing will be affected by the allocation of resources, the extent to which responsibility for marketing is shared throughout an organization, and the way internal processes and procedures are set up. Companies regularly carry out an internal audit in order to assess where they are in the current market, benchmark against competitors and determine future direction and strategy.

The internal audit

The audit provides a company with an opportunity to review its internal procedures, capabilities, resources and marketing strategies. This is known as **situation analysis**, and the internal audit is used to examine the strengths and weaknesses of the organization and assess the efficacy of its current marketing approach. The audit should cover the following:

» Marketing mix

» Target customers

» Positioning strategy

» Differentiation strategy and USP

» Competitors

» Current competitive advantage

One of the first steps is to use a framework known as a SWOT analysis, which is a much-used tool for this type of internal audit.

SWOT analysis

The SWOT analysis provides a framework to collate and review investigative information. It is used to audit the internal strengths and weaknesses of a business enterprise and identify external factors that might provide opportunities within the marketplace and business environment. A SWOT is also used to determine and assess external issues that could pose threats to the enterprise or its brands. Once the strengths, weaknesses, opportunities and threats have been established, they can be presented in a simple overview table. It is important to stress that the SWOT analysis is not merely a list or the chart itself, but an analytical tool that corresponds to four key strategic positions:

1. Strength + Opportunity
Uses internal strengths to capitalize on external opportunity and potential

2. Strength + Threat
Uses internal strengths to overcome external threats

3. Weakness + Opportunity
Works to address or minimize internal weaknesses to ensure opportunity is not jeopardized

4. Weakness + Threat
In this position a company is exposed and at risk. The strategy would be to mitigate weakness and ward off threats

The real purpose of the SWOT is to use the information to determine how to capitalize on a company's internal strengths, using them to create opportunity and potential, or to determine how the strengths could be best employed in order to overcome threats in the market. It is not always easy to assess internal weakness, but facing up to issues that might be holding a business back is vitally important.

SWOT ANALYSIS

A summary of the results of a SWOT analysis can be recorded in a simple table. The example below gives an overview of the issues to consider for each area of investigation.

INTERNAL

EXTERNAL

STRENGTHS	**W**EAKNESSES	**O**PPORTUNITIES	**T**HREATS
» THE REPUTATION OF THE COMPANY, BRAND OR FASHION LABEL	» UNDIFFERENTIATED PRODUCTS WITH NO CLEAR USP	» STRATEGIC ALLIANCE OR OPPORTUNITY TO PARTNER WITH OTHERS	» CHANGES TO FASHION TRENDS, SIGNATURE LOOK GOES OUT OF STYLE
» DISTINCTIVE SIGNATURE STYLE AND USP	» LACK OF SKILLED STAFF OR SUPPORT	» NEW MARKET IDENTIFIED	» NEW COMPETITOR ENTERS MARKET
» EXPERTISE OF STAFF	» WEAK RELATIONSHIP WITH SUPPLIERS	» NEW FABRIC OR MANUFACTURING TECHNOLOGY	» CHANGES IN IMPORT OR EXPORT DUTIES AFFECT PRICING OR SUPPLY
» STRONG RELATIONSHIP WITH SUPPLIERS	» CASH-FLOW OR FINANCING PROBLEMS	» NEW SUPPLY SOURCE AVAILABLE	» RISING OPERATIONAL COSTS
» LOYAL CUSTOMER BASE		» GOVERNMENT TRADE INCENTIVES	» KEY BUYER DROPS THE LABEL

Monitoring the market

The first step is usually to consider the state of the relevant market, be that geographical or product-based. Market research and analysis should be used to:

>> Define the size and composition of a market sector

>> Determine the state of the market, whether it is growing, getting smaller or relatively static

>> Assess trends within the market

>> Establish which brands or competitors operate in the market

This type of research is crucial for those planning to start a venture, or enter a new geographical market. Let's take the example of a luxury fashion brand planning to expand into the Brazilian market. In order for the company to invest in such an initiative and follow through with its plans, it would need to carry out wide-ranging research to assess the potential for retailing foreign luxury goods in Brazil. The following questions should be asked:

>> What size is the Brazilian market and is there potential for expansion into this market?

>> What other foreign brands have already moved into this market?

>> What is the local fashion market like and who are the key players?

To answer these questions, investigations must review market trends and data from the recent past and gauge the current market situation. In addition, forecasting and analysis will need to be employed to determine and predict the future potential of the market. Brazil has a growing market for luxury goods, driven by an expanding middle class and an increasing number of multimillionaires with an appetite for such brands as Chanel, Dior, Louis Vuitton, Gucci, Goyard, Hermès, Burberry and Prada. All these brands have stores in the main cities – São Paulo, Rio de Janeiro and Brasília. High-street giants Gap, H&M and Zara have also extended their operations into the region. Added to this, Brazil has a notable domestic fashion industry. There is São Paulo Fashion Week (SPFW) and Fashion Rio. There are Brazilian fashion brands also looking to expand into Europe and the USA. Osklen, one of Brazil's most notable fashion labels, was established in 1989 in Rio de Janeiro as a lifestyle brand by the Brazilian entrepreneur Oskar Metsavaht. Osklen has a big online presence in the USA and sells online in the UK via Lyst, Farfetch and ShopStyle. So this brand, too, would need to have done extensive market research or relied on research undertaken by its e-commerce partners in order to expand its reach.

Market research into the size and trends within a market does not provide enough information on which to base decisions. Broader marketing research should also be carried out to assess how best to operate in a new geographic market. The process of importing, distributing and selling European-manufactured luxury goods in Brazil is challenging; information on local taxes, import duties and supply-chain logistics will need to be researched. Import duties into Brazil are extremely high, making luxury goods much more costly for Brazilian consumers than if they are purchased abroad, and government procedures are complicated. When extending a business into new territories there will be political, economic, cultural, technological and logistical implications to consider, so PESTEL analysis will also be required (see pages 86–7). The next questions should therefore be:

» What issues will the PESTEL analysis reveal?

» What resources will be needed?

» Are there local business partners or agencies that could help?

There are market-research companies that specialize in providing intelligence on different sectors of the global market, and there are also many auxiliary businesses set up to aid businesses that wish to expand into new markets, such as trading agents, sourcing agents and supply-chain and logistic experts. These companies understand the intricacies of the local market and can help foreign companies wishing to navigate these complexities. For example, the Hong Kong sourcing giant Li & Fung Ltd manages the sourcing and supply-chain logistics for several global fashion brands. In 2009 it entered a long-term sourcing agreement with Liz Claiborne Inc., which owns brands including Kate Spade, Juicy Couture and Lucky Brand. Many of the major foreign luxury brands now trading in China and Asia have formed similar alliances, negotiated business partnerships or entered into licensing deals with local Hong Kong and Chinese trading companies. (For more information on brand licensing, see Chapter 5.)

Working with local partners can help the brand understand and respect the impact of cultural differences, both in the way business is conducted and as reflected in consumer preferences and purchasing behaviour. The hypothetical luxury brand discussed above will require this information so that it can ensure that its approach, products and communication campaigns are sensitive to and suitable for the Brazilian market. This is very important, and without proper knowledge, things can go wrong. This happened when the

British chain-store brand Marks & Spencer entered the Chinese market, opening a store in Shanghai in 2008. The company made assumptions based on its understanding of the Hong Kong market, where it already had ten stores. Unfortunately this did not equate to the realities of China's mainland, where different consumer behaviour and needs applied. One of the problems was that Marks & Spencer had miscalculated the sizing for their clothes ranges, so all the smaller sizes rapidly sold out. Sir Stuart Rose, CEO at the time, said in an interview with the *Financial Times* in 2009, 'We need to get the A to Z of sizing right and we need better market research.'

Market size

The size of a market can be determined in terms of numbers of consumers purchasing within it, or, more commonly, as a figure expressing its financial value. For example, the global apparel market was estimated by a Statista report to be in the region of US$1.7 trillion in 2023. According to the same report, the European apparel market was valued at US$484.2 billion in 2023, of which the largest proportion belonged to the womenswear sector, at US$263.2 billion. A report by Oberlo put the US fashion retail market at US$494.89 billion for the same year.

Each year, analysts publish a range of market reports, detailing the current size and predicted growth of different global and fashion product markets. It is usually necessary to purchase these reports, but some of the headline data can be found online. Across the various reports, the figures don't always match, and this can be because they are compiled for slightly different time frames, for different groupings of market products, such as for fashion apparel, or for fashion and textiles (which may relate to the fashion market specifically, or may include carpets, for example). So it is important to keep a close eye on the small print or detail of the report's approach. Data can be compiled on any of the following:

Location of market: global, international, national

Product category: accessories, leather goods, apparel, lingerie, beauty and fragrance

Who the product is for: women, men, gender-neutral, children, babies

Product type: pro-sport, active wear, sport-luxe, streetwear, denim, formal wear, bridal

Market level: Branded fashion, high street, fast fashion or sustainable fashion, resale or vintage couture, premium, mid-market, value or commodity market

Once the size of a particular market has been established, the next important issue to determine is the direction and trend within the market under investigation.

Market trends

Even though information on the size of a market at a specific point in time is extremely helpful, it is even more useful to track market data over a longer time frame. This helps to reveal prevailing trends, indicating if the market is expanding, stagnant or contracting. If a market is experiencing a period of growth, there is the opportunity for those already operating within that market to increase their business. But market potential may also encourage new entrants. This means that even in good times, existing players cannot become complacent; they must remain competitive or they may lose business to newer market participants. If a market is static or contracting (this could be because of cultural, social or demographic changes, or as a result of an economic downturn), operators in the market will be fighting to ensure they do not lose business or go out of business altogether. Unfortunately, this was the case during the economic downturn caused by the COVID-19 pandemic, and many businesses closed during that period. Gap, for example, closed all its Gap and Gap Outlet stores in the UK and Ireland. However, for others – particularly those focusing on e-commerce and D2C business models – the situation presented an opportunity. They were able to thrive when customers could not shop in store, and brands selling loungewear and tracksuits did well. Sales of the Champion brand, for instance, went up by 21 per cent owing to consumer interest in fitness and comfortable clothing.

Fashion forecasting and market intelligence

An essential element of monitoring the market is keeping abreast of changing fashion trends. It is vital to keep a watchful eye on developments in global fashion culture, catwalk trends, street style and the market in general. But it is not just about monitoring the present or analysing the recent past; the trick with fashion is to try to predict the future. Designers start planning their collections up to a year in advance of when they will sell in-store. Fabric mills develop their ranges at least two years in advance, and fibre manufacturers and colour-prediction agencies work even further ahead of the season. This is why fashion can be such a risky business, and why so much research must be undertaken. Fashion forecasting, market intelligence and trend reporting are indispensable constituents of the apparel and accessory industry. Retailers, design houses and manufacturers use market intelligence and forecasting information to

↑ After-sales service has become a distinguishing factor for fashion brands and retailers to consider. The premium denim brand Nudie Jeans (top) offers its customers a free in-store repair service. Alternatively, the Nudie Jeans Repair Kit containing thread, denim patches and a thimble can be sent to customers. The Japanese retailer Uniqlo (above) offers an alteration service and will hem jeans free of charge.

help them with important product and strategy decisions. The trend-forecasting industry was reported to be worth US$36 billion in 2011, and more recent figures by Statista on the market-research industry as a whole reveal that it was worth more than US$81 billion in 2022. Agencies' services range from specialist consultancy, tailored to meet the specific requirements of the commissioning company, to off-the-peg forecasting, styling and market intelligence reports that can be purchased by professionals in the fashion industry. The US companies WGSN and Stylesight, Trendstop in the UK, and the French companies Trend Union, Promostyl and Peclers are among the best-known. Many of these agencies operate an online subscription service with updates daily, weekly and monthly.

Most fashion-forecasting and intelligence agencies will supply:

» Market intelligence

» Consumer insight

» Information on emerging global trends

» Reports on street style

» Catwalk reports

» Key styles and design ideas

» Colour forecasting

» Fabric trend information

» Information on print and graphic trends

For a larger fashion business, a subscription or bespoke package with a trend-forecasting agency will be affordable, but for an individual or small business the expense may not be viable. It is possible to access relevant information on trends, colour and street style at little or no cost through primary research and observation. Social media and photo-sharing services, such as Instagram, Tumblr and Pinterest, make it easy to monitor trends.

↓ ↘ Thousands of international buyers and designers visit Première Vision in Paris each season. Around 700 textile suppliers from approximately 28 countries exhibit their fabric collections and innovations. Fashion industry professionals use the fair as an opportunity to preview up-and-coming trends and colours, and to place orders for sample fabrics so they can begin the design and development process for the next season.

Fashion designers, manufacturers, retail buyers, merchandisers and brand managers all use a melange of market and trend information as a basis from which to predict the future direction for their businesses. Sales forecasting is a key part of the research and analysis process carried out by buyers, merchandisers and product managers. This type of forecasting uses data on historical sales patterns to gauge potential sales for the coming season. This background data must be used in conjunction with trend-forecasting information so that a design and buying team has the best chance of 'getting it right' when stock finally hits the shops. In fashion retail, sales data is usually reviewed daily and analysed in more depth every week. Major assessment of sales, consumer purchasing patterns and product performance will take place at the end of each season for both retail and wholesale businesses. Designers and product developers will build on this information with research into colour, fabric, design and technical trends so that they can develop appropriate products for the coming seasons.

Life cycle of a fashion trend

An important point about markets and fashion trends is that they change over time; that is why research should be an ongoing discipline.

Fad This is short-lived and usually difficult to predict. A fashion fad can be an individual item, look or style that becomes intensely popular almost overnight, then dies out as suddenly as it came in. A fad might be in fashion for one season only, and definitely out of fashion the next season. A fad generally lasts for a year or less.

Trend The main difference between a fad and a trend is duration. A fashion trend may start slowly with low acceptance in the early stages and build momentum over time. It will peak and then taper off, either disappearing altogether or flattening out and remaining in fashion long enough to be reclassified as a classic. The women's trouser suit has become a classic. The seed of this trend was sown in 1966, when Yves Saint Laurent introduced 'Le Smoking', a tuxedo trouser suit for women. This illustrates how a trend may be initiated at couture or designer level and work its way down through the market levels to be sold in high-street stores; this is known as the trickle-down effect. Trends can also move in the other direction, starting on the street and bubbling up through the fashion hierarchy to be reinterpreted by designers on the catwalks of Paris, London, Milan and New York.

Megatrend A megatrend is a large social, cultural, economic, political or technological change that is slow to form but will influence a market over an extended time frame. Denim jeans could be described as a megatrend.

LIFE CYCLE OF A FASHION TREND

The first stage of the trend life cycle is the introduction stage. The next is growth, then comes maturity, and finally decline, which may tail off to nothing, or (in the case of a fashion classic) remain low and constant. Sales of a fashion fad might take off suddenly. Growth might be rapid, reach a peak, then drop quickly; the fad will die out once everyone who wants the particular fashion has it. Fashion buyers must be sharp when it comes to fads; while they obviously have great potential if you get it right, there is a risk of getting on the bandwagon too late and being caught with stock that no one wants. When a fashion trend reaches maturity, sales flatten out. This is the indication that the market is saturated and sales will start to decline. Declining sales for a specific retailer or supplier could also result when a trend is established, and other competitors offer something similar that consumers prefer.

SALES

FAD

TREND

CLASSIC

TIME

INTRODUCTION | GROWTH | MATURITY | DECLINE

→ SPINEXPO™ Trend moodboards created by the trend-forecasting consultancy Sophie Steller Studio. SPINEXPO™ is an international trade fair specializing in fibres, yarns and technical textiles. Each season SPINEXPO™ publishes information on key trends, colours, yarn developments and fabric concepts in collaboration with Sophie Steller Studio. The studio has worked with brands and retailers including Polo Ralph Lauren, H&M and Gap.

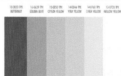

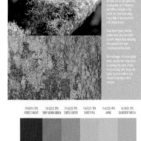

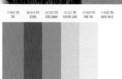

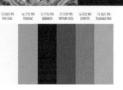

Growth markets

According to figures published by Statista in 2023, the global apparel market is set to increase by US$200 billion, reaching a total of US$1.94 trillion by 2027 and topping US$2 trillion by 2028. These figures highlight how important fashion is as a global value-creating industry. Established fashion brands often consider expanding either by extending the number of regions in which they sell in their own country, or by entering a new global territory. The Japanese retailer Uniqlo has expanded into the USA with stores in New York, San Francisco and Los Angeles, but the parent company, Fast Retailing Co., is reported to have increased its USA marketing budget so that it can extend its reach. The company wants Uniqlo to have the same level of awareness among customers across America as it does in Asia.

↑ The Loro Piana flagship store in the Dubai Mall. The store was reopened in 2023 after extensive renovation, at which point the LVMH website stated that it was the 'first [store] in the world to showcase the new Loro Piana concept and exclusive VIP client salons' so that customers could indulge in an 'unparalleled luxury shopping experience'.

For fashion brands looking to grow, there are several global market areas of interest. The BRIC countries – Brazil, Russia, India and China – have been significant, particularly China. The expansion of European luxury brands into BRIC countries has been driven by the growth of wealthy middle-class consumers and the emergence of such megacities as Shanghai and São Paulo, and such middle-weight cities as Harbin, China. According to a report by the global management consultancy Bain & Company, China is set to become the world's biggest luxury market, with Chinese luxury consumers travelling less and shopping more in their home market in the aftermath of the COVID-19 pandemic. The report predicts that from 2025 Chinese consumers will account for almost half of all luxury spending, and that e-commerce will be the biggest channel for luxury spending globally.

Reports of this kind are only predictions, and market situations do not remain static; they can be affected significantly by global events and economics. Growth into Russia, for example, was halted after the Russian invasion of Ukraine began in February 2022. Key retailers H&M, Zara, Uniqlo, Bershka, Pull & Bear and ASOS pulled out, as did many designer brands, including Alexander McQueen, Hermès, Balenciaga, Brioni, Chanel and Gucci.

The Middle East and Africa are also areas that have been cited for growth. Dubai, the financial centre of the United Arab Emirates, is the location of the world's largest shopping mall. Growth in this region is generated by the high purchasing power of customers. Before the pandemic, this market was growing at 6 per cent a year according to the Dubai Design and Fashion Council, as quoted by the Fashion Trust Arabia. Naturally, most of the world's prestigious luxury and fashion brands are housed there, along with well-known mass-market names H&M, Zara, Forever 21, Banana Republic, Bershka, Urban Outfitters and Victoria's Secret.

The African fashion market is gaining strength thanks to a growing number of high net worth individuals and an increasingly wealthy middle class, with Angola and Nigeria emerging as markets for luxury. African designers are also becoming more prominent on the global fashion stage. International celebrities Naomi Campbell and Zendaya have been pictured wearing the work of African designers. For her film *Black Is King* (2020), Beyoncé showcased outfits by several designers, among them Loza Maléombho from Côte d'Ivoire and Adama Amanda Ndiaye from Senegal (founder of the label Adama Paris and instigator of Dakar Fashion Week).

Expanding into new global market territories is one option for a company looking to extend its business, but not the only one. The marketing tool known as Ansoff's Matrix can be used to identify possible approaches.

Market opportunity: Ansoff's Matrix

Ansoff's Matrix offers four potential scenarios for opportunity that could be used by a company seeking to extend its business:

1. Market penetration

2. Market development

3. Product development

4. Diversification

Market penetration means continuing to sell existing product within an existing market with the aim of capitalizing and improving upon the profitability of the current market proposition. Essentially, this presents several key strategies:

» Increase number of customers

» Increase customers' average spend

» Increase margin (raise prices and buy in at lower cost price)

» Improve product mix and range plan

This first scenario equates to the general situation within fashion. Although fashion product could be considered new each season, many designers and retailers producing their own collections stick to a recognized formula, and it is usual for ranges to include signature or carry-over styles that customers have come to expect.

Market development is also common within fashion, when brands expand their business by taking an existing product to a new market. South Korea has become a new hotspot for expansion.

The Swedish label Toteme, started by Elin Kling and Karl Lindman in 2014, continued its overseas growth with a new store in the Hyundai Main department store, and a second in the Hyundai Trade Center department store, both in Seoul's upscale district of Gangnam. Toteme's first foray into the Asian market was China, opening its debut store in the Taikoo Li Qiantan mall in Shanghai, to sit alongside a raft of fashion and luxury brands including Balenciaga, Dior, Fendi, Giorgio Armani, Gucci, Hermès, Loewe, Louis Vuitton, Moncler, Prada, Saint Laurent and Zegna. Toteme also has a second Shanghai store in the Réel mall.

Expansion into new markets does not have to be physical. In 2021 the Danish fashion brand Ganni, which is B Corp-certified (see pages 74–5), launched in China through a direct-to-consumer e-commerce collaboration with Tmall, part of the Alibaba Group. According to an article on Fashion United by the fashion journalist Danielle Wightman-Stone in 2021, this gave Ganni 'access to more than 800 million active and digital-first consumers on the platform and will allow Chinese consumers to experience the "full Ganni universe"', with events hosted by Tmall and a presence on Chinese social media platforms Weibo, WeChat and Redbook.

↑ The Dior Autumn/Winter 2023 Ready-to-Wear show held at the historic Gateway of India in Mumbai. Maria Grazia Chiuri, creative director of Dior, wanted to highlight the long-standing collaboration and 'creative dialogue' between the fashion house and the Chanakya atelier and school of craft in Mumbai. Chanakya is known for its intricate beading, embroidery and craftsmanship.

← (left to right) Gaeul, Wonyoung, Yujin, Leeseo and Liz, members of the K-Pop girl group IVE, attend a photocall for the RIMOWA event at Rimowa's Cheongdam flagship store in Seoul in May 2023.

ANSOFF'S MATRIX

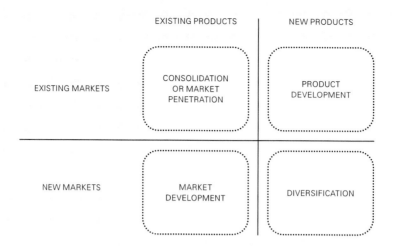

Product development relates to developing new product for an existing market. This allows growth by capitalizing on a brand name to launch a new individual product or branded product range, such as a diffusion line.

Diversification means developing new product for a completely new market, such as homeware or fragrance. This is the most risky of the four options. It usually requires solid strategic partnerships and is most likely to be achieved by licensing the brand name. Licensing is discussed further in Chapter 5.

Degrowth

All the examples on pages 116–18 relating to brand expansion are predicated on the concept of market growth. This is where fashion comes up against an ideological conundrum when considering the effects of constant growth on the environment. By contrast, there is the concept of degrowth. This is a movement of activists and researchers who advocate for the prioritization of ecological well-being as opposed to over-production and excess consumption. The ambition is to balance economics with planetary boundaries by reducing how much we produce and consume. At its heart, degrowth rejects the fast-fashion business model. According to the article 'Degrowth: The Future Fashion Could Choose', published on the app Good on You in 2022, degrowth 'builds on the work of ecological and anti-colonial theorists … the concept of degrowth is closely linked with climate justice, Indigenous rights, and reparations for fashion's extractive and neo-colonial production models.'

What could fashion and degrowth look like? Fashion Revolution poses a new scenario in a piece by Lauren Rees in 2022, 'Slow Down and Scale Back: Degrowth in the Fashion Industry'.

Rees envisions a system where big fashion brands 'slow down their production [and] pay their workers a living wage'. The idea is that garment workers 'make less but earn more'. In order to do this, the end-consumer might have to pay more for the final product. This, however, is not mentioned specifically in the Fashion Revolution vision. What the article does propose is that profits could be spread throughout the entire supply chain, 'supporting clean energy, pollution reduction and fair wages'.

Bella Webb, in 'Degrowth: The Future that Fashion Has Been Looking For?' (*Vogue Business*, 2022), cites Professor Kate Fletcher, who believes that 'fashion needs to reduce its resource use and waste by fourfold to exist within planetary boundaries'. The article explains that the idea of a fourfold reduction comes from the work of Ernst von Weizsäcker, the author of *Factor Four: Doubling Wealth, Halving Resource Use* (1997).

Key to the discussion of degrowth is the concept of the **global north** versus the **global south**. This relates to how countries can be classified geographically by their socio-economic and political characteristics. The global north includes the USA, Canada, the UK, Europe, Israel, Japan, South Korea, Australia and New Zealand. According to the United Nations Finance Center for South-South Cooperation, there are 77 countries classified in the global south. Regions and countries include Africa, South America, Indonesia, India, Pakistan, China, Bangladesh, Vietnam and Sri Lanka. Many of these are significant in the manufacture of fashion products for markets in the global north. Research conducted by the anthropologist Jason Hickel and published in *The Lancet* in 2020 quantifies the 'national responsibility for damages related to climate change by looking at national contributions to cumulative CO_2 emissions in excess of the planetary boundary'. Hickel found that the global north is responsible for 92 per cent of excess. Most countries in this region were found to be within their boundary, including India and China, although Hickel's view was that China would soon overshoot its boundary.

So, are there any fashion brands working towards a degrowth model of sustainability? There are, but each is tackling it in a different way. Some brands and their initiatives have already been mentioned in Chapter 2 in the sections on rental fashion, sustainable fashion, B Corps, the circular economy, slow fashion, and mend and repair.

↓ One of the most famous examples of a fashion brand taking a stand against consumption is Patagonia's 'Don't Buy This Jacket' campaign on Black Friday in 2011. Sales rose by 30 per cent following the campaign, so it could be said that the advert was not successful in its intended purpose, but Patagonia claimed that it did raise awareness of consumption and the resources required to manufacture the garment.

Market research methods

Once research information has been gathered, its relevance can be assessed and the data analysed. The aim is to establish facts that can help with business and marketing decisions. Research data obtained by first-hand investigation is termed **primary research**. New data is gathered to address a specific question, using direct methods, such as interviews, or indirect methods, such as observation. Information gathered through reading reports and surveys compiled by someone else is called **secondary research**. This involves the collation and analysis of found data to explore the question to be addressed.

In addition, research can be either qualitative or quantitative:

Qualitative research investigates the quality of something and provides evidence about how and why the market is the way it is. Qualitative research is exploratory in nature and is useful for gathering facts on what consumers think or feel about particular issues relevant to the investigation. It can be carried out on its own or used as a forerunner to quantitative study. It helps form an overview of a market and assess the need for more in-depth quantitative investigations. Qualitative consumer research usually takes place face to face in small focus groups or individual interviews. Many fashion retailers and design companies invite a selection of consumers to preview a product range and try on garments before the seasonal launch in-store. Alternatively, they may invite influencers to try items in advance so that they can give feedback and share their support with their followers online. These methods help the company to gauge the likely response to the range and to specific products, packaging and marketing materials. Feedback is very useful in working out what might be bestsellers. Buyers have a better chance of determining appropriate quantities for the buy and working out the ratio of styles and colours if they receive pre-season information of this nature. Social media is a great tool in the first instance, since it can provide a starting point for identifying trends and gaining consumer insight. Instagram, Facebook and X (formerly Twitter) can assist the researcher in identifying suitable respondents to invite for face-to-face interviews or to join focus groups.

Quantitative research is numerically orientated. It quantifies the market, and can be used to calculate market share and provide detailed statistics on consumers. Market-research surveys that gather data from a large sample of respondents are quantitative in nature. They can be conducted face to face (either in the street or at home), via online questionnaires, by post or via telephone.

Primary research or **field research** is the gathering of original data by going out into the field. Market-research surveys, questionnaires, **focus groups** and individual interviews are all primary research. Primary research can also be used to collect data on products and to investigate competitors. It does not have to be complicated; visits to the high street or mall, recording information on products, styles, colours, prices, special offers and mark-down, and keeping an eye on fashion all constitute primary research. Research excursions to stores are a quick and simple way to gather current information at first hand. This can be augmented with follow-up online research. If research is conducted regularly, you should notice both subtle and dramatic changes that occur in the marketplace over time.

Secondary research or **desk research** investigates and reviews data published online, in books, magazines and trade journals, or via academic, government or industry sources. It is used to determine the size and make-up of a market sector and get background information and detailed financial data. Much of this information is available free of charge from libraries, but some sources require payment for access to material. Companies that supply industry information as a commercial venture usually charge substantial sums, but the cost is likely to be considerably less than that of hiring a market-research company to conduct extensive primary research.

The approach to primary and secondary research will depend on the exact nature of the project and why the research has been commissioned. Before research gets underway, first determine the aims and objectives of the study. Marketing and market research should be considered when:

» Starting a new business

» Entering a new market

» Launching a new product or product range

» Creating a brand identity or brand redesign

» Adding a new service

» Targeting a new customer segment

» Developing a major promotional campaign

» Reviewing progress or resetting targets

» Researching how to compete in a market

» Responding to changing situations within the market

» Investigating underperformance

» Keeping relevant to and abreast of the market situation

THE MARKET RESEARCH PROCESS

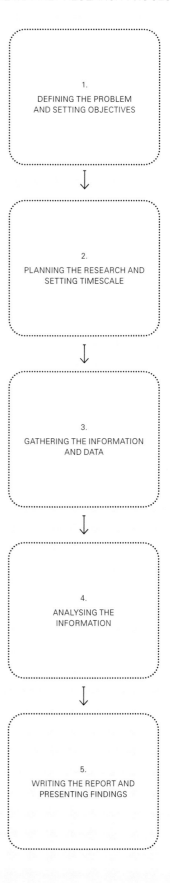

1. DEFINING THE PROBLEM AND SETTING OBJECTIVES

2. PLANNING THE RESEARCH AND SETTING TIMESCALE

3. GATHERING THE INFORMATION AND DATA

4. ANALYSING THE INFORMATION

5. WRITING THE REPORT AND PRESENTING FINDINGS

↑ Trend-forecasting companies, such as Stylesight, use freelance trend scouts to report on street fashions around the globe. Seen here (top) is a street-style photo captured outside the Munthe show at Copenhagen Fashion Week Spring/Summer 2024. Above, a guest wears a Body Butter denim outfit with Loewe sneakers and Moncler glasses outside Pillings in Shibuya at Rakuten Fashion Week, Tokyo, Autumn/Winter 2023.

Once the purpose of the research is clear and the exact aims have been clarified, the next step is to determine who might be most suitable to carry out the research, analyse the findings and produce a final report. Large-scale market-research projects are usually carried out by consultancies or agencies, but it may be possible to farm out some aspects to a number of different specialist companies, or carry out parts of the project in-house. A full-service market-research agency will be able to help you determine the scope of the research and will assist with the development of a customized project. They will be able to carry out quantitative research and provide personnel to design and conduct market-research surveys, questionnaires and interviews. They will also be able to analyse and evaluate data.

Another option is to use a trend and market consultancy. Such firms usually concentrate on qualitative research and provide information on consumer types, lifestyle trends and market trends. Condé Nast (the publisher of *Vogue*), for example, commissioned the Future Laboratory to carry out consumer research so that it could learn more about the motivations and needs of the modern reader of fashion magazines. Condé Nast also has an in-house consumer insight team, who research and report regularly on customer behaviour and engagement with their fashion and lifestyle publications and media content. Consultancy companies are practised in conducting focus groups and running interview panels. They may have viewing facilities where interviews and discussions can be watched or recorded. (It is important to stress that market research is subject to guidelines and laws regarding data protection.) Trend consultancies may use the services of a network of freelance **trend scouts** located in major fashion and trend hotspots across the globe. Consultancies also commission people to go out into the marketplace as a **mystery shopper** or to carry out an investigative procedure called **comparative shopping**. Consultancies of this type may be able to provide additional quantitative research; they may subcontract this to a fieldwork and tabulation agency specializing in data collection and survey analysis.

Another option is to conduct market investigations in-house, or commission one company to carry out fieldwork and engage a data preparation and analysis agency to analyse the results; these agencies have sophisticated software programmes suitable for in-depth data analysis. If the plan is to employ an outside agency to conduct research or analysis, it is important to define the task and brief the consultancy or agency. A brief should contain:

» Information on the company and its current market

» The background for the research

» The topics the research should address

» What the research should achieve

» Detailed time frame for the project

» Deadline for submission of the report

» Available budget and resources

Even if a company wishes to carry out all or part of the investigations itself, it is important to be clear on these points before beginning the project. The next section will take you through basic primary-research methods. While professional market researchers will be able to carry these out in great depth, students, designers, buyers or individuals running a small business can also use most of them just as effectively.

Observation

A great deal of practical and easy research can be carried out simply and at little cost. One of the most beneficial market-research methods is observation of the market. It is fascinating how much valuable knowledge can be gathered at first hand by watching people in the street, perusing the shops and studying consumer behaviour as they browse and shop in-store. Constant observation of street fashion and scrutiny of the fashion retail environment is routine in the industry. Designers, buyers and marketers visit key

← Street style outside the Christian Dior Autumn/Winter 2024 show at Haute Couture Fashion Week in Paris.

↑ Visiting concept stores in top fashion
cities is a must for fashion designers
and buyers tracking trends and looking
for inspiration. 10 Corso Como in Milan
(top) and Dover Street Market in London
are two of the best-known, and both
now have outposts in other cities across
the world.

fashion cities regularly, and check out activity in their local fashion stores as part of their working routine.

Comparative shopping

Manufacturing companies and suppliers send personnel out into the marketplace to visit the stores of key competitors in order to monitor what they are up to and review their product offer. This practice is known as comparative shopping or the 'comp shop'. Comparative shopping is a simple yet important process that involves observing and recording information on the composition of fashion ranges, colours, fabrics, price points, promotional activity and visual merchandising in competitors' stores. Comp shops are a form of primary research. The usual procedure is to visit the stores and look directly at the products, but a great deal of comparative information can also be garnered using the internet. Websites and social-media platforms can themselves be the subject of a comparative exercise; they can be compared in terms of ease of use, technology, service, content, extra offers or discounts, and consumer engagement.

Like-for-like product comparison

The like-for-like (LFL) product comparison is a more detailed investigation into a specific product. This is carried out when a company wishes to investigate in depth how a particular product they currently produce or are planning to develop compares with similar items offered by competitors. LFL comparisons are generally carried out to compare core products or basics. The usual procedure is to purchase the item from several retailers. For example, if the retailer Gap wants to compare its men's basic white T-shirt with those offered by competitors, it may purchase similar product from Uniqlo, J.Crew, Hanes and Calvin Klein. The garments will be compared in terms of price, fabric and make quality, design details and fit, care and performance. It is normal to send the garments to a testing laboratory to check on pilling (bobbling), spirality (twisted seams caused by stress on the fibres) and shrinkage. Obviously, purchasing garments and sending them to a lab for testing will incur some costs, but it is possible to carry out LFL comparisons without purchasing garments, in which case comparisons will be mainly for price, styling, fabric composition and colour options.

Mystery shopping

Many market-research companies employ researchers to enter shops in the role of a potential customer. These undercover observers can monitor and report on their experience of customer service and other retail activities. Retailers may commission mystery

LIKE-FOR-LIKE COMPARISON CHART

PRODUCT MEN'S FIVE-POCKET JEANS	PRICE	FABRICATION » FIBRE COMPOSITION » FABRIC WEIGHT » FABRIC FINISH OR WASH	STYLING DETAILS	CARE INSTRUCTIONS AND AFTERCARE » GARMENT LABELLING	ADDED VALUE (DETAILS OR SPECIAL OFFERS THAT ADD VALUE)
COMPANY A					
COMPANY B					
COMPANY C					
COMPANY D					

A simple table can be used as a framework for LFL product comparisons. The criteria along the top should include price, fabrication, design details, care instructions and additional labelling or product information. A column can also be added to indicate how many colour options the item comes in. Products can also be compared with regards to details that might achieve added value – this could be a unique technology used to enhance the product, or a promotional campaign with a special offer.

WAISTBAND
distinctive, embroidered 1969 stitching

BELT LOOPS
durable tri-fold with a little give

POCKETS
soft, clean finished pockets

HARDWARE
stamped copper rivets

SEAMS
vintage-inspired, busted-side seams

FABRIC
premium, ring-spun denim

STITCHING
heavy-gauge thread and single-needle stitching

shopping as part of their overall market research so that they can analyse and compare the service offered by competitors. In light of the growing relevance of 'process' (see pages 28–9) as part of the marketing mix, and the increasing need for retailers to provide an exciting and engaging shopping experience, mystery shopping should be viewed as a worthwhile investigative method.

Focus groups

Focus groups and discussion groups run by experienced market researchers provide information concerning consumers' opinions, attitudes and purchasing behaviour. A selection of consumers is invited to view the collection and give feedback. Fashion companies often use these groups to gauge the reaction to new marketing campaigns or product ranges before their launch, and the information can be extremely helpful for designers, buyers and merchandisers, who can use the data to determine which styles and colours will be popular. The downside to research of this nature is that the small sample group may not be representative of consumers as a whole. There is also a risk that the results will be

Interviews, focus groups and product testing

ZACARIAS 1925

ZACARIAS 1925 is a contemporary and conceptual brand based in Manila, the Philippines. Launched by creative director Rita Nazareno, it produces exclusively handwoven bags and home accessories at the S.C. Vizcarra workshop. The original workshop was founded in 1925 in Manila by Nazareno's grandmother, and the name ZACARIAS 1925 pays homage both to her grandmother and to her grandfather Zacarias.

Nazareno's coveted designer pieces are inspired by contemporary art, architecture and cinema, references that are reflected in a wide array of colourful, playful and thought-provoking designs. The ZACARIAS 1925 brand is shown and promoted at trade fairs in Paris and Milan, including Maison et Objet Paris, Première Classe Paris, Pitti Immagine Filati in Florence, Super Milan and the Salone del Mobile Milan. The brand sells in fashion and concept stores in the USA, Belgium, Italy, France, Japan and the Philippines.

Before launching a new product, Nazareno conducts research to discover how it is perceived by the target audience. This can include holding a focus group, asking someone to wear-test a bag to see how it feels to wear or carry, getting information on how it performs functionally, and gathering feedback from a selection of trusted reviewers. This type of research allows Nazareno to test ideas and decide whether changes are required to a prototype design.

← Nazareno holding a small focus group in Manila to preview one of the proposed designs for ZACARIAS 1925.

skewed if one person in the group becomes dominant and sways the opinions and responses of other participants. However, if the sample consumer group is selected by a reputable consultancy and the session steered by a professional moderator, a focus group can provide insight into consumer attitudes and help to negate any assumptions that might have been held by a retailer about the customer or the product.

Interviews

Face-to-face interviews are useful for gathering more in-depth consumer information. They can be used to expand on data from questionnaires, and to gather qualitative data. Interviews can be run as a semi-structured discussion where respondents can share their opinions and views. This type of interview allows researchers to gather customers' feedback on a particular brand, and on competing products and services. Generally, an interview lasts 10–30 minutes and can be conducted on any number of selected individuals within the target market. Interviews can be carried out over the telephone, but face-to-face is better for more lengthy discussions,

Nazareno explains that after her North Star bag was wear-tested for several weeks, the feedback led to a slight change in the shape, the opening and the D-rings of the design. Another example was when Nazareno showed a prototype of her pink Be Bag to a reviewer. She was doubting whether to go further in producing it, but the feedback was highly positive. The comments were, 'You must put this out and do a black version as well.'

↓ The Be Bag in pink and black. A review of the prototype led to this bestselling design being produced in two colours.

↑ The North Star bag. This special limited-edition bag was produced in a collaboration between Nazareno, Patrisse Cullors (one of the founders of the Black Lives Matter movement) and the poet Nissi Berry. The bag is square-framed, representing a section of a patchwork quilt. The front is decorated with the North Star, and a poem by Berry is etched into the leather of the back. The North Star bags have poignant significance and meaning. Enslaved Africans followed the North Star when escaping to freedom, and the patterns sewn into quilts hanging along the escape route are said to have held secret messages directing the fleeing slaves to the next safe house. Cullors has travelled extensively wearing this bag – it is a conversation starter – raising awareness of the deep themes of her work: 'ancestry, abolition and healing'. Profits from the bags go to help previously incarcerated Black women – of whom Berry is one.

or if the research requires the interviewee to look at products. The biggest drawback is the time it might take to carry out the interview, particularly if it is done on the street. Busy people do not always want to be stopped or devote time to lengthy questions.

Surveys and questionnaires

Surveys or questionnaires are extremely helpful for collecting quantitative information from a large number of people. It is essential to ensure that questions are not leading or biased in any way, and that they are designed to obtain accurate and relevant information. Questionnaires must also be designed so that the data can be analysed systematically once it has been gathered.

Try to ensure that a questionnaire will not take too long to complete. A short statement explaining the purpose of the study should be included at the beginning – you want to establish a rapport with respondents and engage them with the project. When designing the questions, think carefully about the objective of the survey: what it is you want to know and why. Make sure to:

> » Keep questions short and simple

> » Make questions precise

> » Avoid ambiguity

> » Avoid negatives

Open-ended questions allow respondents to formulate their own answers, while closed-format questions force respondents to choose from prescribed options. It is possible to use a mixture of the two, but it is best to keep open-ended questions to a minimum, since they are much harder to analyse than closed-format questions. The **Likert scale** can be used to gather consumer attitudes to particular statements, for example, 'Sustainable fashion should be fashionable as well as ethical'. The scale offers five positions:

1. Disagree strongly

2. Disagree

3. Neither agree nor disagree

4. Agree

5. Agree strongly

Responses to questions using the Likert scale can be analysed easily using a numerical system that equates to each position: agree strongly = 5, agree = 4, and so on. The format of questions using a five-point system can also be adapted. For example, you could ask

'How important is price to you when you shop for clothes?' and offer
the following options:

1. Of no importance

2. Not very important

3. No opinion

4. Fairly important

5. Very important

It is, however, not good practice to design a questionnaire using
this system alone. Respondents tend to choose one or two of the
five positions and tick them consistently. Another option is to use
questions that offer a checklist from which respondents can choose.
A questionnaire designed to find out if respondents owned clothing
made from sustainable fabrics might offer the following tick list:

» Garments made from hemp

» Garments made from organic cotton

» Garments made from bamboo fabric

» Garments or accessories made from vegan leather

» Garments made from any other sustainable fabric

» Don't know

Respondents are asked to mark as many options as applicable.

Another approach is ranking. This is where respondents are given
a list of options and asked to rank them in order of preference. For
example, 'Please rank the following according to how relevant you
consider them to ethical fashion (1 being most relevant and 5 being
the least relevant)':

» Fair-trade

» Low carbon footprint

» Ethical production and fair wages

» Sustainable or circular design

» Recycling and reusing

When setting out the order for your questionnaire, it is best to
start with general questions. Begin with the easiest and simplest
questions and work through to those that are most particular or
complex. If you are using a mixture of closed-format and open-ended
questions, start with the closed-format questions.

Ethical fashion exhibition and questionnaire

WHAT'S YOUR E-MOTIVE?

When the London College of Fashion ran its first sustainability week it invited industry professionals, lecturers and students to attend seminars, debates and conferences to discuss sustainable and ethical fashion. An exhibition and interactive data-gathering exercise entitled 'What's Your E-motive?' was held as part of the activities. The exhibition aimed to raise awareness of and inform on sustainable and ethical fashion, engage the audience with the debate, and encourage them to share their views. The overall objective was to capture consumer views and understand purchasing decisions and behaviour when it comes to sustainable fashion.

The interactive exhibition showcased garments and products from a broad selection of fashion designers and companies. Adili, Amazon Life, Blackspot Shoes, Del Forte jeans, Howies, Simple Shoes and Terra Plana were some of the companies whose product was featured. Research was inherent to the exhibition; an online 'eco-wardrobe audit' questionnaire was posted on the university website and computers were placed in the gallery so that visitors could answer the audit. The combined results of the interactive exhibition questions and online eco-wardrobe audit provided the London College of Fashion with more than 400 individual responses, and almost 200 people answered the questionnaire. This revealed that 97 per cent of respondents were interested in purchasing and wearing garments that they believed to be ethical and sustainably produced, but that only a third claimed actually to own a garment that was fairly traded or made from sustainable materials.

Respondents were asked the importance of the following criteria when making purchasing decisions about clothing:

» Fashion and style

» Price

» Fabric

» Ethics behind the production of the garment

Sixty-three per cent said that fashion and style were very important when choosing clothes, while the ethics behind the production of garments was judged by 55.6 per cent to be only fairly important. Interestingly, 56.3 per cent of people said that anti-sweatshop was very important in a separate question that asked respondents to compare the importance of:

» Anti-sweatshop

» Fair-trade

» Sustainable fabrics, such as organic cotton

» Recycling and reusing garments

This result highlights the importance of language and context. It may have been easier for people to grasp the meaning behind the emotive, more specific term 'anti-sweatshop' than the idea of ethics.

→ 'What's Your E-motive?' This exhibition at the London College of Fashion provided an opportunity to collect data on consumer attitudes to ethical fashion.

The questionnaire should conclude with questions designed to collect demographic data. You may need to know the age bracket, gender, profession and status of respondents. Think about these questions logically. If you are asking only young women to respond to the questionnaire, it is not necessary to include a tick box for male or female. But you may wish to know their chosen pronouns, depending on the angle of your survey. It is vital to preserve confidentiality and to abide by data-protection laws. Make sure it is clear who is carrying out the research and for what purpose.

It is sensible to test a draft survey on a small sample of respondents before it goes live to a large sample. This will help you to refine questions so that they are not leading, to eliminate ambiguity and to iron out any other teething problems. A well-designed questionnaire should be easy for respondents to answer by themselves online, via email, in response to a survey in a magazine, or if sent in the post. Present the results in a report that outlines the purpose of the study, explains the methodology employed to gather data, summarizes the results, and provides conclusions and recommendations based on the analysis. The main body of the report will analyse the data and illustrate results with detailed charts and tables.

Surveys are easy to undertake using online survey tools, such as SurveyMonkey, Google Forms or HubSpot. These platforms collate the results for you and give you the data in a variety of formats so that you can analyse the implications of the results.

Analysing and using marketing research

Once research has been done, it is important to analyse the results and consider carefully their implications. This should be done for each discrete element, such as the PESTEL analysis and SWOT analysis, as well as overall: what does the full range of research reveal in terms of market opportunity, internal operations, competitors and so on?

The scenario in which marketing research has been done may also support the analysis and direction for its conclusions. This is usually captured in key **takeaways**, which are the main insights the research has revealed, and which inform the decisions that are taken as a result. The standard process is to write a report to describe the methods used for the research, the information and data captured, and the takeaways or conclusions resulting from the research. Next, consider how to enter the planning and implementation stage for the project, and determine the strategy.

Planning and strategy

Strategic planning uses the key marketing and strategic tools discussed in Chapter 1 (the marketing mix, segmentation, targeting, positioning and differentiation) and the research processes outlined in this chapter. With this in place, it is possible to consider the marketing strategy (which could include various promotion and communication campaigns) and write a **marketing plan** setting out the **strategy** and **tactics** so that the plan can be achieved.

At this point it is important to explain the difference between strategy and tactics. Strategy, which comes first, is the plan designed to achieve the business's overarching goal. Tactics, which follow, are the specific actions or steps (the finer details of that plan) that will be undertaken to put the strategy into action and achieve the goals.

The goal or objective/s is the vision. WHERE do you want to get to?

The strategy is the plan. WHAT are you aiming to achieve? WHAT is your overall plan? WHAT resources are needed to get there?

The tactics are the detailed steps. HOW will we get there? HOW will each tactic be achieved?

Most businesses have a business strategy and business plan. Contained within this, or developed from it, are the marketing strategy and marketing plan. An example of a marketing strategy is to shift the perception of the brand and reach a new target audience. Tactics might include:

» Engaging a relevant influencer to front the campaign

» Asking a PR professional to write a press release and get coverage for the new brand concept

» Creating social-media content to attract the new target audience

» Developing a sales promotion campaign offering an incentive for new customers

The planning process

In order to determine the strategy and the plan, a business will go through a process of review, research and planning. The first step is to review and assess the existing circumstances of both the business and the market, to determine the overall business and marketing objectives. The next step is to devise the strategy and write the appropriate business and/or marketing plan. The tool known as SOSTAC can be used to guide this process. It was developed by Paul R. Smith in the 1990s and is still very widely used for strategic marketing. The model has six fundamental facets: **S**ituation, **O**bjectives, **S**trategy, **T**actics, **A**ctions and **C**ontrol.

The first step is what is known as Situational analysis. This is a review that considers such questions as: Where are we now? What is the current state of the market, and what are the market opportunities? This stage will include marketing research and involve SWOT and PESTEL analysis. It may also include a deeper review of the internal marketing environment with the company (see pages 105–7).

Next, use this research and review to set the vision and Objectives. As we have seen, this takes the business from where it is now to where it wants to be. It can be helpful to use 'SMART' objectives: **S**pecific, **M**easurable, **A**chievable, **R**ealistic and **T**ime-based.

With the objectives in place, the marketing Strategy can be developed along with details on the Tactics required to achieve the intended

↓ This diagram shows how the SOSTAC tool can be aligned with the steps of the planning process. Companies can use either of these maps as a framework for their planning processes, or a combination of the two.

THE PLANNING PROCESS

SOSTAC

SITUATION	OBJECTIVES	STRATEGY	TACTICS	ACTIONS	CONTROL
WHAT IS THE CURRENT SITUATION OF YOUR BUSINESS? **QUESTION:** WHERE ARE YOU NOW?	SET THE MISSION AND GOALS **QUESTION:** WHERE DO YOU WANT TO GET TO?	AN OVERVIEW OF HOW TO ACHIEVE THE OBJECTIVES **QUESTION:** WHAT ARE YOU AIMING TO ACHIEVE? WHAT IS THE PLAN?	SPECIFIC DETAILS ABOUT ACHIEVING THE OBJECTIVES **QUESTIONS:** HOW WILL YOU GET THERE? HOW TO ACHIEVE EACH TACTIC?	PUTTING THE PLAN INTO ACTION **QUESTIONS:** HOW BEST TO ACTION THE PLAN? WHO WILL UNDERTAKE EACH STEP?	MONITORING THE SITUATION AND RESULTS **QUESTION:** HOW DO YOU KNOW IF YOU HAVE ACHIEVED THE DESIRED RESULTS?

THE PLANNING PROCESS

MARKETING RESEARCH & SITUATION ANALYSIS

- MARKETING RESEARCH (PESTEL)
- CONSUMER AND COMPETITOR RESEARCH
- PRODUCT RESEARCH AND DEVELOPMENT
- SALES ANALYSIS AND FORECASTING
- INTERNAL AUDIT
- SOSTAC/SWOT

PLANNING

- DEVELOP THE VISION
- SET GOAL AND OBJECTIVES
- ESTABLISH THE STRATEGY

- DETERMINE CORRECT MARKETING MIX
- CONSIDER POSITIONING, USP AND COMPETITIVE ADVANTAGE
- DEFINE TARGET AUDIENCE
- RANGE/PRODUCT/ DISTRIBUTION/ PRICING PLAN
- DETERMINE CORRECT PROMOTIONAL MIX
- SET BUDGETS AND SALES FORECAST
- PREDICT EXPECTED RESULTS

- DETERMINE CORRECT SET OF MARKETING AND PROMOTIONAL TACTICS
- ENSURE CORRECT RESOURCES ARE IN PLACE TO IMPLEMENT TACTICS
- BRIEF AND WORK WITH STAKEHOLDERS, PARTNERS AND SUPPLIERS

IMPLEMENTATION

- CREATE AND ACTIVATE PROJECT-MANAGEMENT PLAN
- PUT MARKETING PLAN INTO ACTION
- MAKE SURE DEADLINES AND TIME FRAMES ARE CLEAR
- ACCOUNTABILITY: WHO IS DOING WHAT?
- PRODUCT AND PROMOTIONAL CAMPAIGN LAUNCH

REVIEW

- REVIEW SALES RESULTS
- REVIEW COSTS
- REVIEW RETURN ON INVESTMENT (ROI)
- REVIEW PROMOTIONAL CAMPAIGN EFFECTIVENESS

MONITOR SITUATION, CHANGE OR ADAPT ACTIONS IF NECESSARY

FEEDBACK ON RESULTS INFORMS DIRECTION FOR NEXT TIME

outcome. The objectives, strategy and tactics form the marketing plan, which can include information on who will undertake the different elements of the plan, time frames and deadlines, required resources, predicted costs and budgets. Expenditure must be carefully researched and calculated, since the proposed tactics and actions required to achieve them will all have a cost. It is important to set a budget and determine time frames to ensure the best use of resources. The key is to keep the plan simple and realistic; the overall vision should be easily understood by everyone engaged in bringing the plan to fruition. The structure of the marketing plan is outlined on page 136.

The next part in the SOSTAC model relates to putting the plan into Action. Who will undertake each step? How will you execute the plan to achieve the best results? The Action element could also relate to project management and setting up specific timelines and accountability for the different aspects of the plan.

The last element is Control. How do you know if you have achieved the desired results? How will success be measured? What is the predicted return on the investment put into the project? It is a good idea to include staging posts for monitoring and reviewing progress, and to consider the metrics you wish to measure to determine success. These are known as Key Performance Indicators (KPIs; see opposite). Aligned with all of this is a final review and feedback, assessing how the strategy performed. The findings can be integrated into marketing research and situational analysis next time.

It is worth remembering key elements from the three chapters so far. See below for those that can be used when carrying out situational analysis and developing the marketing plan.

PESTEL analysis What is going on in the macro-environment that should be factored into the planning?

Market data Information on the size of the market and its current state. For example, is it a growing market? What market opportunities have been identified?

Marketing mix Review the company's marketing mix. Is it right for the circumstances? Should a new approach be considered?

Customers Who are the existing and potential customers of the business? From which brands do they currently buy, and why? Why would they buy from you? Are you targeting them appropriately?

Competitors What brands are in direct competition with the business? What products and services do they offer, and at what price? Where are they positioned in the market? What is their USP? What customers are they targeting and how?

Differentiation and competitive advantage How is the brand, its products and services differentiated within the market, and does this provide competitive advantage?

Positioning Is the brand positioned correctly against competitors in the market? How are specific products or product categories positioned? Does any of this need to change?

Stakeholders, partners and suppliers Are you working with the right people? Are you working in the right way with your partners and suppliers? Are you acting ethically and do you align with partners who have similar values and approaches to ethics and sustainability? Who do you need to engage to support you to achieve your plan?

Return on Investment (ROI)

One of the most important considerations of a marketing campaign and its budget is to evaluate if the money has been well spent. Has the marketing plan improved the financial results for the company? By calculating the intended return on marketing investment (ROI), and later measuring if this was achieved, a business aims to justify its marketing spend and budget allocation for ongoing and future campaigns. The basic equation for calculating ROI is:

Marketing ROI = (sales growth – marketing cost) / marketing cost

However, this assumes that sales growth is directly tied to the marketing efforts and that no other factors contributed. For this reason, the real calculations can be more nuanced and complicated.

Things don't always go according to plan. It is not always possible to predict with accuracy future situations, such as how markets behave, what customers want, what competitors do, or what PESTEL factors may intervene with plans. If things do not go to plan, the strategy may need amending, or specific tactics reassessed and budgets trimmed. Plans can be reviewed regularly to ensure they are on track, or amended if needed, and it is always useful to consider whether more could be done with less.

Key Performance Indicators (KPIs)

KPIs are specific measures that are agreed on within a business. They can relate to all sorts of things across a business, such as how many new customers were gained as a result of a particular strategy, or how well employees perform in their role. For marketing, they are used to evaluate the effectiveness and performance of marketing, promotional, PR or social media campaigns. ROI described above is one such measure. There is more information

MARKETING PLAN

» The market sector, giving figures to show size and financial trends

» PESTEL analysis

» Information on the company's current position in the market

» Information on targeted customers

» Internal audit including SWOT analysis

» Current products, services and USP

» Current marketing mix, including routes to market, distribution and promotion

» Current positioning, differentiation and competitive advantage

» Information on key competitors

» Conclusions and recommendations

» Key marketing objectives, proposed strategies, actions and anticipated outcome

» Timescales, costs, budget and anticipated ROI

» Resources, strategic partners and stakeholders, relevant staff skills and capabilities

on measuring the success of campaigns in Chapter 6. There you will learn about the range of metrics used, including how to gauge audience engagement (determining how many people saw an ad), what was the return on an advertising spend (known as ROAS) and how much press attention a campaign received. Ultimately, all KPIs are used to work out if the money spent or resources used were worth it in comparison to what was achieved.

Structure of a marketing plan

A clear, well-written marketing plan communicates the company's vision and objectives to its staff as well as to strategic partners, investors and stakeholders. It is useful to have a plan so that progress can be monitored and results gauged against targets. Its basic structure should include:

» Cover page with overall title, date, name of author or company

» Contents page listing the sections with page numbers

» Brief introduction setting out the context and purpose of the plan

» One-page executive summary giving key points, key financial data and an overview of objectives, strategy and recommendations

» The main marketing plan

» Relevant references and appendices

The main body of the marketing plan (left) brings everything together. Its structure is open to interpretation, and should be tailored to the type and size of business concerned. The key is to analyse and use the marketing research and internal audit information to produce a cohesive document.

You may have spotted that one of the most important aspects of research and analysis – the customer – has not been covered in much depth in this chapter. Understanding the needs, wants and behaviour of customers, both businesses and end-consumers, is paramount to successful marketing. Since this is so significant, the whole of the next chapter is devoted to it.

4
Understanding the Customer

"I don't have an ideal, just someone who genuinely

likes my clothes, between 18 and 81." Erdem Moralıoğlu

Researching and understanding the customer are central to marketing and promotion, and essential for anyone creating, selling and promoting fashion products. This concerns business at every point in the supply chain, from manufacturer to retailer; without customers there is no business, so detailed knowledge of their preferences, motivations and purchasing behaviour is crucial. This equips designers, manufacturers, retailers and fashion-promotion professionals to design, produce, sell and promote products and services that fulfil or exceed the customers' requirements.

This chapter explains the basics behind consumer or **customer research and analysis**, and outlines the criteria, or **segmentation variables**, used to classify and profile existing or potential fashion consumers. The processes of creating a **consumer profile** or customer persona and writing a **customer pen portrait** are also explained. In addition, the chapter includes information on **mapping the customer journey** and analysing **user experience**, and concludes with simple ways of **analysing business customers**.

Defining the consumer

Before going any further, it is important to establish the difference between the often interchangeable terms 'consumer' and 'customer'. Customers are the people who purchase a product or service. The consumer, or **end-consumer**, is the person who uses or 'consumes' the product: the eventual wearer of the clothes or accessories, or user of the service. Often they are one and the same, in that the eventual wearer of the product was the customer who purchased it. However, a baby or small child, for example, despite being the end-consumer, would not be the purchasing customer. In this case, the retailer must understand not only the special requirements of a baby or child but also the motivations and expectations of the person who purchases the clothes, most generally the mother.

'Customer' is a broader term. It can be used to refer to the end-consumer, who will be a customer of a particular fashion retailer, or to describe a business customer, which could be a business or organization operating within the fashion supply chain. In the first instance the relationship described is **B2C (business-to-consumer)**. When a business is the customer of another business, the arrangement is termed as **B2B (business-to-business)**. A fashion concept store owner or online seller, for example, who purchases collections from a designer brand is a B2B customer. Companies supplying this boutique must have not only a good knowledge and understanding of the boutique owner as their business customer, but also a thorough understanding of the end-consumers or customers who purchase from the boutique. Currently most industry reports refer to consumer behaviour, but as a brand owner it is more useful to think of customers, since they are the people and businesses to whom you sell.

The terminology can be complicated by the growing concern about consumerism and its effect on global resources and the ethics of fashion production. Is it helpful to use the term 'consumers'? Might there be an alternative that would help to shape new, more sustainable behaviour?

It is also possible that new terms could be considered. 'Engager', for example, might be used for someone who engages with branded content but does not actually purchase the brand's fashion products. Engaging with branded content could involve watching online the catwalk show of a major fashion house, or looking at its TikTok channel or YouTube content, such as the behind-the-scenes mini-documentary by the filmmaker Mélinda Triana showing the making of the Dior Spring/Summer 2023 Haute Couture show.

↑ Fashion customers have varying clothing needs depending on their lifestyle and personality. The person illustrated here may be required to wear a traditional suit to work, while outside the workplace they might wish to adopt a more flamboyant or relaxed style.

There are other concepts to consider. The prosumer is a consumer who also produces products or content, whether for their own use or for others to buy into. Makers or upcyclers who sell on Depop are an example. The term 'prosumer' was coined by the futurist Alvin Toffler in his book *The Third Wave* (1980). Another term is **sellsumers**, which indicates that consumers no longer just consume, but also sell creative output to corporations or other consumers. Online democratization means more consumer participation in the world of supply and demand. This can be achieved through **co-creation**, **crowdsourcing** and user-generated online content. Co-creation is when a company creates products or generates content in cooperation with consumers or social-media followers. One form is crowdsourcing: when ideas, services, content or design tasks that would normally be carried out by company employees or suppliers are outsourced to the public, especially the online community, allowing the larger collective or 'crowd' to get involved. Crowdsourcing projects are usually achieved through collaboration, competition or popularity vote. Co-creation of this nature offers fashion brands an opportunity to involve their customers and community in the design and process of product development. This can help them to match supply and demand better, and cut down on overproduction or the production of products that customers fail to buy. This type of interaction is especially important to **Gen Z** (see pages 145–6), a generation that wants to be heard and to influence what brands are doing. According to an article in *Women's Wear Daily* in 2019, '44 percent of Gen Z wants to be in on product design, and 66 percent say it's important for brands to value their opinion.'

UNDERSTANDING CUSTOMERS

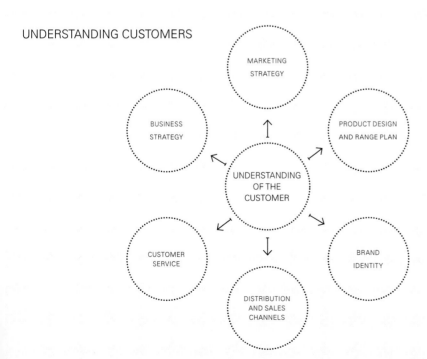

MARKETING STRATEGY

BUSINESS STRATEGY

PRODUCT DESIGN AND RANGE PLAN

UNDERSTANDING OF THE CUSTOMER

CUSTOMER SERVICE

BRAND IDENTITY

DISTRIBUTION AND SALES CHANNELS

Understanding of the customer is central to all aspects of effective marketing. Many businesses become so focused on internal processes or monitoring the activities of their competitors that they fail to recognize the needs or changing requirements of their customers. Solid background knowledge and understanding of customers is essential and should underpin key business and marketing decisions.

SEGMENTATION VARIABLES

DEMOGRAPHIC VARIABLES
GENDER
AGE
GENERATION
ETHNICITY
MARITAL STATUS
LIFE STAGE
OCCUPATION
EDUCATION
INCOME
SOCIAL GRADE CLASSIFICATION

GEOGRAPHIC VARIABLES
REGION
URBAN / SUBURBAN / RURAL
RESIDENTIAL LOCATION
HOUSING TYPE
SIZE OF CITY OR TOWN
CLIMATE

**PSYCHOGRAPHIC AND
BEHAVIOURAL VARIABLES**
LIFESTYLE
SOCIAL ASPIRATIONS
SELF-IMAGE
VALUE PERCEPTIONS
PURCHASING MOTIVES AND BEHAVIOUR
INTERESTS AND HOBBIES
ATTITUDE AND OPINIONS

USAGE AND BENEFIT VARIABLES
BENEFITS SOUGHT FROM PRODUCTS
USAGE RATES
VOLUME OF PURCHASES
PRICE SENSITIVITY
BRAND LOYALTY
END-USE OF PRODUCT

Customer segmentation

Customer segmentation is one of the key functions of marketing. It aims to divide a large customer base into smaller subgroups that share similar needs and characteristics. Not all consumers are the same – each individual will have their own complex set of motivations and purchasing behaviour – but it is possible to group them into clusters of broadly similar characteristics, needs or fashion traits. This process of customer segmentation is a key feature of STP (segmentation, targeting and positioning) marketing strategy (see page 35).

Basic customer analysis can be carried out effectively by a small business or individual designer with a limited budget; an example appears later in the chapter showing the research carried out by someone setting up their own fashion boutique and online shop (see pages 170–1). A national brand wishing to expand into a new global market may require more in-depth and detailed analysis for which the services of a professional market-research consultancy may be necessary.

Typical criteria for classification are age, gender, occupation, financial situation, lifestyle, life stage, residential location, purchasing behaviour and spending habits. Segmentation enhances a company's understanding of its customers so that it can position its brand and offer products and services designed to appeal to the targeted customers. Lifestyle plays a crucial role in segmenting fashion consumers; clothing needs and style preferences will be highly influenced by a person's type of work, peer group, and sporting or leisure activities. Attitudes and opinions on a variety of topics, such as politics, art and culture, or the environment, might also affect someone's choice of clothing. When analysing a consumer's lifestyle and determining what type of customer they might be, the aim is to gain insight into what they buy, why they buy, which companies they purchase from, and how and when they purchase.

Segmentation variables

At the beginning of any consumer analysis it is important to determine the segmentation variables that will be used to classify and characterize consumers. It is normal to use a combination of criteria; the exact mix will depend on the objectives of the research project and the specifics of the company and its market. Traditional segmentation falls into the following main categories: **demographic**, geographic, and a combination of the two known as **geo-demographic**, all focusing on identifying who customers are and where they live; and behavioural and **psychographic** segmentation, which look at the actions and psychology behind consumer purchasing behaviour. With the last type, the idea is to decipher what consumers think, how they behave, why they purchase and what product benefits they require.

Demographic segmentation

Demographic segmentation is one of the most widely used methods of classification. It employs such key variables as age, gender identity, generation, occupation, income, life stage and socio-economic status. Each of these factors is extremely important, but they should not be considered in isolation. Two female or male fashion lovers of the same age may have distinctly different attitudes and purchasing behaviours, which are not fully explained by considering their age as the determining factor. The occupation of a fashion customer may also have an impact, along with the mode of work, such as working from home, being a hybrid worker, or working mainly in an office. Income – most importantly, disposable income – will be a factor, and during an economic downturn or cost-of-living crisis, spending on fashion may be affected. In general men spend less on fashion than women, but this is not always the case. Male consumers can be extremely fashion-conscious and spend a significant proportion of their disposable income on clothing or accessories. At the end of 2022 Capri Holdings, owner of Michael Kors, and Tapestry, owner of Stuart Weitzman, Kate Spade and Coach, announced that menswear would become an important area for growth. The market-research company Euromonitor predicted at that time that menswear would grow faster than womenswear, estimating that it would reach US$547.9 billion by 2026.

Demographics also consider the life stage of a consumer: whether they are still living with their parents, are single, in a partnership or married, with or without children, or with children who have left home. As a person passes through the various phases of life, their priorities are likely to shift and their income and discretionary spend change. Key stages in the life cycle are:

» **Dependent** Children living at home, dependent on parents

» **Pre-family** Independent adults who don't yet have children

» **Family** Adults with children

» **Late stage or empty nesters** Parents with children who have left home, or older people with no children

↑ ↑ Nike sneakers on display at the Niketown store in New York.

↑ Gooey Wong shows off one of his most expensive acquisitions, a pair of Nike Dunk Low Pro SB 'Paris' sneakers featuring artwork by the French painter Bernard Buffet. Only 202 pairs of this limited edition were produced, so they exchange hands for prices in the region of US$4,000.

Market-research companies often attribute names or acronyms to different consumer groups as a way to signify stage in life. Examples are:

- » **DINKYs** Double Income No Kids Yet

- » **HEIDIs** Highly Educated Independent Individuals

- » **SINDIs** Single Independent Newly Divorced Individuals

- » **NEETs** Not in Employment, Education or Training

- » **YADS** Young and Determined Savers

- » **TIREDs** Thirty-something Independent Radical Educated Dropouts

- » **KIPPERS** Kids in Parents' Pockets Eroding Retirement Savings

- » **NETTELs** Not Enough Time to Enjoy Life

- » **Soccer mom** Spends time transporting kids to sports events

- » **School-run mum** Mothers who make an effort to look stylish even for the school run

Consumer generations

Another form of demographic segmentation is to classify consumers by generation. This considers the effect of the political, economic, social and cultural situation into which someone is born. More specifically, it takes into account the period when a consumer comes of age as a teenager or young adult, since this will play an important part in shaping their opinions and attitudes on fashion, style, consumerism, branding, advertising and technology. Generational traits can impact the way consumers shop, how they spend money, the type of item they spend it on, and their allegiance and loyalty to certain brands. The following section provides a snapshot of the key consumer generations from baby boomers to Generation Z.

Leading-edge baby boomers

Baby boomers were originally defined as those born between 1946 and 1964. However, this 20-year generation span was later broken down into two groups: leading-edge baby boomers (1946–54) and trailing-edge baby boomers (1954–65). The name 'boomer' alludes to the birth-rate explosion that occurred during the period of economic stability following World War II. As they came of age, baby boomers challenged traditions and adopted styles of dress guaranteed to upset the Establishment: long hair for men, for instance, and the

shortest of miniskirts for women. Ironically, baby boomers are now part of the Establishment, and wealthy in comparison to other generations. However, they are increasingly being left out in the cold by fashion companies keen to reposition their brands to attract young professional millennials or Gen Z. The boomer generation should not be forgotten; in their heads they are still young, and they want to look current and fashionable. The trick with this group is to provide good service and better quality, and offer stylish clothing with excellent cut and fit. It is worth remembering that baby boomers were reported in a paper by Norstat in 2020 to have 17 times the spending power of Millennials. There are fashion brands that include this generation in their advertising. Seminal campaigns have included Gucci under Alessandro Michele featuring the icon Iggy Pop aged 72 (2020), and Celine championing the 80-year-old writer Joan Didion (2015). The supermodel Daphne Selfe was 86 when she starred in the Vans x & Other Stories campaign in 2015, and Maye Musk became a CoverGirl when she was 69 years old.

Trailing-edge baby boomers (aka Generation Jones)

The name 'Generation Jones' was coined by the American sociologist Jonathan Pontell in 1999. Derived from the slang word 'jonesin', the name relates to feelings of craving, fuelled by unfulfilled expectations. Pontell identified a generation born in 1954–65 that had mistakenly been lumped in either with the boomers for the older end of the spectrum, or with Gen X for those at the younger end of the cohort. By his account they should be considered a separate group with distinct characteristics. A lot was written about this generation in 2009, when

↖ Iggy Pop starred in Gucci's campaign for the Cruise 2020 collection. Shot by the cult film director Harmony Korine, the concept was titled '#ComeAsYouAre_RSVP'. Iggy, who featured along with the actor Sienna Miller and rapper Gucci Mane, was 72 at the time.

↑ Maye Musk walks the runway at the LuisaViaRoma and British *Vogue* 'Runway Icons' show at Piazzale Michelangelo, Florence, in June 2023. Musk started modelling at the age of 15, and is renowned not only as Elon Musk's mother, but also as an older supermodel with more than a million followers on Instagram.

they were between 44 and 55 years old. A survey conducted in that year by the US Department of Commerce's Census Bureau considered Generation Jones to be a powerful demographic representing 26 per cent of the US population, with almost a third of the total spending power. Research carried out by Carat the same year identified that they represented 20 per cent of the UK's adult population. Madonna, Prince and members of punk bands such as the Sex Pistols, as well as Barack Obama, belong to Gen Jones. Generation Jones's attitudes and tastes were shaped by the political, social and cultural events of the 1970s and early 1980s. Financially they were affected by negative equity in the 1990s and the breakdown of the pension system.

Generation X

Generation X is the title of a book by the journalists Jane Deverson and Charles Hamblett in the 1960s, but the term did not come to prominence until many years later, when Douglas Coupland published his novel *Generation X: Tales for an Accelerated Culture* in 1991. Described as a lost generation, this demographic came of age in the 1980s and early 1990s, shaped by the Thatcher and Reagan years in the UK and USA respectively. Affected by escalating rates of divorce, fear of AIDS, recession, job insecurity and the potential of employment in a menial 'McJob', this disaffected generation, also termed 'slackers', sought comfort by creating their own self-sufficient culture and alternative tribal family unit of close-knit friends, as illustrated by the television shows *Friends* in the US and *This Life* in the UK. As Gen X grew up and matured, they cast off their juvenile slacker habits and morphed into 'yupsters', creative urban professionals who endeavoured to balance the personal with wider

↓ This image taken by Josh Meister for *Paste* magazine shows the evolution of hipster subculture. From left to right: The Emo; The Emo Redux; The Ashton; The Scenester; The Twee; The Fauxhemian; The Mountain Man; The Vintage Queen; The Williamsburg; The Meta Nerd.

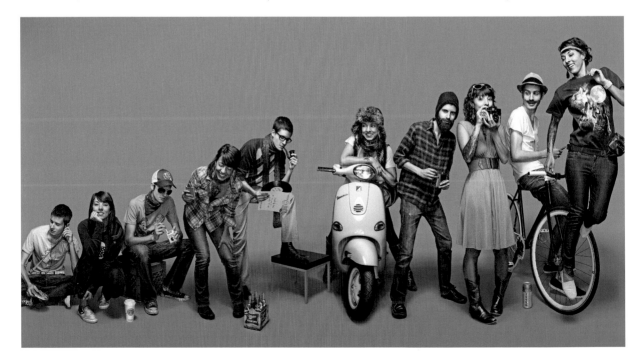

social concerns of family, community and work. This generation can show contradictory traits. They are corporate but have hip individual fashion style; business-minded but independent and entrepreneurial in spirit. They value family time and aim to work smarter not harder.

Generation Y (aka Millennials)

Gen Y, according to Neil Howe and William Strauss, encompasses those born after 1982, although others have classified them as born between the late 1970s and the mid-1990s. This generation are the children of Gen Jones. They have experienced pressure from their parents to succeed and overachieve; money has been spent on their education, and those with a college education are likely to start their working lives paying off sizeable student loans. For this reason Gen Y have also been given the rather depressing title of IPOD generation – Insecure, Pressured, Over-taxed and Debt-ridden – a name coined by Nick Bosanquet and Blair Gibbs in their report *Class of 2005: The IPOD Generation* (2005). This generation also includes the post-1980s children born in China during the one-child policy. Millennials have grown up with technology and increasingly live their lives online; they are plugged in and globally connected. They understand branding and are media and marketing savvy, they communicate using social media, form online communities and are happy to create their own online content. Millennials were the first social-media influencers and were responsible for the rise of lifestyle and beauty blogging and presenting content using the ubiquitous Millennial Pink.

Generation Z

There is still much debate as to the dates and characteristics that define this generation. Some say Gen Z consists of those born after the mid-1990s; others, such as Howe and Strauss, believe it is those born from 2004 onwards; while the research organization McCrindle states that they were born between 1995 and 2009. What can be said for sure is that they are the offspring of Gen X and Y, and their grandparents are baby boomers or Gen Jones. Gen Z are digital natives. They hop easily between the physical and digital worlds, and their online identity is extremely important to them. This is the generation under the spotlight, the one that fashion brands are working hard to attract. Numerous consumer behaviour and marketing reports have been written about this generation. Research carried out by the retail and brand consultancy Fitch discovered that Gen Z have a specific approach to shopping. They like to discover things online by browsing Instagram or Pinterest, and are keen to create digital scrapbooks from images taken in-store. They are careful savers, and will track prices before purchase. Uniqlo tapped into this trend in 2010 with its Lucky Counter campaign. Shoppers visiting the retailer's site could choose from a selection of ten garments that they would like to see discounted. Clicking on an item

"They're looking beyond tangible products and actually trying to understand what it is that makes the company tick. What's its mission? What's its purpose? And what is it actually trying to build for us as a society?

Bo Finneman, McKinsey & Company, *Meet Generation Z: Shaping the Future of Shopping* podcast (2020)

produced a pre-written tweet, and the more tweets generated, the lower the price of the garment would fall. It is worth considering this system of creating discounts by social sharing, because, according to PricewaterhouseCoopers, by 2030 Gen Z and Millennials will make up about 58 per cent of the global workforce.

Sustainability is highly important to this generation. Insights into Gen Z by UNiDAYS revealed that '79 per cent of their survey respondents stated that sustainable fashion is still incredibly important to them and 67 per cent prefer fashion brands who appeal to their social conscience.' An article by *Vogue Business* for Paypal, 'Gen Z Shopping Trends Uncovered' (2021), said that Gen Z don't always buy new and are 27 per cent more likely to shop preloved or vintage, or use such platforms as Depop.

Gen Z subcultures

Analysts do have a tendency to clump all members of a generation together, ascribing similar attributes to the cohort overall. However, there can be several subcultures or alt aesthetics at play. For Gen Z these include: Cottagecore; Dark Academia; Angelcore; Japanese Gothic; E-boys and E-girls; and VSCO Girls. Followers of these niche trends use social media to express themselves and build their community.

Cottagecore
This celebrates the ideal rural life, harking back to a past of long summer days picnicking in a wild-flower meadow or hanging out in a British cottage garden. The ideal is simple living: cooking, baking, drawing, sewing or pottery. Cottagecore life is slow, so things take time and there are no mobile phones – there is time for health and well-being. Vintage clothing, soft summer dresses, florals, puff sleeves and handmade, embroidered pieces typify the look.

Dark Academia
This draws on ideas of traditional or classical academia. Education, the arts, libraries, museums and gothic architecture inspire its dark, moody vibe. The thinking goes that it originated as a response to the novel *The Secret History* (1992) by Donna Tartt, the story of a murder committed by a group of classics students at an elite American college. An article on Bookstr by Karen Reyes in 2022 states that the subculture started as a 'sort of book club thanks to Tartt's novel'. Dark Academia fashion features wool tweed and checks, V-neck knits, neckties, turtleneck jumpers, brown leather belts and shoes, and corduroy. Think Harry Potter and tweedy academics sitting in a dark-panelled study discussing history, the classics and philosophy.

Angelcore
This, as the name suggests, is inspired by angels, particularly those depicted in Renaissance and Baroque paintings, as well

↑ A quintessential Cottagecore look. Shot in a natural outdoor setting, the model wears a soft, floaty dress and wide-brimmed straw hat, evoking the perfect summer.

↗ (Left to right) The Ralph Lauren Fall 2016 show at New York Fashion Week picked up on the Dark Academia vibe with dark hues, tweed, and the preppy styling of a crisp white shirt and tie.

The American singer Poppy attends the Viktor & Rolf Haute Couture Spring/ Summer 2019 show in Paris, resplendent in full Angelcore styling.

Harajuku girls in Tokyo, dressed in Japanese Gothic style.

The Alpha generation

Gen Alpha is generally defined as those born between 2010 and 2024. They will be the first full generation to be born this millennium, and, according to the social researcher Mark McCrindle, they could be the largest cohort ever. A McCrindle report on Gen Alpha states that 'More than 2.5 million are born globally every week … by 2025 they will number almost 2 billion – the largest generation in the history of the world.' The first of this generation were born in the year the iPad was first launched; they have been in front of digital screens from the outset, often using iPads for distraction and soothing, as well as for entertainment and education. They have grown up with social media and streaming. McCrindle has aptly termed them 'screenagers', and some of the effects of this are

as eighteenth-century Rococo cherubs. Pastel pinks and other soft colours, along with an iconography of hearts, clouds, angel wings and halos, are typical of this subculture.

Japanese Gothic

There are certain nuances to this subculture genre, among them J-grunge (a Japanese Goth style) and Gothic Lolita. The look is typified by wearing black lace with ruffles and bows. It can have a Victorian funeral vibe, and these Goths usually found in the Harajuku neighbourhood of Tokyo often embellish their look with net veils, chokers, bonnets and lace parasols.

E-boys and E-girls

Also known as E-kids. The name derives from 'electronic', as in 'electronic boy', and the association with the internet, especially TikTok. The subculture started on Tumblr and gained more mainstream recognition in 2019, linked to the popularity of K-pop groups, such as BTS. An article in *Business Insider*

by Paige Leskin in 2019 explained that the TikTok E-girl is the antithesis of an Instagram influencer, and that the subculture was 'created as a counterculture to the mainstream aesthetic and standards of beauty'. The look is an iteration of the emo subculture. Key points are: two-coloured dyed hair; heavy black eyeliner, often worn under the eye; and pink blush on nose and cheeks. Facial piercings are common, as is the wearing of an O-ring collar choker. E-kids listen to Billie Eilish and other artists producing sad, moody music.

VSCO Girls

This look is very beachy, with the vibe of a laid-back California Girl. The name derives from the VSCO photo-editing app. Key looks include oversized T-shirts worn over shorts, hair scrunchies, Hydro Flasks and instant cameras. White trainers, Vans, Birkenstocks, Crocs and ballet flats are the favoured shoes.

"Alphas are unlikely to view the things they buy as simple commodities and the places they buy from as commercial production lines. The indications are that they will want to know the stories behind what they buy and engage on a deeper level."

Hugh Fletcher, Wunderman Thompson

beginning to be recognized. They have increased digital literacy but shorter attention spans, for example. As a generation they have been shaped by technology, with access to more technology, information and external influences than any generation before them. In research undertaken in 2019 by the marketing communications agency Wunderman Thompson, 63 per cent said they would be 'interested in jobs linked to environmental protection', and nearly one in five said they would 'prefer to buy products from sustainable sources that weren't made from or packaged in plastic'.

Generation Zalpha

Gen Zalpha is a combination of Gen Z and Gen Alpha, capturing those born after 1996. In fashion marketing terms, the interest is in the teens and 20-somethings as they come of age and their spending power increases. Marketers are clumping generations together in the recognition that Gens Y, Z and Alpha will become the biggest buyers of luxury goods by 2030, according to a report published by Bain & Co. in 2023. The report also highlighted how Gen Zalpha's spending was set to grow three times as fast as that of any other generation. This is interesting, since it counters the idea (stated earlier) that Gen Z 'are careful savers, and will track prices before purchase'. An article for *Business Insider* by Nidhi Pandurang in 2022 explains that the trend for young people to live with their parents is freeing up disposable income that can instead be spent on luxury, including fashion. Another article for *Business Insider*, by Dan Latu and Kelsey Neubauer in 2023, reported that 'being back in their childhood bedrooms also gives these young American adults the freedom to splurge on designer handbags, meals at fancy restaurants, bottle service at nightclubs, cameras, and trips to Europe.' This sounds highly individualistic, but a report by the Future Laboratory in 2022 countered this, stating that collaborative thinking was important to Gen Zalpha and that in the UK 'two thirds (67 per cent) of young people would like to live under an explicitly socialist economic system, according to the Institute of Economic Affairs'. The report focuses on how individualism will become less prominent and community values will gain traction.

Anti-demographics

In 2021 an open letter with 200 signatories was sent to the American think tank the Pew Research Center requesting that it drop the use of generational labels. The letter pointed out that demographic labelling of this nature does not align well with the scientific principles of social research, that it causes confusion and is in effect a crude form of stereotyping. This intervention was led by the sociologist Philip N. Cohen, a professor at the University of Maryland, who wrote in the *Washington Post* that 'throwing everyone together by year of birth often misses all the glorious conflict and complexity in social change.' The concept of non-demographic futures was picked up by the Future Laboratory in a report on neo-collectivism. Their proposition was that 'as collectivism takes hold, citizens would see themselves as members of wider, more complex groups,' as opposed to the proscribed generational consumer types. There are several problems with demographic segmentation, the first of which is that not all customers within the same demographic segment or generational cohort have the same needs and values. Second, demographic descriptions are generalizations at best; they describe but are not necessarily a good predictor of behaviour. The global research and consulting firm Strategic Business Insights (SBI) owns the proprietary VALS™ psychometric research method. The VALS types defined for the USA, for example, are:

» Innovators

» Thinkers

» Believers

» Achievers

» Strivers

» Experiencers

» Makers

» Survivors

Information is then given for each generational cohort subdivided into these behavioural types. Experiencers, for example, are found to be sensation-seeking, first in and out of a trend, and up on the latest fashions, and tend to go against the mainstream. Innovators are always taking in information, confident to experiment, sceptical about advertising, future-orientated, and self-directed consumers. In 2018 Patricia Breman, writing on the SBI website, showed how the Gen Z population was broken down into these behavioural categories. Experiencers constituted 52 per cent, while about 40 per cent were Strivers. Strivers tend to have revolving employment; they wish to better their lives but are challenged to achieve this; use gaming as an escape and tend to display their wealth through clothing and fashion. The remaining 8 per cent comprised Innovators, Makers and Survivors.

In 2020 Euromonitor held a consumer types webinar and published the accompanying slides (although note that this research was undertaken before the COVID-19 pandemic). It identified 200 global consumer types clustered into 11 groups. The five criteria used to determine the clusters were:

TABLE OF TWENTIETH- AND TWENTY-FIRST-CENTURY GENERATIONS

BORN	GENERATION COHORT NAMES	DECADE OF INFLUENCE	AGE IN 2030
1946–54	LEADING-EDGE BABY BOOMERS	1960s	76–84
1955–65	TRAILING-EDGE BABY BOOMERS GENERATION JONES	1970s AND EARLY 1980s	65–75
1961–81	GEN X YUPSTERS	1980s AND EARLY 1990s	49–69
1982–2002	GEN Y MILLENNIALS ECHO BOOMERS NET GENERATION IPOD GENERATION	1990s, 2000s, 2010s	28–48
1995–2009	GEN Z	2010s, 2020s	21–35
2010–24	ALPHA GENERATION	2025 AND BEYOND	6–20

GENERATIONAL COHORT OF FASHION DESIGNERS

GENERATION	FASHION DESIGNERS
POST-WAR GENERATION	VIVIENNE WESTWOOD, REI KAWAKUBO, KARL LAGERFELD, YVES SAINT LAURENT, GIORGIO ARMANI, CALVIN KLEIN, VALENTINO GARAVANI
BABY BOOMERS	JEAN PAUL GAULTIER, PAUL SMITH, MIUCCIA PRADA, DONNA KARAN, VERA WANG
GENERATION JONES	JOHN GALLIANO, MARC JACOBS, TOM FORD, DRIES VAN NOTEN, MARTIN MARGIELA, DONATELLA VERSACE
GENERATION X	STELLA MCCARTNEY, PHILLIP LIM, NICOLAS GHESQUIÈRE, ALEXANDER MCQUEEN, PIERPAOLO PICCIOLI, MARIA GRAZIA CHIURI, ALESSANDRO MICHELE, ERDEM MORALIOĞLU, GUO PEI
GENERATION Y	CHRISTOPHER KANE, ZAC POSEN, ALEXANDER WANG, SIMONE ROCHA, ELENA VELEZ, CHARLES JEFFREY, GRACE WALES BONNER, MOLLY GODDARD
GENERATION Z	TIA ADEOLA, KIMINTE KIMHEKIM, HARRIS REED, TYLER LAMBERT, TAOFEEK ABIJAKO, IMOGEN EVANS

» Personality traits and future outlook

» Shopping preferences and habits

» Perception and use of technology

» Attitudes towards global issues

» Health and well-being behaviours

Among the clusters identified were the Impulsive Spender, a 'discount and bargain-oriented consumer, often keeping up with latest trends'; the Empowered Activist, who 'prioritize[s] authenticity and [is] often concerned with global issues', considering their purchases and wanting to ensure that these are in line with their values; and the Undaunted Striver, 'Trendy consumers willing to spend money in order to maintain their status both offline and online. Highly prioritize experiences and leisure activities as well as name-brand and luxury products.'

There is further information about other proprietary segmentation tools in the section on geo-demographic analysis tools (page 152).

Geographic segmentation

Geographic segmentation analyses customers by region, continent, state, county or neighbourhood. It is important to consider this type of information, particularly as fashion markets become ever more global and retailers and brand managers are required to understand the particular needs of customers in each country or region in which they do business. The product offering, marketing and promotional approach may need to be adjusted to address differences of climate, culture or religion. It is also important to consider whether someone lives in a city, a large town or the countryside, since this will affect the physical shopping experiences accessible to them. However, since so many purchases are made online, geographic location in terms of accessibility may be less important than cultural differences.

Geo-demographic segmentation

Geo-demographic segmentation, which makes use of a combination of geographic and demographic analysis, can be effective for understanding the social, economic and geographic make-up of a population. Geo-demographic analysis divides up a country and analyses each geographic subdivision demographically. It is particularly useful for helping retailers determine which locations might be the most profitable or how best to adapt stores to fit with the geo-demographic of a particular place. Research shows that consumers can display a strong attachment to their local area, doing their shopping and leisure activities 5–23 km (3–14 miles) from their home or place of work.

Matches Fashion is a well-known high-end multi-brand fashion e-tailer, selling such brands as The Row, Toteme, Gucci, Jacquemus, Simone Rocha and Zimmermann, to name but a few. It has three boutiques in central London. Each store has its own fashion profile, designed to cater specifically to the unique style characteristics of the local customer. The boutique in Marylebone High Street, for example, is in a locale that is both residential and work-based. There are cafés, boutiques and hip art galleries in the area, so in a bid to attract the art-loving demographic who live and work nearby, the store has been transformed into an innovative retail/gallery space where fashion and art can coexist.

Geo-demographic analysis and consumer profiling can be carried out using the services of a market-research and analysis consultancy, which will have access to sophisticated database-profiling systems. However, a small business can carry out simple but effective research using basic census data, free online postcode analysis, statistics from the local council, and fashion-industry information on market trends. The example on pages 170–1 describes the basic geo-demographic background research carried out by a boutique owner as she prepared to launch her business.

Geo-demographic analysis tools

There are several proprietary geo-demographic neighbourhood classification systems, such as ACORN (A Classification Of Residential Neighbourhoods) and Mosaic. These tools use government census data, postcode or zip code analysis, and a complicated array of demographic and lifestyle variables to segment populations by neighbourhood and social status. The ACORN Classification Map, created by CACI Ltd, divides the UK population into five categories: Wealthy Achievers, Urban Prosperity, Comfortably Off, Moderate Means and Hard-Pressed. These are divided into 17 subgroups, among them Affluent Greys, Flourishing Families, Blue-Collar Roots, Settled Suburbia and Aspiring Singles. These groups are further subdivided into 56 consumer types.

The Mosaic Global system devised by Experian is available in Europe, North America and the Asia-Pacific region. The population is divided into ten neighbourhood types, US examples being Affluent Suburbia, Upscale America, Metro Fringe, Urban Essence and Remote America. These groups are further broken down into 60 subgroups.

Psychographic and behavioural segmentation

Psychographic and behavioural segmentation analyses consumers based on their lifestyle and personality type. The purpose is to determine the underlying motivations that drive a person's attitude or behaviour as a consumer. It is possible for consumers to have similar demographic profiles but entirely different attitudes to clothing and appearance. One person, for example, might believe that they must look crisp, smart and well turned-out for all occasions, whereas someone else might choose to wear expensive branded fashion that looks worn and battered even when new, giving the impression they don't care how they look. Psychographic, behavioural and lifestyle studies aim to gain further insight into consumer attitudes, interests and opinions (known as AIOs) and understand how these influence a person's fashion needs, desires and purchasing choices.

This is a complex topic, especially when it comes to attitudes to fashion or to social media. If you remember, the aim of marketing is to satisfy consumer needs and wants, and while it is fair to say that we may want or desire new clothes, most Western consumers certainly do not *need* more clothes, accessories or shoes. The reality is that many of us have brand-new items in our wardrobes that remain unworn; we give copious amounts of unwanted clothes to charity shops and cast an alarming quantity of surplus clothing into landfill. So what is it that motivates us to continue purchasing even if we do not theoretically need any more or can ill afford it? The answer lies in psychology and the theories of human motivation.

Consumer motivation and behaviour

What motivates us to buy into fashion, what influences our purchasing behaviour, and how do our attitudes, interests and opinions affect our purchasing choices? At a simplistic level it could be said that the motivating force to purchase a garment, handbag or pair of shoes is a real physical need; in other words, we do not have a receptacle in which to carry our keys, money and mobile phone, or a pair of winter boots to protect us from the cold and wet, so to satisfy this need we must purchase the required item.

The reality is that in most cases the motivation is more akin to desire and the need is psychological. The Danish brand guru and futurologist Martin Lindstrom argues in his book *Buyology: How Everything We Believe about Why We Buy Is Wrong* (2008) that the motivation is neurological, and the University of New Mexico evolutionary psychologist Geoffrey Miller contends in his book *Spent: Sex, Evolution, and the Secrets of Consumerism* (2009) that evolutionary biology is behind our need to purchase and display conspicuous consumption. Miller's theory of 'display signalling' proposes that we wear certain fashion styles or brands in order to signal specific qualities of our character to others. Someone wearing an ethical or eco-fashion brand, for example, is at some level trying to communicate that they are conscientious and aware of climate change. A person wearing conspicuously branded designer labels is advertising wealth and desirability, while someone with an active and sporty style is trying to signal their health and fitness. Now that we can post innumerable images of ourselves online and receive responses from a global audience, it could be said that content is the new social currency, and that it has taken precedence over clothing as a method of display signalling.

Consumer purchase decision process

It is evident that fashion purchasing decisions are rarely based on logical criteria alone. The motivations behind our purchasing behaviour are driven by a complex interplay of demographic, geographic, psychological, neurological, economic, social, cultural and personal factors. Research indicates that consumers go through a decision-making process when they purchase a product. The basic steps are as follows:

1. Recognition of need

2. Information search and identification of possible options

3. Evaluation of options

4. Decision and purchase

5. Consumption and use of product or service

6. Post-consumption evaluation

7. Divestment

The decision process starts with the recognition that there is a need. This might be a valid physical need; a person may gain or lose a significant amount of weight, for example, and need to purchase new clothes to fit. A couple may be planning a traditional wedding and therefore need to purchase or hire appropriate outfits and accessories, or someone might be starting a new job for which they are required to dress in a certain way. The need could be cultural: a person travelling to a country where the convention is to dress more modestly, for instance, may need to acquire a long skirt or a top with sleeves and a high neckline. It is more likely, however, that the need

THE CONSUMER PURCHASING DECISION PROCESS

This diagram of the steps for the consumer purchasing decision process is adapted from the EKB model devised in 1968 by James Engel, David Kollat and Roger Blackwell, and discussed by Sethna and Blythe in *Consumer Behaviour* (2019).

This is a linear system that ends in divestment. For fashion that could be: resale, throwing the garment out, giving it to charity or swapping it with someone else. There are serious problems with the disposal of fashion that must be addressed, so divestment is now something that fashion brands should consider and find new solutions for.

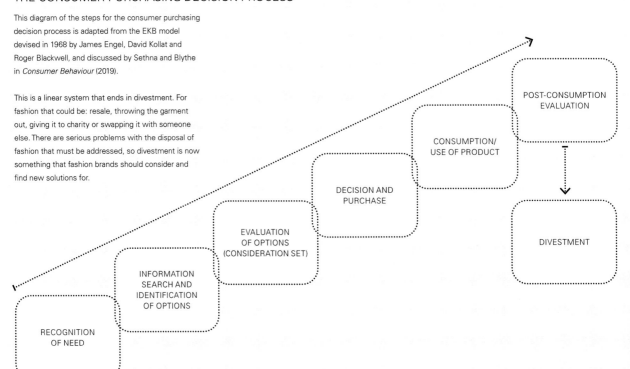

RECOGNITION OF NEED

INFORMATION SEARCH AND IDENTIFICATION OF OPTIONS

EVALUATION OF OPTIONS (CONSIDERATION SET)

DECISION AND PURCHASE

CONSUMPTION/ USE OF PRODUCT

POST-CONSUMPTION EVALUATION

DIVESTMENT

MASLOW'S HIERARCHY OF NEEDS

Abraham Maslow developed his theory in 1943 and proposed a five-tier hierarchy, starting with basic-level physiological necessities, such as food, water and sleep, and progressing up through needs of safety, social belonging and esteem, culminating in the highest level of need driven by the motivation for self-actualization, which could also be viewed as self-realization or self-fulfilment. The original premise was that an individual will attempt to meet their needs at the lowest level before advancing to the next. In reality, individuals attempt to meet a variety of needs simultaneously, and do not progress up the hierarchy in a prescribed manner. In modern society we do have a basic physiological need for clothing to protect us from the elements, but in most cases consumer motivation regarding fashion need is triggered by a diverse set of desires and stimuli. These might relate to social belonging, gaining approval, affiliation with a group, or notions of self-acceptance and esteem. The hierarchical nature of this long-used model has been criticized, however. Marketers now view consumer needs more holistically, with social belonging, esteem and self-actualization linked by a need for connection, with this need being fulfilled through social media.

SELF-ACTUALIZATION

Self-fulfilment or fulfilling own potential. Consumer may purchase equipment or clothing for travel or hobbies. Individual style might be created to express fun or sense of freedom.

ESTEEM

Status, achievement, level of responsibility. Consumer may choose status brands or designer clothing to signify importance or position.

SOCIAL BELONGING

Relationships, acceptance, family, peer group, work group. Dressing to fit into style tribes.

SAFETY, SHELTER, PROTECTION, SECURITY
CLOTHING FOR PROTECTION

PHYSIOLOGICAL: BASIC LIFE NEEDS –
FOOD, WATER, SLEEP

will arise at a subconscious level. If a person thinks, 'I'm not wearing the latest trend, I will be judged and no one will find me attractive,' deep down they believe they lack something. The belief sets up what could be termed a false deficit in their mind. The discrepancy between what they believe is lacking and what they desire creates the sensation of need: 'I need a fresh look. I'd better buy some new clothes.' This thought becomes the motivation, leading towards action and a potential decision to purchase.

Once a need has been established, the next stages are to search for information and check out and evaluate options. This usually occurs by going online, looking at social-media influencers or other sources of opinion and influence, such as the press, or gathering opinions from friends. Prices may be compared and the various benefits of different options weighed up, assuming of course that this is not a spontaneous and rather unexpected

THE MCKINSEY LOYALTY LOOP

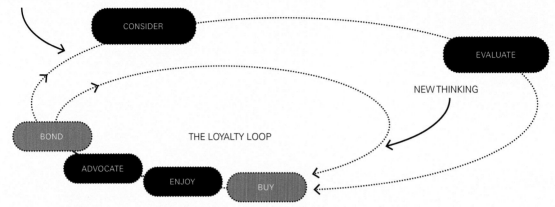

Diagram based on Edelman and Singer, 'Competing on Customer Journeys'

CONSIDER AND BUY
The premise of this model is that marketers mistakenly allocate too many resources to the consider and buy stages.

EVALUATE AND ADVOCATE
The evaluate and advocate stages are increasingly more relevant. Marketing investment that helps consumers navigate the evaluation process, then share positive word of mouth and post reviews advocating for a brand, can build awareness and encourage others to purchase.

BOND
If a customer is loyal to a brand and has a strong bond with it, they are likely to take a shorter purchasing journey for subsequent purchases, cutting out the early stages of the process.

NEW THINKING
More up-to-date thinking proposes that new customers can enter the journey directly into the loyalty loop. The consider and evaluate stages are compressed or removed thanks to the positive word of mouth and loyalty bond of others. This concept was developed by David C. Edelman and Marc Singer in 'Competing on Customer Journeys' (2015).

purchase. There may be several brands or product options under consideration by the potential consumer. This is known as the consideration set.

The next step is the final decision and purchase. Normally, this is where one might consider the process to be complete. However, it is important to take into account steps 5, 6 and 7. The experience a customer has wearing or using their purchase is very likely to be shared on social media, and positive or negative viewpoints could arise. So, for a brand, the story does not end at the purchase stage. Returns and aftercare services may be an important feature of the customer's experience.

Finally there is divestment. This is something that fashion brands must consider in much more depth. The issue of rejected garments ending up in landfill has already been discussed (on page 71 and elsewhere). There is a growing argument that the end of life for fashion garments and products should be factored in from the beginning, at the design stage of the product's life cycle. You can see from the consumer purchasing decision diagram opposite that it is linear. The question is: should this model be redesigned? The circular economy and circular design have been discussed in Chapter 2 (pages 75–7). The diagram on page 76 shows how the product or its constituent materials are fed back into the circulatory system – there is no end-of-life stage in this scenario.

The loyalty loop

There is a lot of debate among marketers and branding professionals about linear models and diagrams of the customer decision-making process, versus the circular system that most now believe to be much more appropriate. In addition, research has shown more clearly where companies should focus their marketing budgets. In an article for the *Harvard Business Review*, 'Branding in the Digital Age: You're Spending Your Money in All the Wrong Places' (2010), David C. Edelman explains that companies traditionally spend the larger portion of their budgets at the 'consider' and 'buy' stages of the journey. However, he writes, research shows that 'the single most powerful impetus to buy is someone else's advocacy.' This thinking is reflected in a model of the process created by David Court and three associates and published in the *McKinsey Quarterly* in 2009. Their Consumer Decision Journey (CDJ) diagram was devised using data from nearly 20,000 consumers. They identified these stages: Consider, Evaluate, Buy, Enjoy, Advocate, Bond. This circular process can be shown in what is known as the McKinsey Loyalty Loop diagram (opposite). This concept was further developed by Edelman and Marc Singer in 2015. They recognized that new customers can enter the journey directly into the loyalty loop. They explain how the 'consider' and 'evaluate' stages are compressed or removed, owing to positive word of mouth and the loyalty bond of others.

We frequently make our fashion choices, whether consciously or subconsciously, based on what peers, friends, colleagues or celebrities are wearing. When consumers promote products or pass on style ideas to each other it is known as word of mouth (WoM), word-of-mouth marketing (WoMM) or peer marketing. It is great news for a brand if its customers, influencers or the public promote the brand's product or services in this way. Known as viral marketing, this often proves to be a far more powerful marketing tool than advertising or promotion controlled directly by a company.

Factors influencing purchase decisions

There is a range of factors that might affect the consumer's choice when purchasing fashion. Some behavioural and motivational factors have already been mentioned in this chapter. Another behavioural model is Rogers' Diffusion of Innovations, developed by the sociologist Everett Rogers in the 1960s. It describes the way in

ROGERS'S DIFFUSION OF INNOVATIONS

Trends originate within the innovator group of individuals, adventurous types who are cutting-edge in their ideas. As the trend takes hold, a tipping point is reached. This is the moment when the trend or idea crosses a significant threshold; the adoption rate increases exponentially and the trend spreads rapidly and reaches the mass market. Eventually the trend will peak and begin its decline. The late majority purchase the trend just as its fashionability and mass-market appeal begin to dwindle. Laggards are those at the tail end who manage to cotton on to the idea when it is already too late and the trend is over.

Source: Everett Rogers, *Diffusion of Innovations* (1995)

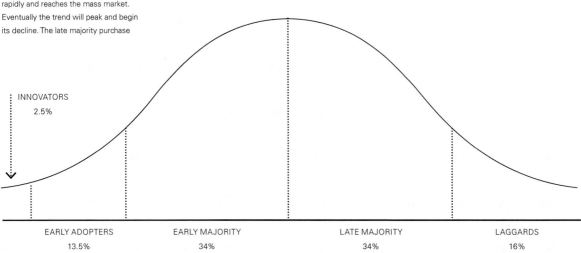

INNOVATORS
2.5%

EARLY ADOPTERS
13.5%

EARLY MAJORITY
34%

LATE MAJORITY
34%

LAGGARDS
16%

which an innovation, new idea or trend is taken up by consumers and moves through a population.

Consumers vary in their response to new trends and ideas. Those who are more conservative or reticent might take some time before they feel ready to buy into a new or developing trend. They might want to feel safe, fit in or not look out of place. Others might feel that an innovation or new style is too expensive. They might wait until the trend hits the mass market and the price comes down; their motivation is to be cautious and spend wisely. There are others who like to be on the cutting edge of style. They may purchase the new-season collections at the earliest opportunity; they want to be the first, be noticed or stand out from the crowd. Rogers identified five types of individual classified by their propensity to adopt innovation:

Innovators A small percentage of adventurous people who initiate trends or adopt innovations before others. They are risk-takers and visionaries, people who buy into designers when they first emerge, or who may be controversial in their approach. Now, this would also include those who innovate and instigate subculture and street trends.

Early adopters People who take up a trend in the early stages, often cultural opinion leaders or those who disseminate fashion, style or artistic ideas. This group accepts and embraces change and enjoys new ideas. They will have the confidence to follow or adapt the trend, mix styles and create the desired look from a combination of designer, boutique, accessible fashion and vintage.

Early majority Represents the bulk of people, who adopt a trend as it gathers momentum and begins to penetrate the mass market. Members of this group are likely to take up a trend after they have seen it worn by others, when it has gained a lot of traction on social media, and when it is readily available at a more reasonable price.

Late majority Those who buy into a trend when it is already very well established and reaching its peak or beginning to decline.

Laggards These people do not take fashion risks, and are the last to catch on to a trend, usually when it is too late.

You will probably notice that there are similarities between Rogers's classifications of consumer types and those identified in the VALS™ system discussed on page 149. Also worth pointing out is more current thinking about trendless and timeless fashion. Are trends themselves part of the problem with consumption? Do they set up the sensation of need, the 'false deficit' mentioned earlier? Early adoption could relate to new, more sustainable approaches to fashion, the system and consumption – not just to seasonal trends or fashion fads. It is to be hoped that such questions will help to challenge the status quo and initiate positive change.

Country of origin

Customer perception of a brand can also affect purchasing decisions. Consumers may have a positive perception of particular goods from certain countries: for example Italian leather, French perfume, Swiss watches, Scottish cashmere and tweed, or British tailoring. Such products are seen as special, luxurious and of high quality. This is known as the **country-of-origin effect** (**COO** or **COOE**). It is not only the country of manufacture that can affect perception, but also the country of design (COD). In this instance the product may be designed in a country renowned for a particular design skill, but manufactured elsewhere: Swedish-designed furniture, for example. Genuine products designed and manufactured in countries or regions renowned for their skill and expertise can demand a premium price, but it is important to point out that there may be strict trade laws concerning country of origin, making it illegal to label garments incorrectly.

The country-of-origin effect in fashion and luxury goods is usually applied to European countries, and this tends therefore to situate the narrative of fashion within a Western context or in what is known as the global north (see page 119). This limits the focus and

→ At Dior Pre-Fall 2023, luxurious
embroidery and beading show off the
heritage craft skills of the Chanakya atelier
in Mumbai. Chanakya is working with Dior
to gain global recognition and highlight its
specialist expertise.

↘ A highly skilled artisan makes a pair of
finely crafted leather shoes for the Italian
brand Tod's.

acts to close out the wider heritage of fashion. India, for example, has exceptional capabilities in luxury embroidery and beading. Chanakya is a family-run business in Mumbai specializing in luxury hand-embellishment and counting Dior, Gucci, Tory Burch and Schiaparelli among its clients. The aim is to preserve the age-old heritage of hand-embroidery, and to be an advocate of this refined craftsmanship. Chanakya is a large company and reasonably well known within the world of luxury fashion, as the list of customers illustrates. Possibly less well known are the many artisans across India and other areas of the globe who are custodians of heritage skills in weaving, dyeing, block-printing, lacemaking and embroidery, who may not be given full recognition or recompense for their work. There are those within fashion who are working hard behind the scenes to get recognition for artisans with specific heritage craft skills. The aim is to ensure that these skills are maintained and passed down to future generations, and that, if they are used in mainstream fashion, this is acknowledged appropriately and the craftspeople are paid fairly. Ideally, their crafts would become designated in a similar way to Italian leather, for example. This topic is discussed in more depth on pages 30–1.

It is possible to create and market a brand with an identity that is suggestive of a particular country, but not from the country or region in question. The UK fashion brand Superdry Japan was set up after an inspirational trip to Japan. Garments are embroidered with Japanese-style writing and given such names as the 'Osaka' T-shirt. This can, however, lead into the dangerous territory of cultural appropriation. This is an area where brands can be called out by consumers who are much more culturally aware and won't tolerate inauthenticity and the appropriation of cultural signifiers used in the wrong way. Two notorious cases are the Tom Ford Romanian blouse worn by Adele in 2011, which was a direct copy of the traditional *blouse roumaine*, and Tory Burch's copy of a Romanian coat for the Resort 2018 collection. Neither brand acknowledged the original source or used traditional skills in the manufacture of the garments.

Heuristics

Heuristics are in essence decision-making shortcuts that someone might use when thinking about what to purchase. They could also be assumptions one makes in order to assist in making decisions, or a rule of thumb applied when making a choice. For example, the country of origin as described above could be important in someone's decision-making process. This would be described as a location or geographic heuristic. Another example is someone who, when faced with two similar garments, always goes for the cheaper one. This would be a price heuristic. Another heuristic concept relates to scarcity. This is why there is a desire for limited editions; knowing that there are only a few of something and that it is hard to get hold of could swing the decision for certain types of customer. This could be labelled an availability heuristic. If someone were to select the brand with the best sustainability credentials in preference to any other, that could be described as a moral heuristic.

Heuristics are related to the discipline of behavioural psychology, so it is important to point out that they are often triggered automatically and unconsciously. This can lead to snap judgements or irrational decisions underpinned by cognitive bias. In an attempt to navigate these complexities, some brands employ the services of a fashion psychologist to help them understand consumer motivation, decision-making and purchasing behaviour.

The customer journey

This follows the stages from a customer's first awareness of a product or service through to purchase and possibly post-purchase as well. Along the way, a customer will experience this journey across all the different steps and interactions with the brand or seller, acquiring either a positive or a negative opinion of the process. This is known as **customer experience (CX)** or, for a journey that takes place online, **user experience (UX)**.

It is usual to create a **customer journey map**, showing all the phases of the journey. These often use a five-point framework: Awareness, Consideration, Purchase, Retention and Loyalty, and Advocacy.

Awareness The particular product must come to the attention of the potential consumer. This could be by a variety of means, some of which are indicated on the customer journey map (page 163).

Consideration As part of their journey to purchase, a potential customer may search online, comparing prices, availability and quality. If several brands are in the running – say Nike, Adidas, New Balance and Veja for trainers – this is termed the consideration set.

Purchase Having investigated and evaluated all the options, the person makes a final decision and chooses to make a purchase.

Retention and loyalty How to keep customers loyal to the brand is becoming ever more important. This is where things like loyalty programmes and receiving a discount when signing up for an email newsletter come in.

Advocacy When someone takes the next step and advocates for the brand or product, on social media, via word of mouth or by leaving a favourable online review. This promotes a more circular

CUSTOMER MOTIVATION AND BEHAVIOURS

GETTING A BARGAIN

» Shops in sales

» Attracted to promotional offers

» Buys second-hand or vintage

» Goes to designer outlets and warehouse sales

» Sources vouchers and deals online

TRYING TO AVOID CLOTHES SHOPPING

» Shops infrequently for clothes

» Purchases mainly for replacement items

» Shops from catalogues or online

» Does not browse – heads straight for required item

» Abandons store if queue to pay is too long

STANDING OUT FROM THE CROWD

» Buys from independent stores and boutiques

» Makes an effort to seek out new trends and ideas

» Makes own clothes or customizes

» Shops in street markets

LOOKING LIKE A CELEBRITY

» Avid reader of celebrity gossip magazines

» Attracted to stores and websites that are current with celebrity fashion trends

» Would queue to purchase special celebrity or designer fashion collections

FITTING IN AND BELONGING

» Buys similar style to friends

» Connected to peers via social media

» Shops where friends shop

» Personal style fits with chosen tribe

CARING ABOUT THE ENVIRONMENT

» Tries to buy from ethical fashion brands

» Recycles and upcycles clothing

» Won't buy 'fast fashion'

» Likes smaller local fashion labels

A consumer's attitudes, preferences and motivations will influence their purchasing behaviour. This table presents possible purchasing behaviours associated with a variety of potential motivations. If someone's motivation is to get a bargain, for example, this will drive certain behaviour, such as shopping during the sales, signing up to a discount website, or scouring vintage stores for that special bargain.

MAPPING THE CUSTOMER JOURNEY

This customer journey map shows possible points of interaction between a customer and a brand, as the potential customer progresses from first awareness to purchase and post purchase. The interaction can be entirely physical or digital, or a combination of the two. The key from a marketing and promotion point of view is to consider the **calls to action (CTA)** that may face the customer as they progress, such as to sign up for a newsletter, click 'Like' or share the information with a friend.

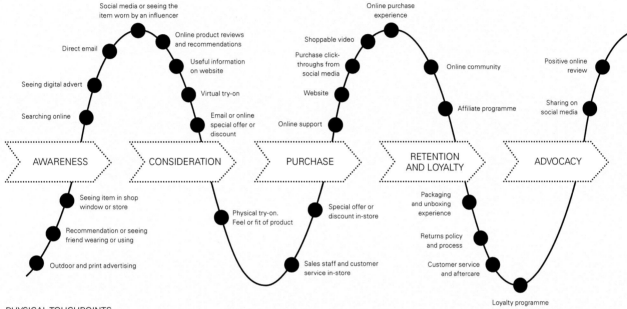

DIGITAL TOUCHPOINTS

PHYSICAL TOUCHPOINTS

process, encompassing a positive feedback loop. In other words, when someone advocates for the brand and spreads the word, that forms the first awareness stage for someone new. This is also known as organic marketing, when the brand did not have to pay directly for advertising or promotion.

The map shows generic journey options that can be used as a template for creating more specific customer journey maps. Different types of customer will gain their first awareness of a brand or product via different channels. For one customer it could be via TikTok, while for another it could be seeing an outdoor advert on their journey to work. Another person might see an item on the shopping page of *Vogue*. Each type of customer, depending on their engagement with social media and their specific interests, will take a different route.

THE AIDA/AIDAR MODEL

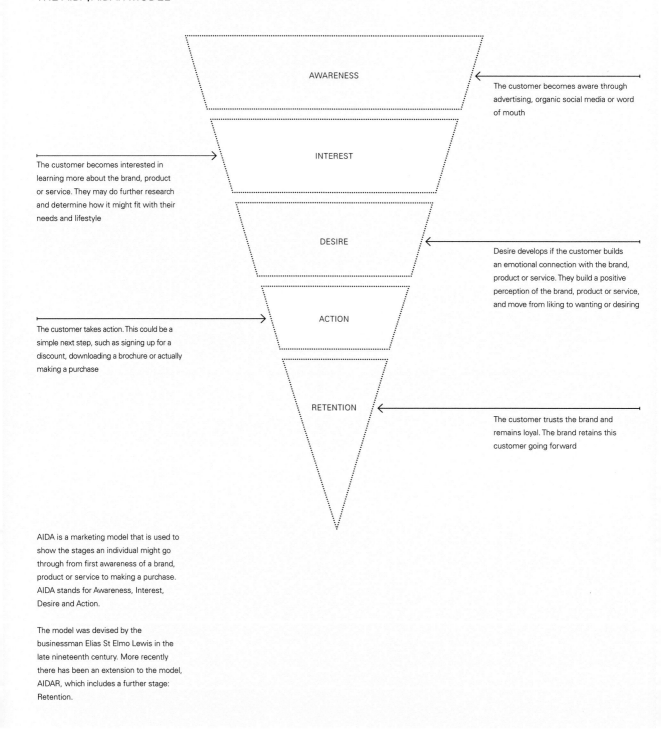

The customer becomes aware through advertising, organic social media or word of mouth

The customer becomes interested in learning more about the brand, product or service. They may do further research and determine how it might fit with their needs and lifestyle

Desire develops if the customer builds an emotional connection with the brand, product or service. They build a positive perception of the brand, product or service, and move from liking to wanting or desiring

The customer takes action. This could be a simple next step, such as signing up for a discount, downloading a brochure or actually making a purchase

The customer trusts the brand and remains loyal. The brand retains this customer going forward

AIDA is a marketing model that is used to show the stages an individual might go through from first awareness of a brand, product or service to making a purchase. AIDA stands for Awareness, Interest, Desire and Action.

The model was devised by the businessman Elias St Elmo Lewis in the late nineteenth century. More recently there has been an extension to the model, AIDAR, which includes a further stage: Retention.

As you will see from the customer journey map, customers can interact both digitally and physically along the journey. When someone tries products in-store but then purchases online, often at a lower price and from another source, it is termed **showrooming**. The opposite of this is known as **webrooming**: when consumers research online and then go to the store to purchase, perhaps because they do not want to pay for shipping or want to purchase that day and not wait for delivery. 'Click and collect' (purchasing online and picking up from the store) could also be considered a type of webrooming.

Consumer trends

Identifying and understanding consumer trends is a vital element of fashion market research. Observing consumers and gathering information from markets around the globe keeps you up to date. The trick is to watch out for innovators and early adopters, since they are likely to be ahead of the curve. Trend-watching helps you to develop intuition, spot new ideas and gain inspiration. Trend-forecasting websites, such as Faith Popcorn's BrainReserve and Trendwatching.com, are excellent sources of information. Remember that consumer needs will alter in response to political, economic and social change. An article by Joan Kennedy in *Business of Fashion*, 'Where Did Luxury's Aspirational Shoppers Go?' (2023), described the slowing demand for luxury goods from consumers who usually buy into a luxury brand via entry price-point products. The article concluded that this was either because of the rising cost of living and pressure on their spending budget, or because of rising awareness of sustainability and the climate crisis, and the associated shame of buying new.

Popcorn and her team have identified 17 global trends that in their opinion predict future consumer trends. The team monitors these over time, since their view is that a consumer trend is a 'deep social and cultural movement' that will shape behaviour over the coming decade. The most famous trend Popcorn identified is that of Cocooning, 'the need to protect oneself from the harsh, unpredictable realities of the outside world'. She identified this concept in 1981, since when it has evolved into several sub-trends, among them:

Super-cocooning Uncertainty and a feeling of vulnerability result in an increase of at-home entertainment with television and movies on demand. Online communication and shopping mean that it is possible to retreat to the safe environment of the home. This prediction became reality during the COVID-19 pandemic.

Regenerative cocooning This is about being in a protective bubble, where products, services or environments foster optimal health and well-being. This concept has been picked up within the beauty industry. ESPA, for example, has a Restorative Cocooning

Try this

Create your own customer journey map, using one of your past fashion purchases as an example. Take a moment to think. What was the very first instant when you became aware of the item you bought? Did you see it on Instagram? Did you see a friend wearing it? Was it in an article in the press or was it recommended to you? Was that first point of awareness digital or physical? Work your way step by step along your journey, writing down each moment you can remember. As you do this, consider if each interaction with the brand, be it physical or digital, was a positive or negative experience. At the end, evaluate whether the overall experience was positive. Did you end up a loyal customer or advocate of the brand? If not, why not?

Body Cream. The promotional copy states that the cream 'hugs the body … to rebalance and comfort'.

Mobile cocooning The original version of this trend was about the security of SUVs insulating a family from 'the dangers of the road'. However, Popcorn sees this progressing in the future to encompass driverless cars or 'on-the-move pods' in which families can travel, work, rest and play.

As society continues to express the need for safety, comfort, protection and privacy, the various forms of this trend are likely to hold sway for years to come.

Further consumer trends have been predicted by Popcorn and others. They are:

Cosy childhood memories Nostalgic items – 1950s florals, tea-time cupcakes, board games, storage tins with 1960s and 1970s branding – remind us of childhood days. Baby boomers and Gen Jones desire to feel cosy and secure in tough times. Popcorn calls this Down Ageing, a desire for a nostalgic, carefree childhood, 'finding comfort in familiar pursuits and products' from our past.

Control the scroll This trend was predicted in 2023 by Euromonitor. People are more selective about screen time, and choosier about how much time they spend on devices. This will result in taking stock of which apps and subscriptions to opt for, and deleting those that don't offer value or genuine engagement. Euromonitor also identified the Eco-economic trend. This is also about cutting back, in this case working to reduce bills and acquiring less.

Crowd shaped Identified by Trendwatching.com. People pool data, profiles and preferences in groups (small and big) to shape new goods and services. 3D-printing communities, such as Shapeways and the Fab Lab movement, are examples, as are clothes-swapping, skill-sharing, freecycling and random acts of kindness (RAK). Popcorn predicts a similar trend, called Clanning. This is about belonging to a group that has common feelings or stands for similar causes or ideas.

Addicted to niche Consumers want to find an intricate balance between being one of a kind and fitting in. Niche brands come with a story, so niche is about the kudos of being in the know, as well as being one of the few. Popcorn describes a trend called Egonomics: when consumers want to be recognized for their individuality as an antidote to a depersonalized society.

← Fashion design graduate Philli Wood won a national design competition in the UK run by the fashion retailer Warehouse in partnership with the British Fashion Council. The collection features images of cable knits printed on to exaggerated tent-shaped padded parkas, within which the wearer can cocoon themselves and retreat from the world.

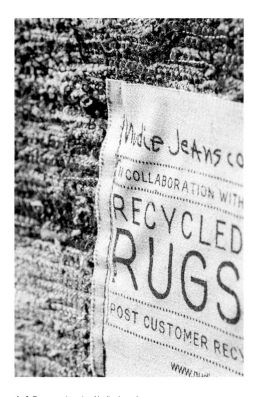

↑ → Rugs made using Nudie Jeans'
recycled denim appeal to the customer
seeking a 'guilt-free' treat.

Small indulgences This is another trend identified by Popcorn:
'Stressed-out consumers want to indulge in affordable luxuries and
seek ways to reward themselves.' The future of this trend is also
seen as mood-enhancing experiences. Overall this trend is about
'elevating the mundane'.

Guilt-free status People aware of the damage caused by over-
consumption look for 'guilt-free' products to indulge their need for
status symbols.

PERSONALIZED PRICING
Spaaza MyPrice

Fashion retail is now a multi-channel, multi-platform
environment, so businesses with retail stores must find
innovative ways of encouraging customers to purchase in-store
to offset showrooming. Spaaza (South African slang for an
informal shop), founded by David Sevenoaks and Sam Critchley
in 2011, is a software company that builds tools to incentivize
modern commerce, and aims to bring a little online wizardry
to the offline world. Spaaza works with many well-known
international brands, including G-Star Raw and Clarks shoes,
to run incentive marketing activities and create customer,
employee and influencer loyalty programmes. Its personal
pricing initiatives can also be designed for online commerce,
and the analytics tools can track the results of promotions in
real time.

Spaaza's mission is to make pricing and rewards more personal;
its MyPrice loyalty programme, available to retailers and accessible
to customers via smartphone app, offers unique ways to reward
shoppers who buy in-store. Trials with Clarks in the Netherlands
and Quiksilver in South Africa showed that Spaaza personal
pricing accounted for 25 per cent of sales in the first six months,
with a 40–50 per cent increase in basket size (average spend
per customer visit) compared to non-Spaaza baskets. The main
benefits of personal pricing are:

» Improves in-store experience for consumers

» Gives the retailer a way to make shoppers happy instantly
  – no delayed gratification

» Allows the retailer to reduce margin loss through targeted
  price promotions

» Gives more accurate understanding of shopper behaviour
  and conversion rates across the shopping journey

← Each product in a store where
Spaaza MyPrice is in operation has
a recommended retail price and a QR
code. Discounts can be applied for
a number of variables, such as purchasing
in-store, consumer loyalty, student
discount or as a birthday reward. The
nature of the rewards is established
between Spaaza and the retailer partner.
Customers never pay more than the
official recommended retail price, and
shoppers get the opportunity to pay
a personalized price based on their own
purchase history and profile.

RESEARCHING YOUR TARGET MARKET

STARBURST BOUTIQUE

Starburst Boutique is an independent boutique in the beautiful, historic coastal town of Dartmouth in southwestern England. It offers a unique blend of womenswear and accessories from a host of international designers, including Day Birger et Mikkelsen, Armor-Lux and Petit Bateau from France, as well as UK labels Marilyn Moore, Pyrus and Saltwater. Running alongside the contemporary womenswear collections are one-off vintage pieces, bespoke jewellery and luxurious lifestyle products. The boutique is in Dartmouth's most exclusive shopping street, and its stylish and relaxed in-store atmosphere is reflective of its coastal setting. It is designed to attract affluent second-homeowners, weekenders and tourists, but also to provide local clientele with a chic destination in which to buy exclusive and desirable fashion brands.

BACKGROUND MARKET RESEARCH

Starburst Boutique's owner and buyer, Hannah Jennings, carried out detailed research in order to set up her business. She investigated the current status, trends and predicted future of the independent retailing sector and the UK womenswear market, and obtained data from trade magazines, such as *Drapers* and *Retail Week*, industry analysts, such as Mintel, WGSN, Fashion Monitor and the British Retail Consortium, and a range of websites, magazines and newspaper articles. Information about the demographic of the local area and tourism was sourced from the local and county councils. Jennings also carried out an extensive investigation of existing independent retailers in the area, including in the nearest city, 40 km (25 miles) away. She also travelled to other cities, such as London, Edinburgh, Winchester, Bath and Brighton, to visit similar stylish independent boutiques.

RESEARCH FINDINGS AND INFORMATION

Tourism makes a significant contribution to the local economy. Pre-pandemic data revealed that Dartmouth attracts 400,000 visitors a year, plus 100,000 during a festive regatta week held in August. Sixty per cent of those visiting the area can be economically grouped as ABC1 (likely to have been to university and have a professional career) according to the social grading system used in consumer classification. Owing to the rising cost of living, there is evidence that an increasing number of UK residents choose to take holidays within Great Britain. The local area also boasts the third-highest percentage of second-homeowners in the UK, and has experienced a net population

"Independent retailers offer a personal service and cultural understanding of the local market."

Hannah Jennings

> *"The customer profiling I did turned out to be very accurate with regards to my core customers. It is fundamental for my business and I now buy with that segment in mind."*
>
> Hannah Jennings

increase of 441,000 since 1996 – a result of people migrating to the area in search of a better quality of life. Jennings found market data from a British Retail Consortium survey that showed a growing proportion of UK consumers preferred to shop in small independent stores than at high-street multiple retailers. The retail expert Mary Portas backed this up with a prediction that customers in their thirties will spend less on fast fashion and transfer their allegiance to local shops, where they can invest in high-quality products and receive better, more personal service. Research also indicates that female shoppers stay 'younger for longer', and that once they have defined their personal style in their thirties they will want to continue purchasing chic, contemporary and stylish clothing through to their sixties and beyond.

CONCLUSIONS: THE STARBURST BOUTIQUE CUSTOMER
Jennings recognizes how important her background research has been in helping her to understand the Starburst Boutique customer and the potential of the market.

The Starburst Boutique target market can be split into two customer profiles. The first represents the core customer to the business, namely women aged 30–45 who are married with small children. They either have a second home in the area or are weekender or tourist visitors who aspire to coastal living. The second profile is represented by slightly older, locally based women, aged 45–60 or over, probably with grown-up children and possibly grandchildren. The 60+ market is also important to the boutique, since this customer might bring along daughters or even granddaughters. They too might love the chance to shop in the store's chic and laid-back environment and snap up something desirable to wear on their holiday or to take back home.

←↑ The visual merchandising and store styling of the Starburst Boutique show a great attention to detail. Chandeliers, flowers and shabby-chic elements create an inviting atmosphere for the boutique's target customers.

Creating a customer profile

Once consumer research and analysis are complete, the next step is to create a customer profile report to describe the customers/consumer groups being targeted. The report should give background demographic, geo-demographic and psychographic data, information on current or emerging consumer trends, current sales statistics and relevant observational data. It is normal practice for such personnel as buyers, marketing or brand managers, or designers to give presentations summarizing the consumer report to other staff members or to suppliers, partners and stakeholders. A technique used to précis the research and describe the customer is known as a **customer pen portrait** or **customer persona**. Usually a written description that represents a customer archetype, it fleshes out the key traits, motivations and behaviours in order to build a fuller picture of this consumer type. It is often helpful to accompany the written portrait with an image depicting the customer and visualizing their lifestyle.

Writing a customer pen portrait

A pen portrait provides a composite picture of the target customer, and should be built up using information gathered from primary and secondary market research. The portrait should present a realistic and factual description of the consumer demographic, age or age bracket, lifestyle, fashion style, brand preferences, purchasing motivation and attitudes towards purchasing fashion.

Traditionally, a pen portrait includes information on age and gender, but this may no longer be the best approach. It could be better to consider attitude, rather than age. Think more about describing their lifestyle and stage of life. You can list the clothing brands that they wear or aspire to wear, and indicate how much they spend on clothing. Also consider which social-media channels they use, and from where they are likely to get inspiration and ideas about fashion.

The problem with pen portraits is the tendency to describe a fantasy life or the aspirational life of the consumer, rather than the reality. It is important, therefore, to reiterate that the portrait *must* be based on researched information and data. Information can be obtained from government demographic statistics, articles in the fashion media, fashion trend publications and websites, and blogs, and by carrying out a customer questionnaire.

The visual depiction of the customer and their lifestyle that is a useful addition to the written portrait can be pictures covering interiors, lifestyle, food, gardening, sport, gadgets or technology.

When creating a visual profile, it is important to ensure that images reflect the consumer's lifestyle and activities, and not just their approach to fashion. Try to use pictures that typify the product or brand choices for that consumer type, such as their car, watch, scent, accessories and clothing. The images should reflect accurately the market level and status level of the customer.

You could also include a customer journey map as an indicator of the way the customer typically gains awareness of fashion and might progress through to purchase. Think carefully about the loyalty and advocacy stages of the journey. Are they a loyal customer, and could they become an advocate of the brand? If, for example, you identify three different core customer types, you could create a specific customer journey map for each.

CUSTOMER JOURNEY

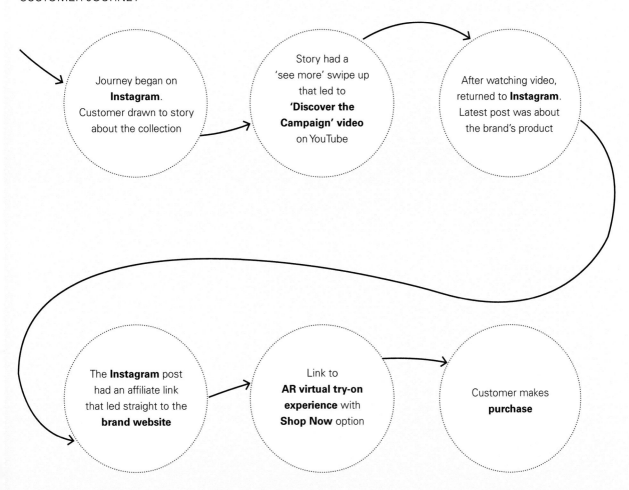

Image: Developed from student work by Charlotte Marsh-Williams

Questions for a pen portrait

» Try to visualize the person, get inside their head and imagine who they are.

» What influences are there in their life?

» What are their key concerns, opinions or interests?

» Think about their routine as they go through the day. Do they have specific clothes or outfits for work, sport or leisure?

» What non-clothing brands are important to them, and why?

Understanding business customers

It is also extremely important to understand business customers. In B2B situations it is normal procedure for a business to analyse its customer base. This is done for two main reasons: first to determine how valuable each customer is to the business, and second to understand how best to meet customer needs and service them effectively. To understand the needs of business customers fully, it also makes sense to have good knowledge of their end-consumers, as well.

An independent designer with their own fashion label, for example, who supplies their collection to approximately 40 stores worldwide, could analyse and classify their customers by country or region, such as Europe, Asia and North America, particularly if end-consumers in each region have differing requirements. The designer may supply independent boutiques that order small quantities from a limited selection of the range, or much larger retailers that take a greater proportion of the collection, so they might want to analyse these customers by the amount they order or by the type of product they order. They may have customers that require little effort to service, others that have input into the design process, specifying colours, styles or fabrics suitable for their end-consumers, and/or others that require exclusivity, requesting certain styles be made available only to them. These more 'high-maintenance' customers might be of great value to the business, even though they require a higher level of service.

B2B customers might be assessed by their financial contribution, but there are other assets of value to consider, such as status and reputation of the customer, publicity potential, partnership or networking possibilities, or their ability to provide access to other organizations. In reverse, large high-street retailers usually analyse their supply base so that they can determine which suppliers provide the best service, quality and prices. A large business, such as a textile manufacturer, for example, might segment its customers by the type of market they represent, separating the companies that purchase for the mass market from other clients who might be at couture or designer level. Here is a summary of the criteria to consider when analysing business customers:

> » **Location** Local, national, international or global
>
> » **Financial contribution** How much they contribute to turnover and profit
>
> » **Reputation** The value attached to their name, the type of end-consumer they attract, and publicity potential
>
> » **Status** New start-up or well established, length of business relationship, loyalty of custom, financial security
>
> » **Type of company** Department store, independent boutique, e-tailer, retail chain. Or manufacturer, producer or designer
>
> » **Market level** Couture or designer level, or retailers that develop own-brand collections

Building a customer profile

THE NICHE DENIM MARKET

Sliced Bread is a denim brand created by James Hayes while he was studying fashion at Plymouth College of Art (now Arts University Plymouth) in southwestern England. The idea was developed in response to increasing consumer demand for authentic, stylish and nostalgic product. The concept is simple: to make high-quality jeans and T-shirts that people will remember. Each piece is handmade in England using the finest materials and production methods. Sliced Bread products are trans-seasonal and 100 per cent fresh!

RESEARCHING THE CUSTOMER

Hayes carried out face-to-face, telephone and online interviews with young men in their early twenties who were potential customers for Sliced Bread jeans and T-shirts. He wanted to gather information on their lifestyles and the type of brand they currently wore, and find out more about the brands they aspired to wear. He discovered how much they spent on clothes, what they did for a living and how they spent their leisure time. After conducting a number of interviews, Hayes noticed commonalities in terms of purchasing behaviour, attitudes and brand preferences that appeared to typify the traits of the sample group. He used this information to compile a customer pen portrait for a character he named 'Selvedge Steve', who would be representative of the target audience for the proposed Sliced Bread brand.

PEN PORTRAIT OF A SLICED BREAD CUSTOMER

Selvedge Steve (as he is known to his friends, or Big Selve or Selvie for short) is a 21-year-old student of architecture at Manchester University. Now in his second year of study, he has rented a student flat with three friends. During the holidays he lives with his parents in Windsor, about 50 km (30 miles) outside London. Big Selve is entrepreneurial and aspires to set up his own design business one day soon. He loves design and the world of Japanese and selvedge denim, and skates at London's famous Southbank skatepark most Saturdays. There he meets other guys who appreciate fashion, but when back home in Windsor, he communicates online and through the platform Discord with other young designers and 'Denimheads' around the world. He follows fashion TikTok pages and sometimes joins in with general fashion and menswear threads on Reddit. He listens to a range of podcasts about denim, such as *Sons of Selvedge*, *NY Denim Hangs* and *The Denimhunters*, and follows Leo Gamboa of Levi's (@leoneski) and Tremaine Emory of Denim Tears (@tremaineemory/@denimtears). He also follows @throwingfits for funny fashion content on Instagram.

Big Selve usually wears T-shirts with his jeans. His favourites are from the vintage clothing Instagram stores @unifiedgoods and @jerks.store, where he has bought various different designs from the 1990s, all of which – despite being bought

AARON WATTS
Age: 20, student
Wears: Adidas Originals and charity shop
Aspires to wear: No particular brand/label

SAM PHILLIPS
Age: 20, DJ
Wears: Levi's, Adidas, Wood Wood, Religion and Bantum
Aspires to wear: Paul Smith, Diesel Black Gold and Vivienne Westwood

ALEX PUGH
Age: 21, student
Wears: Jack Wills, Topman University Gear, Crew Clothing
Aspires to wear: Paul Smith

← Three of the young men interviewed by Hayes during his customer research investigations. He discovered that there was a gap between the brands his target group aspired to wear and those they actually bought. Aspirational brands were Paul Smith, Comme des Garçons, Diesel Black Gold and Dsquared². Labels actually worn were Zara, Primark, charity-shop clothes, Topman, Levi's and Jack Wills. It is important to point out that although Hayes focused on young men aged 20 or 21, the potential market for the Sliced Bread concept is likely to extend to customers aged 30, so research into customers in this age bracket should also be carried out.

↗→ James Hayes' Sliced Bread jeans and T-shirt collection. Selvedge seams and the Sliced Bread leather patch highlight the core concept for the jeans.

in used condition – have held their shape extremely well. With Instagram followers all over Europe, Steve likes to represent the UK through his outfits, and he has lots of great T-shirts from Palace, bought at the store in Soho. He likes to support local, and favours T-shirts that have a quirky appeal. He has a great one from Percival, bought in the store in Hackney. It has an embroidered bowl of ramen on it. He likes the subtle Japanese reference and the way the brand subverts the classics. He paid £27 for this, but has paid £45 for a T-shirt from Carhartt WIP, and £80 for his favourite Studio D'Artisan 9913 Loopwheel Tee that

he got online from Rivet & Hide. It is 100 per cent cotton, with no side seams, and made in Japan. He thinks it is surprisingly soft. His jeans are mostly dark indigo denim, so in general he likes his T-shirts to pop and show personality.

For the all-important denim jeans, Selvie's passion for architecture and design translates into a respect for a product that is well designed but understated: a good pair of jeans from Carhartt (for skating in), Flat Head (a longer-term project, where he's working on the fading and whiskering by not washing them), or OrSlow and Levi's (for everyday use). The brands he likes cost around £90–120; OrSlow cost around £250, so he can't always afford them unless they are on sale, or bought second-hand through Depop. Here he sells almost all his clothes to like-minded members. For rarer pieces he tries Grailed (most members of which are in the USA), but this is mainly for selling, since UK import duties are high.

The brands Steve aspires to most are OrSlow, Auralee, Iron Heart and Levi's Silvertabs. The holy grail are jeans made from deadstock fabric woven at the now closed White Oak Cone Denim factory, then assembled on vintage Japanese machinery for extra strength and authenticity. The Denimhunters blog said that 'Cone is to denim-weaving what Levi's is to jeans-making.' The deadstock cone denim fabric is so rare, Big Selve thinks it's like looking for a unicorn. It is still worth dreaming!

Selvie always pays in cash when he goes shopping for clothes: 'If you haven't got it [money], don't buy it.' For online purchases he uses Klarna so that he can spread the cost. His girlfriend put him on to this, and he was surprised to learn that there was data to show that men were outspending women on Klarna – who knew! He thinks it is best to buy less but to try and buy better.

Knowing your core customers

THE DUBAI CONSUMER

DEMOGRAPHIC VARIABLES
Gender: Female
Age: 23–25
Education: High level of education (international student)
Social status: High
Region: United Arab Emirates

Lifestyle factors: International upbringing, high global awareness, and an affluent and elegant lifestyle

Spending highlights: Investment purchases, quality, modesty, brand loyalty

Key digital touchpoints: Instagram, TikTok. E-commerce and online shopping play a crucial role in the purchasing habits of this demographic. They are comfortable buying luxury items online, and often indulge in virtual shopping experiences offered by high-end brands.

Motivation and behaviours: Trend- and brand-conscious. Prioritizes well-known designer labels and iconic fashion houses, using them as symbols of status and sophistication.

Dubai is a melting pot of cultures, and the young female consumer of luxury fashion reflects this diversity in her style choices. She blends traditional elements effortlessly with modern fashion trends, creating a unique and eclectic personal style. This city-centric demographic travels the world regularly, harnessing an international fluency not only academically but also through her sartorial tastes and experiences. Hailing from diverse cultural backgrounds, the Dubai consumer is always aware of the newest, 'trending' places not only in Dubai but also around the globe. With few monetary barriers, she is characterized by her high disposable income and strong affinity for luxury fashion. Investment purchases are at the heart of her spending patterns, but she also embraces physical experiences – potentially heightened through growing up in a hot environment and therefore pushed towards indoor shopping experiences, what could be described as a thriving 'mall culture'.

← According to Statista in 2024, 'each individual in the United Arab Emirates (UAE) generates revenues of US$56.94 in the Luxury Fashion market'. The report, *Luxury Fashion in the United Arab Emirates*, states that there is a surge in demand for luxury fashion brands in the UAE, with high-end designers opening flagship stores in prestigious malls, such as Dubai Mall.

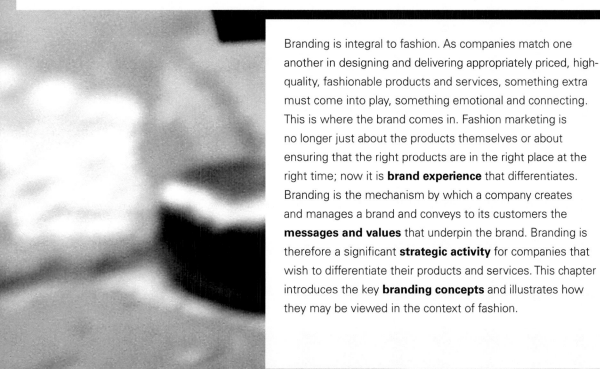

5

Introduction to Branding

"A brand is no longer what we tell the consumer it is – it is what consumers tell each other it is."

Scott Cook, co-founder, Intuit

Branding is integral to fashion. As companies match one another in designing and delivering appropriately priced, high-quality, fashionable products and services, something extra must come into play, something emotional and connecting. This is where the brand comes in. Fashion marketing is no longer just about the products themselves or about ensuring that the right products are in the right place at the right time; now it is **brand experience** that differentiates. Branding is the mechanism by which a company creates and manages a brand and conveys to its customers the **messages and values** that underpin the brand. Branding is therefore a significant **strategic activity** for companies that wish to differentiate their products and services. This chapter introduces the key **branding concepts** and illustrates how they may be viewed in the context of fashion.

Defining a brand

The concrete features of a brand are its logo, strapline, slogan, recognizable brand colour (if there is one), actual products, website, social-media feeds and physical retail environment. But a brand is more than the sum of its parts; most of what constitutes a brand is intangible. In many ways the brand is a paradox, a composite shaped internally by company strategy and externally by consumer perception and experience. Formed from a unique mix of tangible and intangible elements, a brand is created out of a total package, including not only the garments, digital and retail environments, packaging and advertising, but also the meanings, values and associations that consumers ascribe to the brand. Walter Landor, a pioneer of branding, famously said, 'Products are made in the factory, but brands are created in the mind.' In 2007 the branding expert Allen Adamson defined a brand as 'something that exists in your head. It's an image or a feeling. It's based on associations that get stirred up when a brand's name is mentioned.'

Influential and successful brands manage to engender positive or constructive associations in the minds of consumers, triggering emotions and feelings that can be extremely potent and affirmative. However, each consumer forms their own opinion, so there is the possibility that they may develop negative perceptions and beliefs. It is therefore important for those who manage brands to consider carefully the associations that a brand conveys, making sure wherever possible that messages are transmitted by design rather than default. A brand must have clear points of difference, not only in the products and services but also at an experiential level. Consumers need to be aware of the brand's existence, connect with its ethos and value what it has to offer – and, of course, the brand offering should be relevant to the needs, aspirations and desires of customers.

The values, messages and ideas that underpin a brand will be expressed through:

> » The brand name and logo
>
> » The product
>
> » Packaging and display
>
> » The environment in which it is sold
>
> » Social media and online content
>
> » Advertising and promotion
>
> » Company reputation and behaviour

↓ Flags display the brand names of luxury fashion, accessory and jewellery retailers on Old Bond Street, London. The style and design of a logo and the colour of a flag are a significant manifestation of the identity of a brand.

↓ ↓ A trademark Chanel quilted handbag with iconic interlocking 'C' logo on the clasp.

The brand name and logo

The brand name and logo are tangible features that can be controlled from within the company. The logo provides the most fundamental visible element of the brand; the style of this unique identifier should capture and represent the essence or core idea behind the brand. Intelligent or ingenious use of colour, typeface and symbol can help to achieve a distinguishing logo that, it is to be hoped, will stand as an iconic and trusted visual agent of the brand. Some luxury fashion brands, such as Gucci, Prada, Fendi and Chanel, use upper-case letters to create an aura of authority and tradition. Some brands add a crest or cartouche to enhance the logo and bestow an air of grandeur or heritage. Sports brands design their logos with the aim of generating a sensation of movement, speed or direction. Brands that wish to convey elegance or femininity tend to use lower-case script with flourishes and tails.

A well-designed and powerfully recognized logo is a great asset to a brand. The logo can be formed using the brand name, such as Gucci or Prada; Paul Smith uses his signature as the brand logo. Initials and letters can be exploited to construct a brand name, such as DKNY (Donna Karan New York), or to form a secondary logo, as with the interlocking letters of Fendi, Chanel or Gucci. There are, of course, legendary brands, such as Nike with its iconic Swoosh, with symbols so powerful that they instantly identify the brand without the need of accompanying name or words. Similarly, the crossed arrows of Off-White and the Lacoste crocodile act as iconic emblems for their respective brands.

Trademarks

Brand logos, symbols, slogans and straplines can be registered. It is also possible to register elements of a design that are specific signifiers of a brand. Levi's, for example, has registered the marketing slogan 'Quality never goes out of style'®, and the iconic Burberry camel, black and red check became a registered trademark in 1924, when it was used as a lining for the Burberry trench coat. A registered trademark gives the brand company exclusive rights over the use of the registered article. This helps to protect the brand from piracy or unauthorized use of the trademark. Once a mark is registered, it can be identified by the ® or ™ symbol.

A small business intending to trade in its home market can register its mark for exclusive use in the national market. But to ensure more comprehensive protection, it is sensible to be internationally registered if that is an option the brand can afford. Hermès, for example, challenged Dog Diggin Designs for its use of similar brand

CLASSIC LUXURY

Feminine Boutique

modmode

↑↑ The international sports brand Adidas has an instantly recognizable logo, featuring its quintessential three-stripes motif. The classic Adidas emblem has been modified to create logos for the sub-brands.

↑ When creating logos it is important to consider the underlying message and choose a typeface accordingly. The stretched font and forward direction of the 'Sport Fashion' logo creates a feeling of momentum. An upper-case copperplate Gothic Light typeface communicates the timeless authority of heritage and indulgence (Classic Luxury). The italicized Edwardian Script adds a feminine touch to a logo (Feminine Boutique). A contemporary modern look with a retro feel is created using the Bauhaus 93 typeface (Modmode).

> *"Branding is the process by which brand images get inside your head."*
>
> Allen Adamson

identifiers on pet cushions. These were orange and had a HAIRMES logo and brown ribbon with white writing and outer dashed white line – all redolent of the Hermès logo and brand identity. In 2021 Hermès initiated a lawsuit in Japan, but the Japan Patent Office (JPO) dismissed it, stating that there was unlikely to be confusion between the two brands. In 2023 the JPO reversed its decision, this time siding with Hermès. Its view was that Dog Diggin Designs' use of a similar logo showed an intention to 'free-ride and dilute' the value of the famous French fashion house's brand.

Brand colours

It is possible for a brand to register its trademark colour. In 1995 the US Supreme Court ruled for the first time that a colour could be a legal trademark and could therefore become the property of a single brand. The colour must, however, have a secondary meaning; in other words, consumers must recognize and link that shade to one and only one brand. Tiffany blue, Hermès orange and the red on the soles of Christian Louboutin shoes are examples.

There can be challenges to the trademark, and certain colour trademarks may not be recognized in all global territories. For example, the Louboutin 'red sole mark', described as the lacquered red sole on footwear, has been contested several times. The most famous case was in 2012, between Christian Louboutin and the French fashion house Yves Saint Laurent (YSL), when an 18-month legal tussle was concluded. The Manhattan Federal District court in New York ruled that Louboutin had the right to trademark protection for its red soles and that other companies, including YSL, might sell shoes with a red sole *only* if the entire shoe were red. Another case occurred in 2018 between Louboutin and the Japanese Eizo Collection Company. The JPO had refused to agree to a single-colour

↓ Colours that are iconic to a brand are usually trademarked to ensure exclusivity. The distinctive orange of the Hermès packaging is copyrighted in many territories, including America and France. In 2023 it gained trademark status in Japan, having initially been rejected by the country's Patent Office.

↘ The robin's-egg blue of Tiffany packaging is in the registered Pantone colour 1837 Blue, after the date the company was founded. Known as Tiffany Blue®, this iconic colour is integral to the brand's recognition and allure. According to the Tiffany website, the Tiffany Blue Box® is 'regarded as the most recognizable and coveted packaging in the world'.

status trademark when Louboutin brought a case against Eizo for the black shoes with red rubber soles produced by the latter. Louboutin argued that Eizo did not ask permission to use the red sole mark, and that this was an infringement under Japan's unfair competition law. The court in Tokyo found that shoes with red soles had been sold previously in Japan, and that the red in question was an available stock Pantone colour and not one developed uniquely by the Louboutin brand. The court also ruled that consumers would not confuse Louboutin's significantly more expensive luxury red lacquered sole with the lower-priced red rubber sole of the Eizo shoe, and that red was a common colour in Japanese fashion, especially for women.

Brand canvas

Fashion product provides a fantastic canvas for branding. Logos can be emblazoned boldly on T-shirts or used more subtly in placement embroideries. Denim brands use trademark stitching on back pockets to identify their jeans, or use labels, such as the iconic Levi's red tab. When designing branded product, think about how to incorporate brand insignia. Clasps, clips, buckles and zips can all be developed so as to include recognizable and identifying symbols or emblems, and fabrics can be woven or printed with trademark stripes, checks and patterns. Overt logo branding tends to go in cycles. During an economic boom, consumers like to show off, displaying clearly visible logos on clothes and accessories. During an economic downturn, ostentatious displays can be frowned upon, so brands tend to produce collections with more discreet logos. Fashion brands often choose to make their higher-priced product more discreet, appealing to those who want luxury but do not want to broadcast their status with flashy logos. It is often on the entry-priced products that the logos are more obvious, targeted at those customers who want to tap into the brand and signal to others that they have the money to do so.

Types of brand

Brands exist at every level of the fashion industry. There are branded fibres and textiles, such as Naia™, a cellulosic fabric by the chemical company Eastman in collaboration with DuPont biomaterials; DuPont's Sorona® brand, made from 37 per cent renewable plant-based ingredients; and Piñatex®, a vegan leather by Ananas Anam, made from pineapple waste. There are sports brands, such as Adidas, Nike, Lululemon and Gymshark; streetwear brands, including Supreme, Patta, Off-White, Daily Paper, Aimé Leon Dore and A-Cold-Wall*; designer brands, such as Thom Browne, Erdem

↑ The Adidas Originals by Originals (ObyO) collection, created by Adidas in 2009 in collaboration with the New York fashion designer Jeremy Scott, exemplifies how a logo can be integrated into the design of a garment to create effective branding. Scott took an inventive approach by partly concealing an oversized Adidas Originals emblem with layers of fringing.

↑ Burberry's distinctive check is used by
the brand for many of its products. Here
it appears in a menswear collection. The
scale of the check has been enlarged
significantly but it is still instantly
recognizable as a signifier of the brand.

↗ The Fred Perry tennis sweater is
branded with an embroidered laurel
wreath – the label's signature trademark.

and Alexander McQueen; and luxury brands, among them Louis
Vuitton and Hermès. In addition, there are fashion retail brands and
department stores that have achieved brand status. Defining types
of brand can be complicated, but they can be categorized as follows:

A **corporate brand** is an organization with one name and one visual
identity across its brands. The corporation is the brand. An example
is the Sri Lankan manufacturing corporation MAS Holdings:
MAS Intimates produces lingerie and intimate apparel for global
customers, such as Marks & Spencer, Gap and Victoria's Secret;
MAS Active is a supplier of active sports and casual wear to Nike,
Adidas, Reebok, Gap and Speedo; and MAS Fabric develops fabrics,
elastics, lace and other garment components.

Manufacturer brands are created and marketed by producer
companies, which choose a name for their branded product. These
brands are prevalent in the fibre and textile industry. where chemical
manufacturers brand their fibres. The science-based company
DuPont, for example, used to manage the well-known fibre brand
Lycra®. Another DuPont brand is Kevlar®, which is used in garments
that protect from a variety of hazards, including abrasion and heat.
NatureWorks LLC, a joint venture between Cargill and PTT Global
Chemical, produces Ingeo™, a fibre made from renewable corn-

based resources. The avant-garde French fashion label Marithé + François Girbaud selected Ingeo™ for its first eco-inspired designs.

Private label brands are also known as own brands, store brands, retailer brands and own label. An article on Forbes by the retail analyst Walter Loeb in 2022 explained that private-label fashion was a growing area for US stores and department stores. Stores were pinning their hopes on these collections in a bid to counter the tough post-pandemic economic climate and offer attractively priced, well-made collections. The department store JCPenney launched Everyday Marilyn, a 12-piece collection for spring and summer in a palette of black, white, coral and navy. Macy's carries the private-label brands I.N.C. and Style & Co. In the summer of 2021 it introduced 'And Now This', a ready-to-wear collection for women and men consisting of trend-forward pieces at affordable price points.

An **endorsed brand** is created when a parent brand gives its name to or endorses one of its own sub-brands. The names of the parent and sub-brand are linked. Examples are Polo by Ralph Lauren and the perfume Obsession by Calvin Klein. The endorsement gives credibility to the sub-brand while capitalizing on the status and reputation of the main brand.

Co-brands or partnership brands are created when two brands join to develop a new brand. Adidas Y-3, the collaborative project between the Japanese designer Yohji Yamamoto and Adidas, is a good example. The name comes from the 'Y' of Yamamoto and the three stripes of the Adidas logo.

When a company has a **brand portfolio**, the aim is to maximize coverage of the market without the individual brands within the portfolio competing with one another. The various brands within the company are designed to address specific needs across different key segments within the market. Kering's brand portfolio includes prestigious and clearly defined luxury brands, including Gucci, Alexander McQueen, Stella McCartney, Balenciaga, Bottega Veneta and Saint Laurent, and the sports and lifestyle brands Puma and Volcom. The Adidas Group has a brand portfolio that includes Reebok, the shoe company Rockport and the golf brand TaylorMade.

The purpose of branding

The purpose of branding is to establish a clear, distinctive identity for a product, service or organization, to ensure that the brand offers something distinguishable from competitor brands. Branding should also add value or increase the perceived value of a product, allowing a company to charge a premium for its branded merchandise.

On a more complex level, branding works to create emotional connection between customers and the brand. It not only raises the consumer's potential financial outlay but can also affect their emotional investment in the brand. A pair of Nike trainers, for example, is not just a pair of running shoes but 'my Nikes', imbued with additional associations and meaning. In a pair of Nikes 'I can do it'. This is why a brand can be so powerful and influential. The Nike wearer might feel more committed and better able to get up early and run; they might believe themselves to be more sporty, active and alive when they wear this particular brand. Consumers are therefore more likely to engage constructively with a brand and purchase its products if the brand satisfies several criteria: the brand's products and services must be relevant to their life and needs; the consumer should identify closely with the brand ideology and style; and their association with the brand should trigger positive or affirmative feelings and emotions.

Branding should reassure and create a sense of security and trust for customers. If they connect emotionally with a brand and want what it has to offer, the hope is that they will be loyal. It is important, therefore, that the brand remains consistent and continues to deliver the values and promises that customers expect.

Brand continuity is extremely important in the fashion industry. This is because two contrasting factors – newness and consistency – must be integrated season after season. Customers naturally demand choice and want to be tempted with fresh merchandise each season, but they also require some stability. This presents a challenge to designers who must create and develop new product collections regularly. They must ensure the integrity of the brand remains intact and create the sensation of permanence for customers, even when the products in-store change frequently. The theme, concepts, colours and fabrics might be different in each seasonal collection, but the overarching branding, **brand message** and **brand values** must remain consistent. To take an example from a very old brand, Virginie Viard has kept the Chanel brand and aesthetic consistent since taking over the reins after the death of Karl Lagerfeld in 2019.

There are instances when a brand decides it is time to revamp, perhaps by modifying the brand logo or hiring a new creative director, who shifts the style and perception of the brand. This can work successfully – or backfire, as was the case in 2016, when the Italian menswear brand Brioni, owned by the Kering group, hired the Australian designer Justin O'Shea. At the hands of O'Shea, Brioni – previously known for its classic style and for making the suits for James Bond in the film franchise – underwent a radical makeover, including the brand logo and advertising direction. The Autumn/

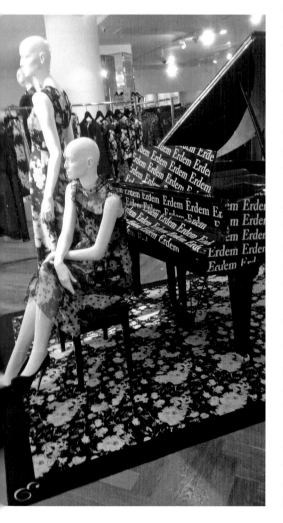

↓ An in-store display and matching floral carpet promote an Erdem collection.

Winter 2017 collection featured the rock band Metallica and the new logo in a large, heavy gothic font, a radical change from the previous smaller handwritten script-style typeface. It did not take long for the brand to realize its unfortunate mistake – that it had alienated its traditional customer base – and O'Shea left after only seven months in the post. It was not until 2018 that Brioni began to get back on track with the appointment of Norbert Stumpfl. The Austrian creative director restored the brand logo, established a look of classic modernity and brought in Brad Pitt as the face of the brand for 2021, and Jude Law with his son Raff Law for the Autumn/Winter 2022 and Spring/Summer 2023 campaigns (see page 261).

In marketing terms, branding is essentially about building a relationship between consumer and brand. This is why a thorough knowledge and understanding of consumers are so vital, and why companies invest so much time and money in consumer and market research. The more intimately a company understands its customers, the better able it is to develop products, services, retail environments and marketing strategies that encourage engagement, promote loyalty and foster trust in its brand.

To summarize, the purpose of branding is to:

» Tap into values and beliefs

» Create connection

» Generate emotional response

» Provide reassurance

» Ensure consistency

» Build loyalty

» Add value and charge a premium

At the business level, branding is about building what is known as brand equity. The aim is to build the commercial value of the brand, which is based not only on the actual financial value of the company but also on the extra value that the brand name itself brings. This derives from consumer awareness and perception of the brand. A model devised by Professor Kevin Lane Keller in 1993 and known as the Customer-Based Brand Equity (CBBE) model is explained in his celebrated book *Strategic Brand Management* (2003). As you go through the CBBE module, you can see how it relates to the purposes of branding listed above.

The CBBE pyramid has four steps and six building blocks that must be in place in order to establish brand equity, working from the bottom towards the top of the pyramid:

Step 1: Salience or brand awareness 'Salience' means being noticeable or prominent in customers' minds. For a brand to gain customer awareness, it must develop and establish a clear brand identity. This is one of the foremost tactics for achieving the emotional connection with a target audience that is so vital to the concept of branding. A clear and recognizable brand identity helps to make a brand stand out from competitors and to raise customers' brand awareness. It is also important that customers' perceptions of the brand, or brand image, is in alignment with the brand identity. (There is more on this later in this chapter.)

Step 2: Brand meaning The goal is for the brand company to communicate what the brand means, and what it stands for. According to Keller, there are two key areas: performance and imagery. Performance defines how well your product meets your customers' needs. This can be viewed across a range of criteria:

• primary characteristics and features

• product style, design and price

• product reliability, durability and serviceability

• service effectiveness, efficiency and empathy

KELLER'S CUSTOMER-BASED
BRAND EQUITY OR CBBE MODEL

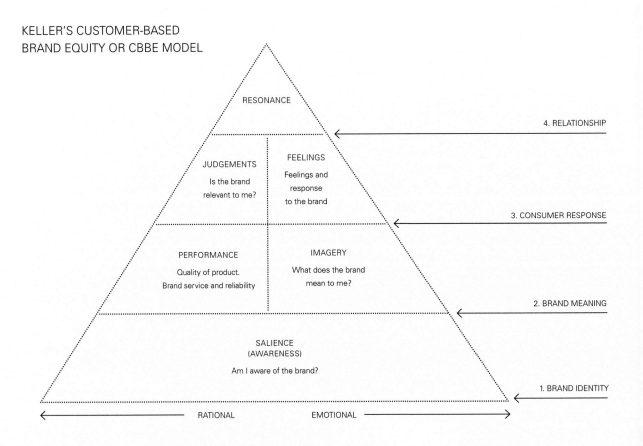

Imagery in Keller's model relates to consumers' image of the brand – how well the brand meets customers' needs on a social and psychological level.

Step 3: Brand response This is the customers' response to the brand. This falls into two categories: judgements and feelings. Customers judge a brand, its products and services on its quality or perceived quality; on its credibility – how trustworthy the brand is; on the expertise of the brand in its market and product area; and on superiority – how good the brand is compared to competitor brands in the market.

Step 4: Brand resonance This relates to the relationship between customers and the brand. This sits at the top of the pyramid and is the most difficult level to achieve, but also the one that achieves the highest brand equity (when customers feel a deep psychological bond with the brand). Keller breaks it down into four areas:

• behavioural loyalty: making regular repeat purchases, for example

• attitudinal attachment: loving the brand and seeing it as a special purchase

• sense of community: feeling a sense of community with the brand and with people associated with the brand

• active engagement: actively engaging with a brand even if they do not purchase it. This can include engaging with brand social media or online forums, participating in brand events or activities, joining a brand-related club, or promoting the brand to others via word of mouth. This is the strongest level of brand loyalty and advocacy.

Brand identity

Brand identity is controlled from within an organization and should relate to how the company wishes consumers to perceive and engage with the brand. People use brands – and fashion in particular – to make statements about themselves, so the meanings and associations consumers foster about brands will be closely connected with how they want to feel, how they want to be seen and how they wish to be perceived by others. Consumers are more likely to connect positively with a brand if they associate closely with its overall identity and ethos. It is extremely important, therefore, for an organization to develop a compelling and engaging identity for its brand. The identity will be built up using the following:

» Logo

» Product and services

» Packaging

» Retail or online sales environment, including windows and visual merchandising, and/or website

» Promotion, advertising, PR and social media

» Inherent values of the brand, what it stands for and how this is communicated in all brand messaging

Brand image

Each expression of the brand listed above will work towards building up the brand identity. It is important to point out, however, that consumers will interpret all a brand's signifiers and form their own impression of the identity. For this reason it is vital that each and every manifestation of the brand uphold the identity coherently and consistently. The image of the brand from a consumer perspective is known as the brand image.

The image of a brand differs depending on whether it is formed by a brand-user or non-user, or someone who has a business association with the brand, such as a supplier or stakeholder. Someone who is a devoted customer of a brand would compose their image based on experience. Take someone who regularly purchases from Ralph Lauren. They may visit the same flagship store frequently, be served consistently by a specific staff member, and build up a very personal relationship with the brand and its products. Another person may aspire to the Ralph Lauren lifestyle, but believe the designer clothes to be expensive or extravagant. They might buy into the brand on a rare occasion by purchasing sunglasses, perfume or homeware from a department store, such as Bloomingdale's or Selfridges.

One way that consumers form their image of a brand is through viewing branded content. This might be adverts or fashion spreads in magazines, via social media or by watching brand-produced video content.

BRAND IDENTITY & BRAND IMAGE

BRAND IDENTITY	INTERNAL COMPANY-DEFINED	EXTERNAL CONSUMER-DEFINED	BRAND IMAGE
	Brand strategy	Consumers and brand engagers make up their own minds and form a personal image of the brand, its products, services and communications	
	Marketing strategy		
	Promotion strategy		
	Communication strategy		

A growing trend is for fashion brands to release films. The New York designer Thom Browne, for example, produces film content each season to accompany his collections. This helps the brand to gain global attention and bring viewers into the unique and wonderful world of Thom Browne. The Autumn 2021 show had to be cancelled because of the COVID-19 pandemic, so Browne's creative approach to content saved the day. For this season the brand collaborated with Drive Studios on a film directed by Carissa Gallo and shot in the mountains of Utah. The concept featured the legendary Olympic ski champion Lindsey Vonn in a fantastical snowy dream world of haute couture. The ten-minute film, shot in black and white with small flashes of gold, references Hollywood and the classic movie *The Wizard of Oz* (1939). The opening sequence starts with an illustration of a mountain scene and the words 'the most angelical and fantastical dream that led me home'. The main portion of the film has Vonn swooshing down the slopes sporting a Thom Browne jacket with the iconic four white stripes on the left sleeve. She weaves her way elegantly between men and women dressed in the most exquisitely detailed haute couture. They stand like sentinels representing the gates of an Olympic ski course as she slaloms past, her eyes widening at the avant-garde beauty of their Thom Browne attire. At the end, she wakes up from her dream wearing beautiful golden boots, with the closing text 'I love being home … I love being home.' '*Bravo merci thom browne*' was one of the comments posted on YouTube at the time.

The power of a brand rests in its relationship with consumers. Every interaction a customer or potential customer has with a brand is important, since it will contribute to their brand experience, either positively or negatively.

The company behind a brand must ensure that there is a close match between the identity they control and the brand image as perceived by outsiders and consumers. A large gap between identity and image can result in catastrophic problems for a brand. There have been cases where companies have lost control of their identity. This happened to Burberry when consumers it had not intended to attract started purchasing both legitimate Burberry product and counterfeit products. The skewed image of the brand affected its identity, which no longer related to the company's strategic intentions.

↑ Stills from the film for the Thom Browne women's and men's Autumn 2021 collection, featuring the Olympic skier Lindsey Vonn. The concept was inspired by Dorothy's journey in *The Wizard of Oz*.

Developing and managing brand identity

Developing and managing the brand identity is an extremely important aspect of **brand management**. A brand is a precious commodity and a valuable asset for a company, and a powerful brand name, brand logo and brand identity, as well as the accumulated goodwill that exists towards the brand, all contribute to the brand equity (the total worth of the brand as an asset). A brand with high equity and a strong identity can command a price premium for its product, which is one of the main purposes of branding. Those managing a brand must ensure that there is a close match between the brand identity created and managed within the company and the brand image held by consumers and others outside the company. In order to develop and manage an identity effectively, it is important to understand that it is formulated from three key constituents:

> » Brand essence

> » Brand values

> » Brand personality

These three elements govern the overall character and feel of the brand; they give the brand its meaning and uniqueness, and serve to differentiate it from others in the marketplace. They are vital components of the identity and should be reflected in the outward manifestations of the brand: its symbol or logo, product, packaging, display, promotion and website.

Brand essence

The first step in defining brand identity is to determine and establish the brand essence, the essential nature or core of a brand. It could be described as the brand's heart, spirit or soul. It is extremely important to understand what lies at the heart of a brand and to be able to articulate it concisely. Nike's statement 'Just Do It' is an example, perhaps even accompanied by the Swoosh. The statement and the Swoosh brand signifier sit right at the heart of everything Nike does. It identifies the fundamental aim of the brand, marks out its central proposition and sums up its essence. This articulation of the essence could also be described as the **brand proposition**, which is a succinct expression of what the brand intends to offer or promise its customers.

Different brands may alter the terminology slightly, and you will hear such terms as brand proposition, brand message and brand promise. Take the Japanese retailer Uniqlo. Its essence or brand proposition could be described as 'high-quality, performance-enhanced, universal, basic casual wear at affordable prices'. Its 'Made for All' brand philosophy positions its clothing so as to 'transcend age, gender, ethnicity and all other ways to identify individuals'. One could combine these two fundamental descriptions to form one central statement that sits at the core of the brand: High-quality, performance-enhanced, universal, basic casual wear at affordable prices – Made for All.

The brand also states its value propositions:

1. Apparel items treated as components (to be worn with other items on offer, all featuring a basic design)

2. High quality at a significantly lower price

3. Apparel proposing new performance features, including such signature fabric innovations as HeatTech, LifeWear and AIRism

Value propositions could also be considered core values. As you can see from the example of Uniqlo, the essence proposition (or promise) and brand philosophy explain the *raison d'être* of the brand and clarify the motivation for the business. A genuine brand essence in combination with an achievable and deliverable proposition will contribute to creating a well-defined brand identity, which can in turn act as a potent force for marketing and set the tone for communication and promotion. If essence is considered to be the heart of a brand, then **brand values** (sometimes referred to as core values) are its foundation stones, often referred to as the pillars of the brand.

Building brand loyalty

Brand identity and the brand values upon which it is built are important tools for establishing **brand loyalty**. Authentic brand values and an engaging brand identity are powerful communication tools, but if consumers engage with a brand because they respect what it stands for, they will want to feel confident that the values will be upheld over time. A company managing a brand must ensure that customers' loyalty and trust are honoured and that the brand identity and values are maintained and remain consistent. This topic has been discussed in Chapter 4 in relation to the loyalty loop and the customer journey (pages 155–6, 161–3). Overleaf is a similar circular diagram that shows the topic from the viewpoint of branding and the importance of brand values for building brand loyalty.

Brand values

Brand values build on and expand the central theme of the brand essence. They are the core values or pillars by which a brand

BUILDING BRAND LOYALTY

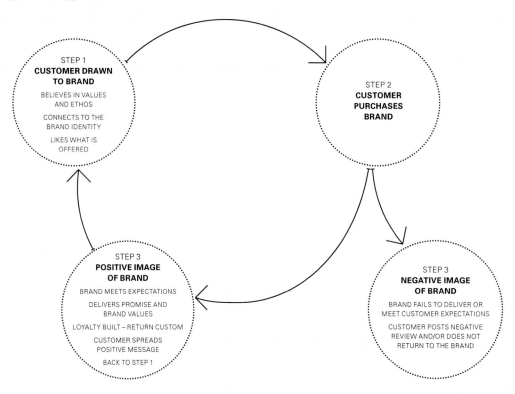

organization operates. The values should inform all aspects of how the company runs its business, designs and develops its products, delivers its services, and markets and promotes its brand (see diagram above). Consumers are more likely to engage with a brand whose values they respect and connect with, as evidenced by the title of Martin Butler's book *People Don't Buy What You Sell: They Buy What You Stand For* (2005).

The Japanese brand Sacai, the brainchild of Chitose Abe, has three core values that Abe has talked about in interviews. The first is 'elegant practicability'. Sacai collections are designed for real life, combining avant-garde innovation with wearability. Abe started the brand in 1999, when she was pregnant. Disappointed at the available clothes options, she designed her own capsule collection of pieces she wanted to wear. As she explained to Olivia Singer in an article for *AnOther Magazine* in 2015, these included a tuxedo cardigan and a sweater combined with a shirt. The second value that Abe upholds for her brand is 'creative freedom'. Abe owns 100 per cent of the business, and is both designer and president of the company. This, she believes, is 'the single most important reason why Sacai can remain free'. This freedom allows her to design based on her creative instincts, knowing that well-designed products at the right price can allow her business to flourish. The final value is that 'fashion

Adding the personal touch

THE CASTLEFIELD BRIDAL COMPANY

Sophie Taylor's wedding-stationery business targets 20–30-year-olds looking for quality and distinction with a personalized touch. Castlefield's brand values include quality, service, communication, distinction and enchantment. While the appearance of the final product is important, Taylor believes that what happens behind the scenes is also a vital part of the brand: 'Without a positive relationship with the client, the Castlefield experience would not be complete.'

DEVELOPING A MOODBOARD

Taylor always starts by making a moodboard and developing a logo. For the Castlefield Bridal Company she researched images of castles, early twentieth-century couture, vintage-inspired bridal gowns, royal jewels, vintage perfume bottles, mythical creatures and similar themes. The final logo design, with its elegant but clear type, flowing scrolls and crown, fits with the ideal of 'grandeur and grace' that Taylor wanted to convey; the warm gold on white keeps the overall look clean with a touch of glamour.

CONSTRUCTIVE FEEDBACK

Taylor sought feedback during the branding process, speaking to a variety of people of different ages, ethnicities and genders. The most frequent comments were that the name and logo sounded and looked sophisticated, regal with vintage glamour and ideal for a bridal company. Taylor thinks 'stylistically the brand appeals to couples who want to feel like royalty on their wedding day, as well as those who just want simple elegance.'

THE FINISHED PRODUCT

The final brand identity balances grandeur and grace, giving the products drama and ornate elegance. Taylor wanted a vein of soft vintage glamour to run through the graphics. She says, 'I have always loved the aesthetics of the 1910s, 1920s, 1930s and 1940s, and wanted the branding to reflect a sense of vintage femininity along with a regal touch.'

is a business'. This links strongly to the second, but is core to why Sacai has been so successful. Abe said in *Vogue* in May 2023 that 'a designer's job isn't just about designing clothes.' While this value may not directly affect customers, it is a rock on which the brand stands, and one that can help to ensure its success and longevity.

Brand personality

Brand personality works on the premise that brands can have personalities, much as people do. Professor Philip Kotler, when describing the differences between the computer brands IBM and Apple, suggested that Apple has the personality of someone in their twenties and IBM the character of someone in their sixties!

When related to fashion, the issue of brand personality needs careful thought. It is all too easy to say that a brand is fashionable, stylish, modern or luxurious. But do those characteristics really capture the flavour of its personality or distinguish the brand clearly from any other? Probably not. The Vivienne Westwood label could be described as British fashion with a twist, but so could that of Paul Smith, so it is vital to take time to delve deeply and define other, more descriptive qualities that capture the unique nature of a brand's persona. Westwood is also anarchic, irreverent and perhaps a little subversive, whereas the Paul Smith brand augments its British style with quirky elements of the unexpected.

↓ Beauté Prestige International (BPI) creates, develops and markets fragrances for Jean Paul Gaultier, Issey Miyake and Narciso Rodriguez. BPI worked with the branding consultancy Interbrand to define the personality for Jean Paul Gaultier's perfume Ma Dame (2008), inspired by Gaultier's vision of the perfect woman. Ma Dame's personality is described by Interbrand as a 'trendy tomboy with classy sex appeal'.

When a brand is built around the distinctive personality of an individual designer, its personality is likely to closely resemble that of the designer in question. The New York fashion designer Betsey Johnson has variously been described as exuberant, whimsical, over the top and fearlessly eccentric. Her dramatic personality permeates her fashion empire, with collections noted for colour, capriciousness, sexy silhouettes and whimsical embellishment.

Maison Margiela sits at the opposite end of the personality spectrum. This French fashion house was started by the Belgian designer Martin Margiela in 1998. In 2014 John Galliano became its creative director, carrying on the house aesthetic and brand personality. The brand is described on its website as unconventional, daring and ambiguous. The journalist Mark Tungate wrote in his book *Fashion Brands* (2005) about a well-known journalist who packed two jackets for a trip to the Paris collections: one from Margiela, the other from Zara. The Margiela jacket cost around five times the price of the Zara garment, but the journalist did not mind paying this premium because, as they explained, 'I like what Margiela stands for. I'm paying for the person, not the article.'

Although this anecdote is from the time when Margiela himself was at the helm of his brand, it illustrates the potential of brand personality as a tool for building relationships between a brand and its customers. This connection can be achieved more effectively if consumers perceive the product as a visible symbol and physical manifestation of a brand's personality. Social media can play a vital role in this regard. The marketing professional Elizabeth Schofield says, 'A living, breathing personality is created on social media and brands must have a content strategy in place to control how people receive the brand personality.' If a brand's personality could be described as edgy, modern, intellectual, beautiful, ethically conscientious and socially aware, it should appeal to consumers who connect with these traits; they are likely to be socially aware, ethical customers who wish to feel edgy and intellectual or modern and beautiful.

↑ A look from the Japanese brand Sacai's Spring/Summer 2023 show in Paris. Chitose Abe, the designer behind the brand, aims to communicate her values of 'elegant practicability' and 'creative freedom' through her clothing.

Carrying the brand

The carrier bag is a highly visual symbol of a brand. This simple item is often overlooked as a marketing tool, but just think about it – every time a customer leaves a store carrying their purchases in a distinctive and recognizable carrier bag, they become a walking advertisement for the brand. For many customers, the bag is an important element of the shopping experience and deemed just as much of a status symbol as the garments or product it contains. It is an amazingly democratic device, available to all who purchase, irrespective of the amount of money they spend.

Brand touchpoints

Fashion product is one of the most important vehicles through which a brand transmits its message, values and identity to customers. The product can be described as a brand touchpoint, which is a point of interaction between a brand and consumers, employees or stakeholders. The concept of brand touchpoints was first published in 2002 in *Building the Brand-driven Business* by Scott M. Davis and Michael Dunn. A brand has between 30 and 100 potential touchpoints, and each touchpoint has the potential to make either a positive or a negative impression. Touchpoints affecting consumers can be categorized into those that occur before, during and after purchasing (see diagram opposite).

Think about all the possible interactions a consumer could have with a brand along each stage of the customer journey. Each touchpoint offers the potential for someone to be converted either for or against the brand. Take, for example, the pre-purchase stage. A person who is not aware of a particular brand or fashion label could see something on TikTok or Instagram, or receive a targeted advert from the brand on their Facebook feed, and thus become conscious of it. Someone who is already brand-aware may visit the website or store and take the next step towards actually purchasing. During the purchase stage the potential customer may be converted and make a purchase, or they may be put off in some way by their experience and decide not to buy and not to interact with the brand again.

Analysing brand identity

Brand touchpoints could also be considered as the brand in action, in other words, the way in which a brand expresses its ethos and identity in actual strategic actions. This brings us to a tool used in brand management: the brand identity onion.

A brand identity onion is used to analyse and map the brand identity and show it in diagrammatic form (see page 200). The onion represents the layers of a brand from its inner essence, or core, to the outer personality layer and brand in action at the surface. The object of the exercise is to summarize the brand identity, capturing the essence, values and personality traits that differentiate the brand from competitors. The real benefit of the tool is its use in establishing how the identity should be made manifest in reality, represented by the 'actions and behaviours' section of the diagram. You could, for example, substitute the outer ring of the onion for the relevant brand touchpoints, since these are the brand in action at the interface of the brand and its customers.

BRAND TOUCHPOINTS

○ PRE-PURCHASE
ADVERTISING
SOCIAL-MEDIA CONTENT
WORD OF MOUTH
WEBSITE
MOBILE APP
DIRECT MAIL
EMAIL MARKETING
PR

○ PURCHASE
STORE AND WINDOW DISPLAY
IN-STORE AMBIENCE AND SERVICE
SALESPERSON
UX AND ONLINE PURCHASING PROCESS
PRODUCT LABELLING AND INFORMATION
PACKAGING
VISUAL OR DIGITAL MERCHANDISING
PRODUCT FIT AND QUALITY

○ POST-PURCHASE
RETURNS POLICY AND PROCESS
POST-PURCHASE CUSTOMER SERVICE
ALTERATIONS AND REPAIR SERVICE
CUSTOMER REVIEWS AND FEEDBACK
PRODUCT PERFORMANCE AND AFTERCARE
LOYALTY PROGRAMME

There are many touchpoints that affect a consumer when they interact with a fashion brand during the pre-purchase, purchase and post-purchase stages. There can be between 30 and 100 touchpoints, according to authors Scott Davis and Michael Dunn.

It would be impossible for a company to focus on them all effectively, so a limited selection must be identified: ideally those that are most relevant to the company, its business and brand.

For a retailer with a physical store, the in-store experience and interaction with sales staff are important touchpoints. For an online retailer,

digital content, user experience (UX), ease of navigation and effective sales platforms are key.

As you can see from this diagram, the brand sits at the core. The brand identity in terms of the core essence, values and brand personality should emanate outwards and be reflected in the touchpoints. You could, if you wished, put the whole Brand Identity Onion (see page 200) in the centre, with the touchpoints in the outer brand-in-action circle.

Diagram adapted from Scott M. Davis and Michael Dunn, *Building the Brand-driven Business* (2002)

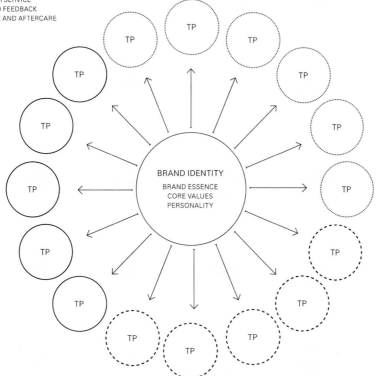

The brand identity prism

Another model for analysing brand identity is Jean-Noël Kapferer's and Vincent Bastien's brand identity prism, introduced in 1992. This six-sided model (see page 202) aims to capture the complexity of brand identity, and the concepts behind it are perhaps harder to pin down than those of the simpler brand onion. Both systems of analysis attempt to depict the internal and external aspects of brand

← The carrier bag or brand tote is often overlooked as a marketing tool. But it can also carry an activist message. In 2007 the accessories designer Anya Hindmarch offered customers a limited-edition 'I am not a plastic bag' reusable cotton shopping bag, developed with the not-for-profit organization We Are What We Do. In 2020 Hindmarch followed up with 'I am a Plastic Bag', made from an innovative fabric formed of recycled plastic bottles.

Creating a brand identity onion

When analysing a brand and developing a brand identity onion, it is often easiest to start with the personality layer. Look at brand social media, the brand website, in-store promotional material, carrier bags, labelling, window displays, in-store ambience and advertising. What kind of personality do you think they convey? How do you feel when you connect to the brand, or how do you think customers feel when they wear the brand?

Work inwards through the brand identity onion diagram and determine the brand values and the essence. Finally, don't forget the actions and behaviours section. Try to determine how the brand essence, values and personality are put into action, and record your findings in the outer section of the onion. The brand-in-action portion of the model is really important, since this is how a brand really can make a difference. It translates mere words on a page of a branding manifesto into reality. These actions form the key interactions between the brand and its customers or stakeholders. Each of these connections is known as a brand touchpoint.

identity. Kapferer and Bastien's model does this by dividing the diagram on a vertical axis, whereas in the brand onion the internal elements are placed towards the centre, and external aspects, such as 'actions and behaviours', are on the outer layer.

Physique equates to the essence of the brand as well as its physical features, symbols and attributes. At a symbolic level, Nike is signified by the Swoosh and Levi's by a red tab, while Ralph Lauren is epitomized by polo. The physical facet also comprises iconic products, such as Levi's 501 jeans or Yves Saint Laurent's 'Le Smoking' dinner jacket.

Personality is the character, attitude or personality of the brand. Kapferer believes a brand should have a unique personality. In *Strategic Brand Management*, he modifies the definition of USP to become 'unique selling personality'.

Culture is the brand's distinctive approach and brand values. At Hermès the culture is built around luxury, craftsmanship and exceptional quality; at Ralph Lauren it is formed from a unique blend of preppy American, rugged outdoorsy casual and classic English tweed.

Relationship relates to the beliefs and associations connected with a brand. What does the brand promise? How is the brand perceived in the outside world? What does wearing a particular brand say

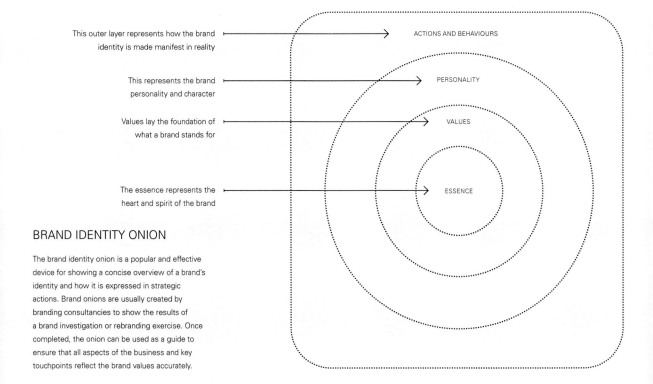

BRAND IDENTITY ONION

The brand identity onion is a popular and effective device for showing a concise overview of a brand's identity and how it is expressed in strategic actions. Brand onions are usually created by branding consultancies to show the results of a brand investigation or rebranding exercise. Once completed, the onion can be used as a guide to ensure that all aspects of the business and key touchpoints reflect the brand values accurately.

A new fashion brand and collection

GRANDMA'S TRUNK

The brand proposal showcased here was part of a project undertaken by a fashion student at an art college in the UK. The student set the scene and outlined the concept for the brand: Grandma's Trunk.

Grandma has a hidden trunk full of secret treasures. Dresses, brooches, old ribbons, buttons and scented love letters have remained preserved and undisturbed for decades. It's a girl's dream to rummage through this treasure trove and unearth vintage gems that could inspire new ideas or spark a trend. Grandma's Trunk transforms faded treasures into delightful, edgy new garments with a surprising, vintage, rock-chic feel.

The girl who wears this quirky new brand is adventurous, eclectic and confident. She radiates happiness, is admired as a trendsetter and experiments with creating her own special style by mixing vintage with raw classics.

→ The concept board for Grandma's Trunk. The imagery gives a visual feel for the brand and the customer.

↓ A brand identity onion showing how the personality of the Grandma's Trunk brand closely matches the personality of the targeted customer. The brand onion also shows how the potential customers might feel when they connect with the brand's quirky mix of vintage and modern.

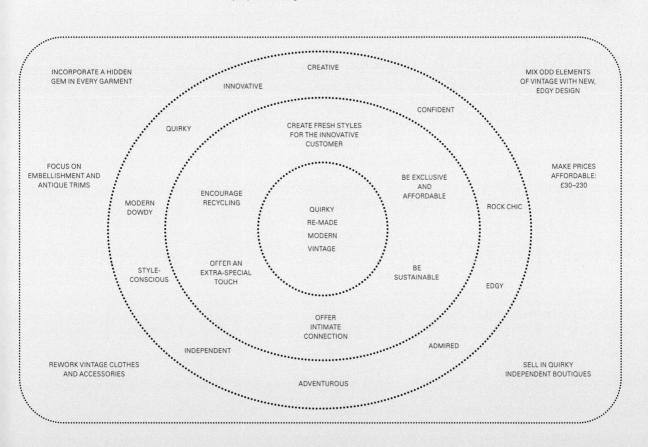

THE BRAND IDENTITY PRISM

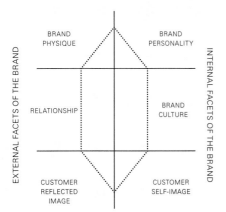

CONSTRUCTED SOURCE (BRAND)

EXTERNAL FACETS OF THE BRAND

INTERNAL FACETS OF THE BRAND

BRAND PHYSIQUE

BRAND PERSONALITY

RELATIONSHIP

BRAND CULTURE

CUSTOMER REFLECTED IMAGE

CUSTOMER SELF-IMAGE

CONSTRUCTED SOURCE (CUSTOMER)

Source: J.N. Kapferer and V. Bastien,
The Luxury Strategy (2009)

about someone? This concerns social communication and the idea of using brands to belong to a style tribe or group.

Reflection is the idealized image of the consumer as reflected in brand advertising. Kapferer describes this facet as the 'external mirror' of the brand. In a short film advertising Chanel No. 5, for example, the actor Nicole Kidman reflects the allure, sophistication, elegance and mystery of the Chanel brand.

Self-image corresponds to the mental image consumers have of themselves when wearing the brand. Kapferer refers to this as the consumer's 'internal mirror'. Someone who wears Ralph Lauren might aspire to live the American dream, while a person wearing Chanel may wish to feel independent and classy.

Branding: emotion and feeling

Branding aims to create connection by generating an emotional response. Brand personality and brand values are instrumental in achieving this. Teri Agins writes in her book *The End of Fashion* (2000): 'Fashion happens to be a relevant and powerful force in our lives. At every level of society, people care greatly about the way they look, which affects both their self-esteem and the way other people interact with them.' The brand prism takes this into account by including relationship and self-image among its six dimensions, while the brand onion positions the personality layer as the interface between brand and consumer. Both models can be used to analyse why consumers might connect with a particular brand and how they might feel when they do so. Bernd H. Schmitt includes a chapter entitled 'Feel' in his book *Experiential Marketing* (1999). He explains that the aim behind the marketing and promotion of fashion and fragrance is to evoke certain types of emotion or feeling likely to make a customer want the brand; this is what he calls 'sense marketing'. The naming convention for fragrances illustrates this concept: for example, Joy by Patou, Happy by Clinique, Pretty by Elizabeth Arden and Beautiful by Estée Lauder.

Brand strategy and management

Establishing a brand is a long-term and costly process, and companies do not take on this risky task lightly. Creating a brand with a clear identity takes time; it usually takes several years or decades to achieve brand status. Orla Kiely, for example, started her business in a small way, working from home. It took approximately ten years for the company to expand and morph into the modern accessory and lifestyle brand that is so loved today. The luxury brands Fendi, Gucci and Prada started out as small family businesses. Fendi was a furrier and Gucci a handbag manufacturer, while Prada designed and sold handbags, shoes and luggage. It was not until Mario Prada's granddaughter Miuccia took the helm in 1978 that Prada started its journey to becoming a global fashion brand. Once a brand is recognized and valued by consumers, opportunity arises to capitalize on the power of the brand name and leverage the brand identity in order to take the brand forwards. While it could be argued that a brand is formed in the minds and hearts of consumers, it is a valuable business asset that must be managed effectively from within the organization. Two of the most widely used strategies used in brand management are brand extension and brand licensing.

Brand extension and brand stretching

Brand extension and brand stretching relate to Ansoff's Matrix for growth, discussed in Chapter 3 (see pages 116–18). Brand extension allows a brand company to capitalize on the power of an existing brand's equity and value to launch new products in a broadly similar market. This relates to product development in Ansoff's Matrix. Brand extension exploits a brand's identity, associating the meanings and values behind it with new products. An apparel supplier that manufactures a branded range of men's performance and outdoor apparel, for example, would be extending its brand into another area of the apparel market if it launched a similarly branded womenswear collection or gender-neutral collection. The benefit of brand extension in this case is that distributors and buyers are likely to perceive less risk when taking on the women's or gender-neutral version of the brand if they have had success selling the menswear, and end-consumers will have existing **brand awareness**.

If the company decided to use its established brand name in a completely different and unrelated market, such as hotels or hospitality, this would be termed brand stretching ('diversification' in Ansoff's Matrix). In 2023, for example, the fashion brand Elle opened the Maison Elle Paris, its first foray into the hospitality business. When considering a brand-stretching strategy, it is important that

CORE AND PERIPHERAL
FASHION MARKETS

BRAND STRETCHING

A fashion brand extends its
offer into an unrelated market,
such as hospitality

BRAND EXTENSION

A fashion brand extends its
offer into peripheral markets,
such as perfume, cosmetics
and homeware

UNRELATED MARKETS

PERIPHERAL
FASHION MARKETS

CORE
FASHION
MARKETS

BRAND EXTENSION

A fashion brand extends its
offer within the core fashion
markets:
Womenswear
Menswear
Childrenswear
Sportswear
Accessories
Footwear
Lingerie

there is a strong conceptual fit between the original brand and the new market. For *Elle* magazine, this extension is a good fit, the hotel walls being adorned with artwork from the magazine's archive. The liaison between fashion and hospitality is not a new concept. Bulgari, the luxury jewellery and accessory brand (and part of the LVMH brand stable), has hotels in Rome, Milan, London, Paris, Tokyo and Shanghai, and resorts in Bali and Dubai. The Bulgari hotels and resorts were set up in partnership with Ritz-Carlton, which is part of the Marriott Group. When a brand decides to enter a new business area, it often does so in collaboration with a business or brand that is well versed in the specific sector into which it wants to expand. Such collaborations are commonly achieved via licence agreements.

Brand licensing

Brand licensing is a strategy that can be used by a business for brand extension. **Licensing** is a business arrangement whereby a brand company sells the right to use its name to a brand operating in that business area, or to a manufacturing company that can develop, manufacture and market specified branded merchandise under licence. Brand-owners use licensing as a way of extending their brand into other product areas, such as accessories, eyewear, intimate apparel, footwear, fragrances, beauty products, watches and homeware, to reach a broader audience, or to expand into new geographic territories. Fila Luxembourg, for example, signed an agreement with the US company Berkshire Fashions for the design, manufacture and sale of Fila-branded accessories in the US market. The Italian company Luxottica is one of the foremost manufacturers of branded eyewear. It has the licence for Chanel, Coach, Prada and Miu Miu. Marchon Eyewear, with headquarters in Amsterdam, New York and Hong Kong, holds the licence to design, manufacture and distribute eyewear for the Victoria Beckham brand, Lanvin, Karl Lagerfeld, Nike and Lacoste. In 2023 the fashion brand Jil Sander announced its ten-year strategic partnership and licensing agreement with Coty, one of the world's largest beauty companies, so that the Jil Sander brand could step into the world of premium fragrances. Coty also works with Burberry, Gucci, Hugo Boss and Chloé, as well as consumer brands CoverGirl and Bourjois.

This type of arrangement is known as **licensing out**, and the manufacturing or distributing company (the **licensee**) pays a royalty fee to the brand-owner (the **licensor**). Royalty rates vary. The exact percentage is dependent on the time frame of the agreement, the type of product involved, the financial investment, the time it takes to develop the product, and the volumes of merchandise predicted to sell. The general view is that less financial risk is attached to licensing compared to brand stretching, because the brand company is not responsible for the capital investment or the costs involved in producing, distributing or marketing the licensed product. It is important therefore that licensing agreements are signed with companies with the correct expertise in manufacturing and marketing specific products.

Fashion licensing is meant to be invisible to the consumer, who should not know or notice that a licensee is making the products that carry a designer's name. However, a lack of control over the licensing can damage the identity and value of a brand. Calvin Klein and Burberry have suffered from this in the past, when they entered into myriad agreements that diluted the cachet and desirability of their brands. One of the first things Angela Ahrendts did when she took over at Burberry in 2006 was to review the company's licensing strategy. At the time it had 23 licences around the world, including kilts for the London Bond Street store, and dog coats and leashes. Burberry was becoming ubiquitous, and that can be a killer for a luxury business.

Another growing licensing model is when two trademark-owners collaborate to create a new product with shared brand values. Examples include the collaboration between Harris Tweed and Clarks shoes; the French designer Christian Lacroix launching a furniture collection with the Italian art mosaic manufacturer Sicis; and the Spanish designer Agatha Ruiz de la Prada designing vacuum cleaners for Dyson.

The most common form of licensing is the licensing out model, as explained on page 205. There is another approach, known as **licensing in**, whereby a fashion brand pays for the rights to use the recognizable designs, images or intellectual property of another brand. An example is a clothing company buying the rights to use a Disney character on a T-shirt. This type of licensing is most common at the lower end of the market, but a new trend of licensing in is gaining momentum at the higher end. Givenchy partnered with Disney to launch a capsule collection starring Oswald the Lucky Rabbit. This was launched to celebrate 100 years of Disney and to bring in the Lunar New Year of the Rabbit in 2023. Givenchy's creative director, Matthew M. Williams, worked with Disney to create a capsule collection that fused Oswald's mischievous, high-energy spirit with the directional aesthetic of Givenchy. This was not the first time that Givenchy had teamed with Disney; it featured Bambi in 2013 and the 101 Dalmatians in 2022.

Kith, a multifunctional lifestyle brand for men, women and kids, was established in 2011 by Ronnie Fieg. The brand has entered into several licensing collabs, the most significant being with Disney Marvel Studios for Spider-Man's sixtieth anniversary. Fieg has a deep connection with Spider-Man; both he and 'Peter Parker' are from Queens in New York, and, as a child, Fieg collected Spider-Man products. Licensing agreements must be considered with care, because you are selling the right to use your brand name. If your business is own-brand jeans and T-shirts and you sell the rights to use your brand name to a big manufacturer in this product area, it would be shrewd to retain the rights for other products, such as dresses or accessories, leaving your options open for other deals in the future.

↓ Prada's move into hospitality is an example of brand extension. The brand acquired a majority stake in the Pasticceria Marchesi, Milan, and opened the Prada-Marchesi pastry shop in 2015. Decked out in Prada's signature green, the elegant eatery was the brand's first foray into the culinary world. In 2023 the brand launched Prada Caffè in Harrods, London (below left). A cake is presented on a Prada plate (below right). All details are branded, including the cake itself and the sugar sachets.

Marketing fragrance as an accessory

BY FAR AND VINCENT VILLÉGER

In 2022 the cult accessories label BY FAR expanded into the beauty sector with the launch of its debut fragrance collection 'Daydream'. Key to this brand extension is the award-winning design of the fragrance bottle, which can be worn as a charm on bags. The scent bottle, envisioned and designed by the luxury packaging designer Vincent Villéger, is an accessory in its own right. Customers can choose the colour of the outer casing, opt for gold or silver hardware, and select a carabiner or leather strap attachment. Sustainability is at the forefront of the design, and each refillable charm contains a 20 ml (¾ fl oz) bottle made from 15 per cent post-consumer recycled glass. The refill bottles are also recyclable and in 100 per cent recyclable paper packaging. The paper is FSC-certified, meaning it is from responsibly managed sources.

BY FAR, the brand known for its 1990s-inspired shoes and bags, was launched in 2016 by the sisters Valentina Ignatova and Sabina Gyosheva, along with Denitsa Bumbarova. They set a brief for Villéger to create a playful product, with consumer interaction at its heart. The aim was for the perfume to contribute to the overall brand success, and not just to create an additional product category. Villéger's solution is not a perfume bottle; it's a refillable, customizable and portable bag charm – a unique idea that reflects the personality of the BY FAR brand.

↓ The award-winning refillable BY FAR fragrance bottle designed by Vincent Villéger. The accessory brand wanted to create a playful fragrance product, with consumer interaction at its heart.

→ The BY FAR Baby Cush faux-fur bag with the BY FAR bag charm fragrance bottle attached.

There were two principles guiding the creative process:

1. The new fragrance had to be a fashion accessory, giving a valid reason for BY FAR to enter the beauty market.

2. It should be a modular design, making the design interactive. Customers could pick their scent, the colour of the charm and the different elements of the design, such as the strap. This also gives the brand the opportunity to launch new accessory designs regularly, injecting newness into the collection without the need for new scent developments. The other genius idea was to make the bottle a charm with a smaller fill capacity, but to sell larger refill bottles.

The choice of designer for the project was a key factor in its success. Villéger is an award-winning product, packaging and retail designer with a career-long focus on the luxury and beauty sectors. His understanding of form, materials and processes imbues his work with structural and tactile qualities, helping his clients achieve emotive brand experiences enhanced by his packaging concepts. Villéger worked at Burberry with Christopher Bailey, and his achievements there include the designs for fragrance bottles and packaging for Burberry Body, My Burberry and Burberry Bespoke. Villéger's more recent clients include the British beauty brand Molton Brown, the luxury menswear label Dunhill, the exclusive fragrance house Clive Christian and the sustainable fashion pioneer Pangaia.

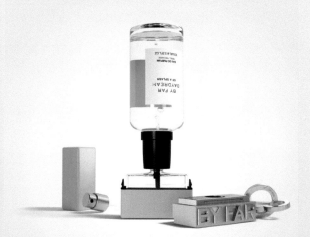

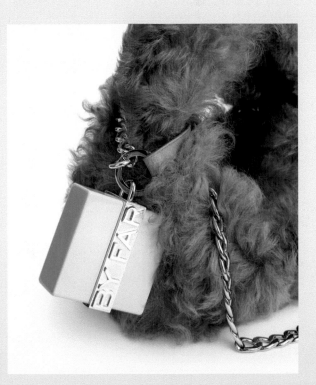

Brand repositioning

Brand repositioning is the process of redefining the identity of an existing brand or product in order to shift the position it holds in consumers' minds relative to that of competitors. A brand organization may decide to alter its strategic direction and reposition a brand if the current brand positioning is no longer relevant or effective. This decision might be a response to:

» A brand losing market share

» Changes in the macro or micro marketing environment

» New brands entering the market

» Repositioning of competitor brands

» Shifts in consumer demand

Repositioning does not usually entail a change of brand name, but it might include updating and modernizing the existing logo. The strategic repositioning of a brand is initiated from within the company through an internal review and analysis of the current market and competitor positioning. The brand managers then determine where the brand currently sits in the market, and where they wish to reposition it. Gucci, for example, embarked on a repositioning strategy when it engaged Alessandro Michele in 2015 to refresh the brand and help it to move forwards. The Gucci image did not appeal to Millennials, so the task was to reposition to suit a more contemporary audience.

↓ The window of the Longchamp store on the Champs-Elysées, Paris, displays the Longchamp x Pikachu collaboration in October 2020, named after the mascot of the Pokémon brand. The collaboration is an example of brand licensing known as licensing in, when a brand pays for the rights to use the recognizable intellectual property of another brand.

Rebranding

Rebranding is a type of brand repositioning, but it goes further to encompass either a new or refreshed logo or a complete change of name and logo, usually underpinned by a significant change in ethos and business strategy. This usually occurs in response to a company takeover, and could include radical internal restructuring. Total rebranding generally occurs in such industries as banking and insurance; it is unusual within fashion, although it can occur in garment manufacturing or in the chemical-fibre industry. One notable example, however, is the transformation of the French fashion conglomerate PPR into a new brand named Kering in 2013. This was one of the most significant rebrands in the industry. Another example is when Riccardo Tisci took over at Burberry in 2018. He instigated a revision of the logo and introduced the new Thomas Burberry TB monogram. When Daniel Lee arrived at the company in 2022 as chief creative officer, it set the wheels in motion for another rebranding exercise. A serif font was reintroduced for the Burberry brand name, and an original Burberry Equestrian Knight logo was revamped and given new prominence. The original motif of a knight on horseback carrying a pennant flag emblazoned with the word *prorsum* (Latin for 'forwards') was the winning entry of a design competition open to the public back in 1901.

The rebrand was launched with a campaign shot by Tyrone Lebon, featuring the musicians Shygirl, Skepta, John Glacier, Liberty Ross and Lennon Gallagher, and an 86-year-old Vanessa Redgrave. The images were augmented with either the new serif font logo or the simpler updated version of the knight in white or royal blue charging across the campaign imagery.

The year 2023 seemed to be a big one for rebranding. The luxury house Paco Rabanne announced that it would be dropping the Paco and going by just the name Rabanne. In the same year, the American designer Jonathan Simkhai jettisoned his forename, rebranding as Simkhai, with a new font for the logo.

↑ An advert for Prada eyewear in *Paper* magazine, 2014. The eyewear is made under licence by the Italian eyewear company Luxottica.

A thread of creativity –
creating a new brand identity

ELIZABETH EMANUEL

Royal College of Art graduate Elizabeth Emanuel came to the world's attention when she was commissioned, with her husband at the time, David, to create the wedding dress for Lady Diana Spencer when she married HRH The Prince of Wales (now King Charles III) in 1981. Since then, Elizabeth Emanuel has been firmly established as one of Britain's leading couturiers, her individual and instantly recognizable style appealing to a wide range of clients of all ages and backgrounds. Over the years she has dressed members of the British royal family, as well as many of the world's best-known celebrities, including Elizabeth Taylor, Joan Collins, Madonna, Cher and Charlize Theron. More recently, with the launch of a new collection and an exquisite new brand identity, Emanuel has attracted a new generation, including Rita Ora, Christina Aguilera, Priyanka Chopra and Raye.

At a certain point, Emanuel realized she had a name but not a brand, so she called on the expertise of Timothy Rennie, who specializes in art-direction, design and branding, to create her new brand identity. The aim was to find a visual identity that would communicate the fact that Emanuel and her couture atelier had a history and heritage, and to establish the contemporary relevance of the brand. The process went through several stages. First Rennie developed the groundwork for the logo with the name 'Elizabeth':

Then he removed the central bar of the E and replaced it with the clever addition of the thread, which looks as though it is being drawn by a needle through the letter. This is what Rennie called 'the thread of creativity'. It was important, he felt, to reflect the hand-finished quality of couture. The addition of a strapline brings further expressiveness and clarity to the message.

As the brand moved forwards, it was decided to add the word 'Atelier' to its name. Rennie had to assess the best way to keep the overall brand identity consistent and retain the thread concept. The resulting logo became more than the sum of its parts: a beautiful expression of Elizabeth Emanuel, her work and the concept of a couture atelier. Rennie sums this up: 'I wanted the name to have an independent voice with a personal touch. It was important that the name would become as recognizable as Emanuel's designs. The logo must also stand the test of time.'

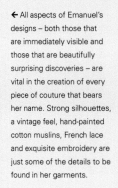

← All aspects of Emanuel's designs – both those that are immediately visible and those that are beautifully surprising discoveries – are vital in the creation of every piece of couture that bears her name. Strong silhouettes, a vintage feel, hand-painted cotton muslins, French lace and exquisite embroidery are just some of the details to be found in her garments.

↖ Design work by Timothy Rennie for the Elizabeth Emanuel logo.

←← A look from the 'Paris 1902' collection, showing Emanuel's use of beading and tulle.

← A piece from the Elizabeth Emanuel bridal collection.

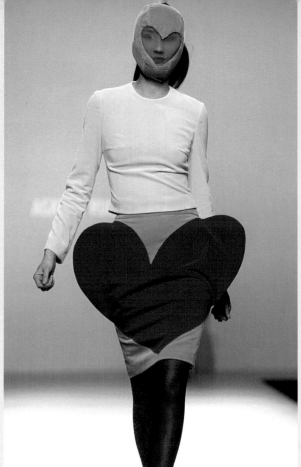

Designs for a colourful world

AGATHA RUIZ DE LA PRADA

The Spanish fashion designer Agatha Ruiz de la Prada (no relation of Miuccia Prada) is known for her vibrant use of colour, bold graphic prints and for the extraordinary funky shapes shown in her catwalk collections. Early in her career, de la Prada realized that she could not build her brand without collaborating with a big-name company. The breakthrough came with a deal to design a collection under her name for the Spanish department-store chain El Corte Inglés. Since then, the Agatha Ruiz de la Prada brand has expanded into a wide array of product areas through partnerships and licensing agreements with a range of manufacturers and globally renowned brands. The heart motif has become a distinctive trademark and has been used in many collaborations, including a chemical-free dress for Greenpeace, a special crocodile logo for the French leisure-wear brand Lacoste, and a brooch for the carmaker Audi. Such collaborations have provided de la Prada with the investment required to expand her branded empire, while at the same time enabling her to focus on design.

↑ The Spanish designer Agatha Ruiz de la Prada.

↗→ The heart motif is a signature of the brand and is used in wonderfully surreal ways in the collections. The heart also features on a wide range of other Agatha Ruiz de la Prada products, such as sunglasses, stationery and kitchenware.

6

Fashion Promotion

"Half the money I spend on advertising is wasted; the trouble is I don't know which half."

John Wanamaker

Fashion promotion is a key element of the marketing mix. It is used to build a brand's status, enhance perception of a brand, increase desire for products, raise awareness of what's on offer, and inform consumers about benefits or services. The ultimate aim of promotion is to support sales and persuade consumers to purchase. Promotional activities, such as **advertising**, **public relations** and **sales promotions**, have become increasingly engaging and interactive. Having decided on a marketing strategy, product design, price points, market positioning, target market, distribution channels and so on, the focus must move to how to advertise and promote the products or services. This chapter outlines and works through the components of the **promotional mix**. The final section is on **planning advertising, promotion and PR campaigns**, and **measuring their effectiveness**.

The promotional mix

The promotional mix refers to the combination of promotional tools used by a company to promote its brand products and services, and communicate its message to consumers. The four standard elements of the mix are:

1. Advertising

2. Sales promotion

3. Public relations (PR)

4. Personal selling

Similar to the concept of the marketing mix, the promotional mix simplifies a vast array of potential promotional possibilities into four overarching headings. This simplification masks the full range of promotional opportunities that might be employed, especially the wide variety of interactive social-media campaigns, contests and promotions that invite consumer participation. These campaigns often generate a global audience and can help consumers to feel as if they are shaping the story behind the brand. In addition, there are specific promotional channels unique to the fashion industry: the fashion press, seasonal fashion weeks and catwalk shows, window displays and visual merchandising. This next section will discuss these, then outline the promotional mix, taking you through the four key areas that constitute this mix.

The fashion press

The press plays an important role in fashion promotion. Fashion magazines, both print and digital, and respected fashion influencers perform a vital role in fashion promotion in terms of advertising and editorial. They report on the designer collections and premier new season styles in their fashion editorial or social media posts; give details of key fashion looks; and profile hot trends for the season. Important to fashion promotion is the press obsession with celebrity. Acres of print are devoted to celebrity goings-on. Weekly celebrity gossip magazines keep readers updated with the latest celebrity news, fashion trends and must-have items available in-store and online. National newspapers also cover celebrities, the designer catwalk shows and report on seasonal and day-to-day developments within the industry.

Fashion shows

Fashion shows are an integral part of the industry and provide significant PR and publicity for designers. The major international designer catwalk shows take place twice a year during London, Paris, Milan and New York fashion weeks, when design houses, designers and luxury fashion brands show their ready-to-wear collections for the forthcoming season. There are also fashion weeks in India, Sri Lanka, Indonesia, Brazil, Australia, China, Nigeria, Ethiopia, South Africa, Germany and Spain, among many others. While these might not be as well known as those in London, Paris, Milan or New York, they are gaining global recognition and are equally important for the relevant regions' designers, press and buyers.

A catwalk show is expensive to produce, and only a selection of designers will be invited to join the schedule for Fashion Week, but for those who show, it is an important opportunity. A fashion show is a great occasion for promotion, and many brands are now gaining press coverage for the ingenuity of their digital presentations. Shows used to be invitation-only events. Now designers can connect with their customers using live-streaming and updates from the show. Burberry was a pioneer of live-streaming, when back in 2011 it broadcast its show for London Fashion Week on a giant screen in Piccadilly Circus. It then went global with outdoor screens in New York, Hong Kong and Beijing. The show, with additional content, was disseminated via Instagram, Facebook, Twitter (now X), Google+, YouTube, Pinterest, LinkedIn, Japan's Sumally and China's Sina Weibo, Douban and Youku.

For Spring 2021, Burberry live-streamed its show via Twitch. Necessitated by the COVID-19 pandemic, this had the advantage of offering an immersive, interactive experience. Using Twitch Squad Stream, guests could see multiple perspectives of the show and communicate using the chat function. Shanghai Fashion Week also went digital in a partnership with Alibaba's Tmall. According to an article by Piers Butel for Mintel in 2020, 'Is Digital Live Streaming the Future of Fashion Shows?', visitors were able to purchase the current-season clothing via Tmall, turning the Shanghai week into a more retail-focused event. That year, too, Helsinki Fashion Week experimented with 3D fashion shows, cyber networking and interactive live-streams.

One of the most inventive shows for Spring/Summer 2021 was Jeremy Scott for Moschino, entitled 'No Strings Attached'. The 40 styles from the collection were presented on puppets designed by Jim Henson's Creature Shop, creator of the Muppets. Also in puppet form were the front-row audience, featuring Anna Wintour, Hamish Bowles and Edward Enninful of *Vogue*. This was a fun and ingenious solution to the situation, and one that garnered much press attention.

↑ The Moschino Spring/Summer 2021 show during Milan Fashion Week in September 2020 featured puppet mannequins. In the background of the lower photograph, the puppet version of *Vogue*'s Anna Wintour sits in the front row.

↑ Speech bubbles created a strong visual image for the summer sale at DKNY London in 2009. The window emphasizes that DKNY is selling colour; the sale plays a secondary role. The graphics also alert customers to the fact that there will be more colours to come for the new season.

Retailers might also choose to put on a fashion show as part of their PR campaign or press day, or they might hold a special in-store event and fashion show to reward loyal customers and social-media followers. Fashion shows are often the favoured choice of those organizing charity fundraiser events, especially if high-profile retailers, designers and models lend their support, which helps with publicity and ticket sales.

Window displays

Windows provide a fantastic canvas and major marketing opportunity for retailers investing in bricks and mortar. Inspirational and eye-catching windows act as a powerful magnet, drawing customers in and enticing them to visit the store or website. Displays can be used to reinforce brand identity, attract press attention or provide information on products, prices and promotions. Zara, for example, does not advertise, preferring to use its expansive windows and stylish displays to promote the brand. Windows can be used to promote special seasonal events, the holiday season, lunar New Year and Christmas usually being the most important. Or they can be used to tell a fashion story showcasing a hot new seasonal trend or designer collection. Many retailers use digital media in their displays. This can include real-time streaming of a fashion show, interactive touchscreens or other interactive features, such as virtual try-on.

Kalogirou is a well-known luxury designer shoe and accessory store in Greece. It worked with the tech company Atcom to install Greece's first interactive fashion window in 2015. The aim was to promote Kalogirou as a forward-looking, innovative company, and to empower the relationship between customer and retailer. The Atcom website details this case study, explaining how visitors to the store were able to try on designer shoes virtually. Microsoft Kinect sensors captured the shopper's movements and matched them exactly with those of a model on the screen wearing the pair of shoes that were on display physically in front of the visitor. To make the experience even more interactive, visitors could vote for their favourite styles by raising their hand in front of the style they liked best. This provided useful direct customer feedback for the brand. The window, which was big enough to handle interactions with several customers at the same time, increased in-store traffic by 40 per cent and resulted in 35,000 interactions.

A really notable window display was for the Louis Vuitton x Yayoi Kusama collaboration in 2023. This was the second time that LV had collaborated with the celebrated Japanese artist, who is known for using spots in her work. This activation featured animatronic versions of Kusama in store windows, mimicking the act of painting spots, and 3D anamorphic billboards in major city locations.

Visual merchandising and signage

Once a customer is inside a store, it is visual merchandising (VM) and signage that become important for communication, promotion and visual drama. VM is used to create internal displays, put key looks together and build outfits. It should be used to highlight specific looks and products that store owners or buyers wish to promote, and it is important that visual merchandisers are aware of products that are scheduled to be promoted in the press so that these items are given prominence. Signage can be used within the store to guide customers and identify departments, zones or specific collections. Externally, signage can be used to indicate which brands and labels are carried. Some retailers use windows or an internal wall near the front of the store to promote what is inside.

Fashion advertising

The first of the key components of the promotional mix is advertising. Traditional advertising is considered a non-personal form of promotion; in other words, it is a one-way communication from a brand to its audience. The principal objectives of advertising are to raise awareness, inform, persuade and encourage consumer

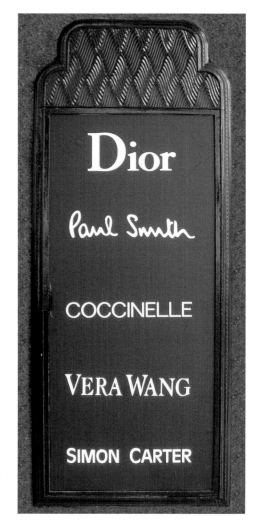

↑ Signage on the outside of a department store is used to indicate noteworthy brands carried on the fashion floors inside.

← In May 2023 the Louis Vuitton flagship store in Shanghai displayed a simulation robot of the artist Yayoi Kusama and a 'dancing pumpkin' artwork to promote the second Louis Vuitton x Yayoi Kusama collaboration.

Towards carbon-neutral

ALLBIRDS CARBON CONCEPT STORE

Allbirds is a B Corp footwear brand that launched in San Francisco in 2016. Its overarching ethos is to use natural materials to create the world's most comfortable shoes. With carbon reduction as its North Star when it comes to tackling climate change, Allbirds is paving the way for a more sustainable approach to business.

In July 2023 Allbirds launched a special pop-up store in the Wonder Room at Selfridges, London. The theme of the display was carbon reduction and visualizing the carbon footprint of Allbirds shoes. The space also served as a signal to other fashion businesses to join Allbirds to make carbon accountability the norm, because ultimately, everything with a price tag comes at a cost to the planet. To highlight this point, each shoe has a carbon-footprint label, with mini-signage spheres used to show the carbon emissions of each shoe.

When Allbirds conducted a poll of close to 600 of its customers on the topic of sustainability, it found that only 35 per cent were confident explaining what carbon means. Using Selfridges – renowned for its environmental commitments – as a platform, Allbirds spotted an opportunity to contextualize carbon and make it more tangible for consumers. As the hero of the pop-up, a large black sphere took centre stage, representing what 1 kg (2¼ lb) of CO2 looks like. The space was designed in partnership with the creative agency HarrimanSteel and production partner Practical Minds. The pop-up used locally sourced, low-carbon and circular materials, such as FSC-certified plywood, recycled wool and recycled bouclé, as well as Allbirds' Plant Leather, a 100 per cent plastic-free, 100 per cent vegan alternative to leather. The 3D-printed balls representing carbon were made from plant-based materials, derived from such crops as corn.

The pop-up was also used to showcase the Allbirds M0.0NSHOT prototype, its biggest innovation breakthrough to date, boasting a landmark carbon footprint of net 0 kg CO2. Carbon-negative, regenerative wool wraps the entire high-top. This product gave shoppers a glimpse of how the future of fashion might look, as the shoe has been completely reimagined with a carbon-first approach.

↗ → The Allbirds Carbon Concept Store in the Selfridges Wonder Room, July 2023. The black sphere represents 1 kg (2¼ lb) of carbon. Along the back wall, a timeline shows the key milestones achieved by Allbirds in its quest to reduce carbon emissions. Signage indicates the carbon footprint of each shoe, and an explanation of that information is included in a carbon-footprint label.

engagement with the brand. The ultimate aim is, of course, to
generate sales, but under the surface advertising endeavours to:

» Reinforce a brand's image

» Communicate a brand's position in the market

» Embed specific meanings into the consumer psyche

» Tap into consumer aspirations

» Create desire for the brand and its products

» Generate conversation and consumer engagement

Traditional advertising can be an expensive mode of promotion, but
for big global brands with sizeable budgets, it is an important and
highly visible facet of a promotional campaign and one of the primary
methods used to transmit brand identity and communicate brand
message. This can include advertising in public spaces on posters,
billboards, taxis or buses, showing advertising films in cinemas
or on television, taking out adverts in magazines, or broadcasting
adverts via social-media platforms. Social media works to support
smaller brands or those with more restrictive budgets with their
advertising. Digital campaigns also offer the potential to be more
interactive and participatory.

Most adverts developed to promote fashion aim to generate desire
and tap into consumer aspirations. Traditionally, they did this by
reinforcing stereotypical ideas that you will be desirable, sexy,
beautiful and alluring, or young, cool, hip, cutting-edge or part of
a like-minded group or community, if you buy into a brand and
purchase its clothing, accessory, fragrance, jewellery or make-up.
For men, the most common messages related to being successful,
attractive, powerful, sexy, rugged, cool and so on. This type of
messaging is now under scrutiny and being challenged, and some
brands are aiming for more inclusive messaging that encompasses
a much wider range of viewpoints. One area under the spotlight in
this regard is childrenswear. There has been a backlash from children
and parents fed up with the pink and blue stereotyping for girls
and boys. In 2021 PacSun opened its first kids' store in the Mall
of America in Bloomington, Minnesota; the brand's kids' label is
genderless so that customers are free to express themselves and
choose what they want to wear without boundaries. In 2022 Banana
Republic launched its gender-inclusive 'BR Athletics' collection.
The campaign, shot by the American photographer Micaiah Carter,
featured up-and-coming New York artists who brought their own
individual style to the collection.

Representing a diverse society

ZEBEDEE TALENT

Zebedee is a specialist talent agency created to increase the representation of people who would in the past have been excluded from the media and fashion advertising. Established by sisters-in-law Laura Winson and Zoe Proctor in 2017, Zebedee looks after over 500 models and actors worldwide who have visible or non-visible disabilities or alternative appearances, and/or are trans or non-binary.

Winson and Proctor recognized that disability is often left out of the diversity debate: 'We were talking about opportunities (or lack of) for disabled people in the media … and it was just a lightbulb moment – if no one is out there representing people with disabilities or differences, why don't we do it?' They want *real* diverse casting to become commonplace in the fashion and advertising industries. Zebedee Talent is already making a global impact; it operates in the UK, Europe, the USA, Australia and Japan, and its models have been cast in a wide range of campaigns for Hugo Boss, Adidas, Nike, Burberry and Gucci Beauty, to name just a few.

Zebedee represents Ellie Goldstein, who has Down's syndrome and who rose to fame when she was featured in a Gucci beauty campaign and as a cover star of British *Vogue* in May 2023. The 'Reframing Fashion' issue had five different covers to highlight a new vanguard of disabled talent. These starred the Hollywood actor Selma Blair, who was diagnosed with multiple sclerosis in 2018; the disabled trans American-Antiguan model Aaron Rose Philip; the broadcaster and disability campaigner Sinéad Burke;

the American Sign Language performer Justina Miles; and, of course, Goldstein. Musa Motha, a South African contemporary dancer and choreographer with the Rambert company in London who lost his leg as a child, is also represented by Zebedee. He too was featured in the special edition of *Vogue*.

In his editor's letter, Edward Enninful wrote, 'Disability should feel personal to us all … The time has come for us to get real about who we are as a society, and for fashion to build a better, more accessible and inclusive industry.' This mirrors Winson and Proctor's vision.

Alongside its work in successfully placing talent in paid work opportunities, Zebedee has also built a real community. It offers regular workshops, as well as running its own catwalk shows and socials. These opportunities ensure that the agency's talent can increase their confidence and skills so that they can deliver on set. Zebedee also campaigns to raise awareness of the conditions and differences of its talent.

....

"We hope that the work of Zebedee, our talent, and the clients we work with, will impact on the wider society – changing attitudes and developing people's understanding of disability and diversity."

....

Laura Winson and Zoe Proctor

→ Five of the models represented by Zebedee Talent featured in Australian *Vogue*. Back row, from left: Rhianna J, whose difference is ADHD and who is non-binary; AlicJa W, who has albinism. Front row, from left: Iona H, who has limb difference; Maya P, whose difference is Down's syndrome; and Jasroop S, whose difference is vitiligo. The image was shot by Zebedee's in-house photographer, Emily Bloomer.

Decoding the image

Semiotics is an investigation into how meaning is created and communicated. It is a way of analysing meaning by looking at the signs (words, pictures, symbols, colours) that communicate it. We receive and decode fashion messages even when we are walking down the street, in the form of adverts, shop signs or displays in shop windows. Even the people we pass generate meaning through the kind of clothes they're wearing, or their make-up and hairstyles. Semiotics relates to the work of three theorists: Ferdinand de Saussure (1857–1913), Charles Sanders Peirce (1839–1914) and Roland Barthes (1915–1980). It was Saussure who came up with the concept of the sign being broken down into two parts: the **signifier** and the **signified**. The signifier is the vehicle that expresses the sign (the fashion image, the words we read, or colours and shapes), while the signified is the concept or meaning that the signifier calls forth when we perceive it. The signifier plus the signified is the sign.

Peirce's concept was that a sign consists of three interrelated elements: a sign, an object and an interpretant. The interpretant – the most distinctive feature of his approach – referred to the understanding we have of the relationship between sign and object.

A key semiotic principle is that of **denotation** and **connotation**, which means that semiotics digs for meaning beyond the immediate, surface level. Denotation is the first layer of meaning. It is literal and informational. This links back to Theodore Levitt's 'total product concept' (see pages 17–18). This would be the generic or core product: a coat, for example. The second layer of meaning in this semiotic principle is connotation. This is the suggestive or metaphorical meaning. This could be likened to the total or augmented product in the Levitt model. Where extra meanings and associations have been layered on to the basic coat – if, for example, the coat were a Burberry trench – it might signify a different set of meanings. This idea is also discussed on page 20.

Barthes, a French literary theorist, suggested that all images are polysemous; that is, they have more than one meaning. He theorized that an image is an 'open text' and that the more you look at it, the more meaning you will make from it (because as one meaning is uncovered, a new one opens up). He called this a chain of signifiers. However, he said that if you add text to the image, it becomes 'closed', shutting down the number of possible interpretations.

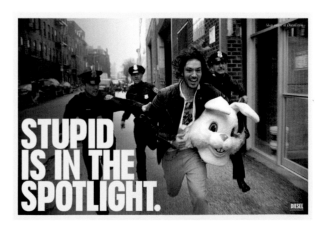

↓ Diesel brand campaigns generally feature an image and the Diesel logo, but for the 'Be Stupid' campaign in 2010, the text adds context to the image. The irreverent campaign imagery was conceived by the London agency Anomaly and shot by the photographers Kristin Vicari, Melodie McDaniel and Chris Buck.

Components of an advertising campaign

Advertising comprises several components. There is the **advertising message** being communicated, the medium or **channel** used to display the advert, and the timing and **exposure** of the advert or campaign. The following section explains each element, with particular focus on the message and the medium, which are of key importance to any campaign.

The message

It should already be apparent that the message is a crucial element of any advertising campaign. It is therefore vital that the purpose of the advert and its overt and subliminal messages are considered carefully. Who is the advert aiming to attract, and what is it trying to communicate? What type of message will be relevant to the audience but also coherent with the purpose of the campaign and the values of the brand? Seth Godin, author of *Purple Cow: Transform your Business by Being Remarkable* (2002), believes that marketing ideas must be 'remarkable' in order to stand out and get a foothold in consumer consciousness. Malcolm Gladwell takes this further in his book *The Tipping Point: How Little Things Can Make a Big Difference* (2000), writing that the message itself or the product it is promoting must be 'memorable'. Gladwell introduces what he calls the 'stickiness factor', the idea that for a concept or marketing message to spread, it must 'stick'. Something about the message, its content or how it is delivered must remain active in the recipient's mind; it must be remarkable, memorable and worth talking about. The mantra is 'ideas that spread win.' When deciding on the message, consider the following points:

> » What is the purpose of the advert? Is it to inform, raise awareness, reinforce brand values, provoke action?

> » What is the most important message it should convey?

> » Will the message be communicated directly or indirectly?

> » What media would be best for communicating it?

Consider if the message should be direct and to the point – 20 per cent off all products in a forthcoming sale, for example – or more subtle, provocative and challenging. Also consider how the message will be conveyed visually: via video, photographic image, fashion illustration, product illustration or other graphic image. Will the advert need additional written information to get the message across? Should there be a slogan, strapline or written text to accompany the image? Could the message be communicated without any image at all, or perhaps just with some written text?

Miscommunication

Creating a global campaign is not always easy. It is essential to consider differences in culture and context in different parts of the world, since campaigns and messaging that are acceptable in the USA or Europe may not translate well into other territories. One highly reported incident was the Dolce & Gabbana campaign that was released on the Chinese social media platform Weibo in 2018. The aim was to promote D&G's forthcoming fashion show in Shanghai. However, the visual content showing a young Asian model in a red sequinned Dolce & Gabbana dress, eating a pizza with chopsticks, and the voiceover by a male narrator were highlighted by the Chinese audience as racist and disrespectful. The campaign was removed within 24 hours, but that was not the end of it.

According to an article in *Jing Daily* by Yiling Pan, 'Is it Racist?: Dolce & Gabbana's New Ad Campaign Sparks Uproar in China', in November 2018, 'Many social media users in China labelled this video stereotypical, racist and disrespectful for Asian female[s].' The incident impacted not only D&G's consumer sentiment in China, but also sales, and D&G's products on the Chinese e-commerce sites Tmall, JD.com and Secoo were removed from sale. In an article by Tiffany Ap entitled 'YNAP Drops Dolce & Gabbana Following Major Chinese Retailers' (2018), *Women's Wear Daily* reported that Yoox Net-a-porter was 'the first global retailer to pull Dolce & Gabbana products off its Chinese platforms'. In addition, Dilraba Dilmurat, the D&G brand ambassador in China, pulled out of the fashion show, and other celebrities and models followed suit. Finally, the show was cancelled on the orders of the Chinese government.

In November 2022 Balenciaga launched a holiday campaign featuring two young girls (children) holding stuffed teddy bears dressed in bondage outfits. According to an article by Danya Issawi for *The Cut*, 'What to Know about the Balenciaga Ad Scandal' (2023), 'the backlash … was swift, with the hashtag #cancelBalenciaga trending across Twitter [now X] and TikTok.' A second advert released later in the month also caused controversy. Creative director Demna Gvasalia, the Balenciaga brand and the parent company Kering all issued apologies. For the Winter 2023 show, Demna wrote a note that was placed on every chair, saying that fashion had become a kind of entertainment and that this has overshadowed its essence, which 'lays [*sic*] in shapes, volumes and silhouettes'. The note continued: 'This is why fashion, to me, can no longer be seen as entertainment, but rather [as] the art of making clothes.'

Brands must also be very wary of false advertising. In May 2023 *The Fashion Law* reported on a lawsuit filed in the United States by

Advertising features and benefits

BLACKSPOT SHOES

Based in Vancouver, Canada, *Adbusters* is a not-for-profit magazine with a circulation of about 60,000. The activist magazine offers its readers philosophical articles and commentary that address global social, cultural and economic issues. The aim is to promote change in the way business is conducted, and to create a stronger balance between economy and ecology. To that end, in 2003, *Adbusters* decided to do something concrete that could challenge the status quo – so it became the first magazine to manufacture and sell a shoe.

The classic V1 Blackspot sneaker and V2 Unswoosher boot were marketed as 'The most earth-friendly shoes in the world'. The soles were made from recycled car tyres and both styles had organic hemp uppers. The shoes were ethical, anti-sweatshop, anti-logo and pro-environment, as well as

what *Adbusters* called 'pro-grass roots capitalism'. Every pair came with a Blackspot Shareholder Document. The certificate, included in the box with the shoes, had a unique login number that allowed the purchaser to log into the members' zone on the *Adbusters*/Blackspot website and participate in shareholder online forums. Anyone buying a pair of the shoes automatically became a member of the Blackspot 'Anti-corporation' and received the right to vote on a selection of company issues.

→ The Blackspot sneaker was a deliberate subversion of the Converse Chuck Taylor All-Star. The advertisement drew attention to the specific features and benefits of this ethical, anti-logo sneaker.

Maria Guadalupe Ellis against Nike. The article, 'Nike Deceptively Markets "Sustainable Wares", Per New Lawsuit', explains the claim by Ellis that Nike took advantage of consumers' desire for sustainable and environmentally friendly products through 'greenwashing' and marketing products in such a way as to give a false impression of their sustainability. The article states that Ellis was challenging Nike regarding its use of recycled polyester and recycled nylon, which, Ellis claims, 'are not sustainable and/or environmentally responsible materials'. In addition, 'only a limited number of products actually contain any recycled materials.' At the time of writing, the outcome of the case was yet to be decided, but it is worth pointing out that the US Federal Trade Commission's Green Guides warn against overstating a product's environmental attributes, and misrepresenting that a product, package or service offers a general environmental benefit. In January 2024 members of the European Parliament voted to adopt a new law banning greenwashing and misleading product information, requiring more reliable and accurate advertising, and outlawing generic environmental claims. It is important to bear all this in mind when creating advertising and marketing materials.

The advertising medium or channel

Once the message and purpose of the advert are established, the next element to consider is the medium, or channel – the vehicle by which an advert is presented and reaches the public. In the early days of mass-media advertising, the channels were print, cinema, television, outdoor advertising and radio. Now, of course, the most prominent advertising medium is digital. Most fashion brands use a combination of channels, either traditional *and* digital, or an array of digital platforms, depending on their budget, who they are targeting and the best communication channels for reaching that audience.

Traditional advertising channels

Cinema This mainstream channel is expensive, so it is generally used only by global luxury brands. While cinema advertising may represent just a small proportion of overall ad spend (according to research, it was 2 per cent in 2023), it does have several advantages. Many cinema-goers consider the adverts an integral part of the viewing experience, and, once seated in a dark auditorium, are a captive audience. Another advantage is that brand adverts are not likely to be placed next to inappropriate content, which can be a risk with digital advertising. Before the COVID-19 pandemic, in 2019, ads shown in the cinema were set to generate US$4.6 billion in global revenue. The post-pandemic recovery of cinema is being threatened by the cost-of-living crisis and rising ticket prices. However, Motivate Val Morgan Cinema Advertising in Dubai, a company that represents the cinema advertising interests of leading cinema chains in the Middle East, believes that cinema is an important touchpoint for affluent consumers in the UAE. This coincides with a rise throughout the region in luxury cinema complexes that provide reclining armchairs arranged in pairs, each with private table, drinks and snacks on demand throughout screenings, and exclusive lounge facilities.

Television There are two routes for advertising on television: linear TV and connected TV. Linear TV is traditional live television. It is called 'linear' because viewers watch the show at the scheduled time via the specific channel on which it is aired. Connected TV refers to devices that are used to stream internet content and digital video, for instance smart TVs, Roku, Apple TV, Chromecast and gaming consoles, such as the Xbox and Nintendo Switch. The view among advertising professionals is that there is a move in advertising spend from linear to connected TV.

An article by Danny Parisi on the daily digital publication *Glossy*, 'Fashion Brands Are Experimenting with Linear and Connected

TV Advertising' (September 2021), gives the example of the D2C footwear brand Birdies. The founders, Bianca Gates and Marisa Sharkey, starred in three 15-second linear TV ad slots to promote their brand and talk about its history. The article explains that during 2021, ad costs on Instagram rose by 42 per cent, while the cost of TV ads in the USA rose by just 5 per cent. In the same year, the retailer Neiman Marcus used linear and connected TV to carry ads for its 'Re-Introduce Yourself' campaign, targeting lapsed customers and aiming to bring them back to the brand.

However, in June 2023 an article by James Davey for Reuters, 'Retail Media Ad Revenue Forecast to Surpass TV by 2028', stated that GroupM, the world's largest media buyer, expects advertising revenue from retailer-owned e-commerce sites to exceed that of television by 2028.

Radio This is a less favoured choice for fashion, which is more suited to visual media. However, adverts on local radio stations are a cost-effective way to advertise sales or promotions, store openings, local fashion events or celebrity appearances.

Outside media Outside media, also termed out of home (OOH) or ambient advertising, refers to billboards, large-scale building wraps, posters and adverts on the side of buses or taxis. OOH media is often used by large global fashion brands. Armani, for example, is famous for its 310-sq-m (3,337-sq-ft) billboard at the junction of Via Cusani and Via Broletto in Milan, which the brand has owned since 1984. During the pandemic, Giorgio Armani used this site to display posters with his personal signature, supporting the health system of Italy and the city of Milan. His messages of encouragement were also posted on digital billboards on Corso Garibaldi and Piazza San Babila, and at transport stops around the city.

↓ In May 2020 Giorgio Armani used its famous billboard in the centre of Milan to communicate a message dedicated to healthcare workers in Italy, thanking them for their service fighting against COVID-19.

↘ A 3D anamorphic billboard in Times Square, New York, promoted the Balenciaga x Fortnite collaboration in September 2021.

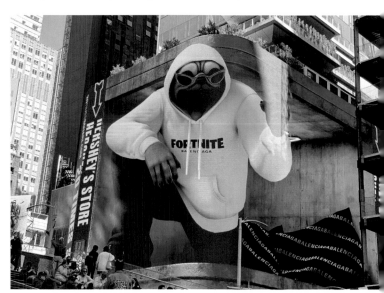

Outdoor and offline advertising that uses digital technology, such as digital billboards or digital screens on public transport, is termed digital out-of-home advertising (DOOH). An exciting new development in this area is 3D or anamorphic billboards. This technology has been used by such brands as Louis Vuitton, Nike, and Balenciaga x Fortnite. Anamorphic billboards trick the eye using stereopsis and forced perspective to create stunningly dramatic, ultra-realistic images and effects. A study in 2020 by the global data firm Nielsen found OOH and DOOH advertising (which includes 3D billboards) to be the most effective offline medium for driving traffic online. An impressive 52 per cent of the target group engaged on their smartphones after seeing an OOH or DOOH advert. 3D billboard campaigns are extremely attention-grabbing, with viewers sharing the content online, which drives organic engagement and creates a conversation about the brand and its advert.

Print media Fashion magazines are the main focus for print media, and titles make their profits by selling page space to advertisers. The amount a magazine can charge for advertising is determined by the size of its circulation, made up of subscription sales and retail sales. The September issue of any fashion magazine is usually the largest of the year, with many more ad pages, because it features the launch of the autumn or fall collections and marks the start of the Christmas shopping season. The premium spot for print advertising is the back cover, also known as the **fourth cover**. This is because many people carry a magazine rolled up, with the back cover on show, and when a magazine is placed on a table there is a 50 per cent chance that the back cover is uppermost. The next most prominent position is inside the front cover.

In March 2022 the *Business of Fashion* reported that the revenue from digital magazine ads would overtake that of print in 2023, coming in at US$11.3 billion versus US$10.3 billion for print. Print advertising still has a place, however; it feels much more luxurious, and the *BoF* article was headed with the statement that 'publishers say the glossy format still has a role to play in telling stories – and driving revenue'. One way for magazines to maintain print revenue is the advertorial. This is more detailed than an advert, and often looks like a short article written by the magazine's editorial team. However, an advertorial is usually written by the brand team or an ad agency, and displayed in the magazine in space purchased by the brand.

Another option is advertiser-sponsored content. This is a more comprehensive editorial-style article that is created jointly by the brand and the magazine's editorial or creative content team. The June 2023 edition of *Vogue*, for example, carried what it called a '*Vogue* Advertisement Feature' entitled 'One of a Kind', about Levi's 501 jeans.

This advertiser-sponsored content celebrated the 150th anniversary of the iconic 501. A similar feature for Pandora jewellery was photographed by Daniel Benson and styled by Julia Brenard. Condé Nast, the publisher of titles including *Vogue*, *GQ*, *Tatler* and *Wired*, has its own in-house global creative studio, CNX. The creative team acts like an agency to create branded content and experiential brand activations. These can be print or digital, or real-life experiences and events.

Digital advertising channels

Whatever the channel chosen for digital advertising, the key is for the advert to be seen by the target audience. This is one of the biggest challenges, since there are so many adverts out there. The role of the marketer is therefore not only to determine which is the correct advertising channel, but also to create memorable digital advertising with strong imagery, messages and calls to action. Any digital content that is used for paid social-media advertising must by law be labelled clearly as 'sponsored' or 'promoted' content.

This section outlines the key online and social media advertising channels. It gives some of the basic information, but – since advertising features on social-media platforms are updated regularly, and different platforms fall in and out of favour, or new ones enter the market – covering all the specific details and keeping up to speed can be challenging. Each platform offers lots of information on how best to use its advertising tools.

Pay per click There are numerous digital channels a brand or fashion company can use for advertising. Many of these use pay per click (PPC) advertising, where the advertiser pays a fee every time someone clicks on its ad. This model is most commonly used on search engines and digital platforms such as Google, YouTube and Facebook, or on such sites as Amazon. Payment can be at a flat rate, whereby a fixed fee is paid for a set number of clicks or 'impressions'. An alternative arrangement is when brands bid for the use of specific keywords relevant to their market and target audience. Brands with the most successful bid and well-targeted advert using the keywords effectively are displayed at the top of the search results, and each time a user clicks on the advert, the brand pays a fee. The term 'cost per click' (CCP) is also used; this is the amount paid for every click in a PPC campaign. PPC is the mechanism; CCP is the cost.

Display ads, which include banner ads, show up on websites when the user clicks through from a search engine, or on any kind of website a user visits. Display ads and banner ads are useful for building brand awareness and promoting products and services.

Typically, display adverts incorporate a call to action, inviting the consumer to click through to the website of the brand advertising. Ads of this kind are usually text, a combination of image and text, or a video. The goal of a banner ad is to attract attention, so it is important to place it at the top of the screen or down the right-hand side of a digital page. This is known as 'above the fold', which means the advert is viewable without the user having to scroll down. The challenge for digital developers is the need for content to fit the screens on a range of devices of different sizes. The goal is to produce 'device-neutral' solutions so that digital content works well on every device.

Social-media ads and sponsored posts Data published by the advisory firm Kepios in 2023 showed that there were 4.8 billion social-media users globally, representing 60 per cent of the global population. This highlights why social media is one of the most important advertising and promotional channels used by fashion brands. When brands and businesses spend money to promote their content to target audiences on social-media platforms, it is known as paid social-media advertising. The choice of platform will depend on the brand, its target audience, and what the brand wants to achieve and communicate through its advertising. According to research carried out by Statista in the United States in 2021, the Meta platforms Facebook and Instagram were the most commonly used social networks for fashion. Statista reported that consumers used these platforms to 'learn about, discover, and buy' fashion.

Meta allows a variety of ad formats, including photo, video, stories, messenger, carousel, slideshow, collection and playables. There are also boosted ads and what are known as dark post ads.

Photo This is a still image, so it must be eye-catching to gain attention. The image can include text, as well.

Video A great tool for capturing attention, raising brand awareness and storytelling. According to Meta's Facebook data, video makes up about half the time that people spend on Facebook, via Stories, Reels or Feed. The length of videos can vary from one second to four hours, depending on the platform and ad type. Viewers generally have short attention spans, so videos of 15 seconds or less are the best for captivating an audience and keeping them engaged. Video ad content does not have to be complicated; it can consist of simple features, such as moving text on a static image or a slight zoom in on an image. Videos can be clickable, encouraging viewers with 'Swipe Up', 'See More' or 'Shop Now' buttons.

Stories People hold their phones vertically about 90 per cent of the time, so Stories are optimized for vertical full-screen viewing. According

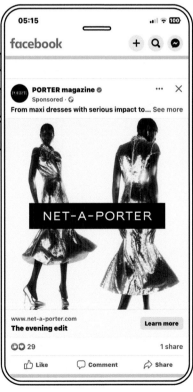

↑ Sponsored social-media ads for the Chanel Cruise Collection 2023–4 campaign (top) and *PORTER* magazine/Net-A-Porter Evening Edit, December 2023.

to Meta, in 2019 more than half a billion people viewed Stories every day across Facebook, Messenger, Instagram and WhatsApp.

Messenger These ads help people to start a conversation with a business or company, and are viewable via the Chats tab in the Messenger app. When someone taps on the ad, they are sent to a detailed view within Messenger, with a call to action that will take them to the brand website.

Carousel These ads can showcase up to ten images or videos. This allows a brand to highlight different products or develop a brand story that progresses across the set.

Slideshow Facebook Slideshow ads are a more affordable option that, as Meta states, makes 'a video-sized impact without a video-sized budget'. These ads use images and text in motion that load quickly and play well across different connection speeds.

Collection These ads have a shopping feature and make it easier for people to browse and click through to purchase. The ad format has one main video or image, with three smaller images below that can be used to highlight specific products. Available on Facebook and Instagram newsfeeds, these ads are best for encouraging viewers to visit the brand website, and for sales campaigns.

Playables This is a try-before-you-buy experience. Playables offers people an interactive preview before they download an app.

Boosted A brand can pay to boost an earlier post that appeared on its Facebook or Instagram feed, turning it into an advert that will appear to a wider audience, beyond those who already follow the brand's social-media page. Instagram posts that include product tags can also be boosted. (There is more information on shoppable social-media content later in this chapter.)

Dark post A targeted ad that appears on the newsfeeds or Stories of a targeted audience is known as 'dark'. What makes it different from standard ads is that it doesn't appear on the advertiser brand's timeline or in the feeds of those who follow the brand on social media. Dark posts can blend in with the brand's organic posts, so they must be labelled clearly to indicate that they are sponsored content. The advantage of these posts is that they can be customized for commercial advertising and differentiated from the brand's organic content, and they can be tailored to a specific audience.

TikTok, owned by the Chinese company ByteDance, launched as Douyin in China in 2016 and went international as TikTok the following year. By 2022 it was the fourth most used platform, behind Facebook, YouTube and Instagram, according to data published by the Influencer Marketing Hub in 2023. It even beat the other social-media platforms

↑ The American actor Maya Hawke at the Prada Fall/Winter 2023 show. As a Prada ambassador, Hawke features on the brand's Instagram and TikTok channel.

for the average time users in the United States spent on it. Douyin and TikTok started out as a place to share short-form videos that were generally lip-synching and dance clips, but they have now evolved into an essential marketing channel. By 2023 TikTok had over 1 billion users across 150 countries, according to data published by Wallaroo Media, a full-service digital marketing company in the United States. Data from the TikTok Marketing Science Global Community and Self-Expression Study 2021, conducted by Flamingo, showed that 73 per cent of people feel a deeper connection with brands they interact with on TikTok, and 93 per cent of users take action on the content they see in the 'For You' feed.

TikTok was ad-free when it launched, but in 2019 and 2020 it began to test its advertising capability, and it launched personalized advertising in 2022. TikTok Pulse landed that same year, and Pulse Premiere in 2023. TikTok Pulse allows advertisers to position their brand next to the top 4 per cent of trending videos on TikTok so that they can be closer to the everyday trends that engage the community. Pulse Premiere lets advertisers place their ads adjacent to content produced by premium publishers. Half of the revenue from these adverts is shared with the publishers. Inaugural publishing partners included Condé Nast, Hearst Magazines and Dotdash Meredith. This concept is essentially similar to a brand paying to take out advertising in a magazine. On the TikTok website, Pamela Drucker Mann, global chief revenue officer and president of US Revenue & International at Condé Nast, stated that Pulse Premiere enabled 'clients to match media buying with how consumers are consuming our brands, like *Vogue*, *GQ* and *Vanity Fair*, on TikTok'.

TikTok has been adopted by fashion brands large and small, from global designer names to indie labels. This includes such mass-market brands as Zara and Abercrombie & Fitch; luxury brands, including Gucci, Prada and Dior; global sportswear brands, such as Nike; and smaller independent brands, among them Snag tights and the French label Sézane. In 2022, for the launch of the second Gucci x North Face collaboration, Gucci cast the TikTok trainspotter Francis Bourgeois for its advert released via Highsnobiety in January 2022. Bourgeois posted trainspotting videos on TikTok during the pandemic, garnering over 2 million followers at the time. Dior, meanwhile, uses TikTok to show video clips of its fashion shows, as well as exclusive ads and content showcasing celebrity collaborations. The Prada TikTok channel has very short clips (7–10 seconds) featuring film stars and celebrities wearing Prada, among them the American actor Maya Hawke, the Chinese singer-songwriter Cai Xukun and the American actor Gabrielle Union with her husband, the former NBA star Dwyane Wade.

↓ A still from the North Face x Gucci video ad of January 2022, in which the TikTok sensation Francis Bourgeois starred as a train conductor. The brands tapped into the zeitgeist, picking up on Bourgeois's huge social-media following as 'Train Guy' with his successful trainspotting videos. Highsnobiety partnered with the director Tom Dream to produce the whimsical film, which was set on a steam train travelling through an alpine landscape.

TikTok has an internal tool that allows brands to create ads in the style of user-generated content. Sézane uses real people for its TikTok campaigns, which are usually filmed on the streets or in one of its stores (Paris, New York, San Francisco, Los Angeles and London). The videos consist of an interviewer asking such questions as: 'Do you speak Sézane?', 'What piece of clothing is the most French to you?' or 'What's your favourite piece in this boutique?' In other videos, they gift Sézane pieces or a bunch of flowers to those whom they interview.

For TikTok campaigns, being genuine and getting it right is important. Snag tights was launched in Edinburgh in 2018 by Brie Read. Catering to customer needs and championing inclusivity are key values of the brand. Snag's TikTok channel shows wearers of all different body types, highlighting the brand's inclusive approach. The marketing approach is also strongly data-driven. For example, the sales figures show that 10 per cent of sales are to men who wear tights, so 10 per cent of the models used in Snag advertising campaigns are men.

There are various advert formats within TikTok:

In-feed ads These brand ads appear as a user scrolls through user videos on the 'For You' page (FYP). These ads can be from five seconds to a minute long. It is important to make them catchy and find ways for them to stand out, otherwise they can be easily missed as a user scrolls through their feed. These ads include a call-to-action button linking to a URL, so they are great for sending users to a landing page.

Brand takeover ads These ads take over the full screen for five seconds when a user first opens TikTok. They are unskippable, so the user has to watch them. The ad, which then converts into a normal in-feed ad – as a video, GIF or still image – can include a link sending users to the brand website or keeping them in TikTok, driving them to a brand hashtag challenge (see below). Brand takeover ads are exclusive and therefore expensive, since TikTok ensures that users won't see more than one a day.

Top-view ads These are similar to takeover ads but appear in the FYP three seconds after the app is opened. They can be from five seconds to a minute long. TikTok suggests that 15 seconds is the best length.

Branded hashtag challenge These ads displayed on the TikTok Discovery page invite users to participate in a trend they create through a branded hashtag. TikTok offers 3–6-day packages with media placement and creative guidance, so this is an expensive option – but worth it for brands that want to encourage user-generated content and brand engagement, and have the budget for it. The aim is for the challenge to go viral; the more people using the hashtag, the more exposure the brand will get. Clicking on a branded hashtag takes the user to a branded landing page on TikTok with a description of the challenge, videos of people doing the challenge, and a link to the brand website.

Branded effects This option allows a brand to design its own custom interactive filter, lasting for up to ten days. This approach is great for boosting user-generated content, and can include shareable stickers, augmented-reality filters and lenses.

Between September 2020 and January 2021 TikTok commissioned Kantar, a data insights and consulting company, to undertake research. The aim was to understand how audiences perceived ads on TikTok compared to those on other platforms. Kantar surveyed more than 25,000 participants across 20 different countries, and the results – which were published on the TikTok website – showed six specific insights, of which the top four were:

> » TikTok ads inspire people. 72 per cent of participants agreed that they perceived ads on TikTok as inspiring. TikTok users are receptive to new and inspirational videos from creators and brands.

> » Trendsetting sets TikTok ads apart. Respondents to the survey believed TikTok ads to be 21 per cent more trendsetting than ads on other platforms. Innovative ad formats, such as the branded hashtag challenge, contributed to this sentiment.

> » Ads on TikTok are viewed as enjoyable and optimistic.

> » TikTok ads capture people's attention. 67 per cent agreed that ads on TikTok capture their attention, a 10 per cent lead compared to other platforms.

Social-media advertising is affordable when compared to some other options, such as outdoor advertising, and there are other social platforms not described above that can be used, including X (formerly Twitter), Snapchat, Reddit, Twitch, Pinterest and LinkedIn. For social-media marketers, the other advantage of social-media advertising is that the results can be measured easily. It is possible to know how many people saw an advert, who engaged with it and clicked through to the brand website or product, and how much was generated in sales through that advert. It is also possible to gain insight into the brand's target audience. The ways of measuring advertising effectiveness are discussed later in this chapter.

THE DIGITAL MARKETING MIX

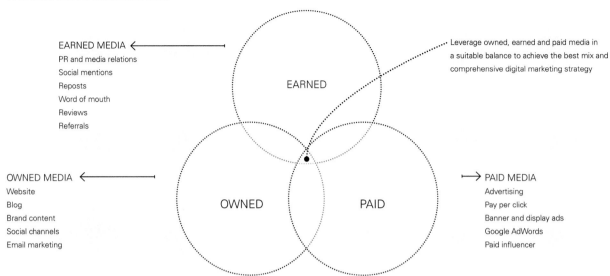

EARNED MEDIA
PR and media relations
Social mentions
Reposts
Word of mouth
Reviews
Referrals

EARNED

Leverage owned, earned and paid media in
a suitable balance to achieve the best mix and
comprehensive digital marketing strategy

OWNED MEDIA
Website
Blog
Brand content
Social channels
Email marketing

OWNED

PAID

PAID MEDIA
Advertising
Pay per click
Banner and display ads
Google AdWords
Paid influencer

It is important to note that the owners of social-media platforms constantly update their advertising formats, as well as the way that certain algorithms work, so social-media marketers must keep up to date. The world of digital is moving very fast, and platforms can gain or lose popularity among users, and new platforms – such as Discord, Clubhouse and Caffeine – emerge and gain traction.

All of the above refers to what is known as **paid social-media advertising**. The brand or company in question has paid to get its advertising spot on to its chosen digital channel. If content is paid for, by law it must be clear that this is the case. This is achieved by the use of the word 'sponsored' or 'promoted' in the ad.

There are other ways to promote on digital without paying an advertising fee. This is known as **organic media**, and it refers to any free content shared by a brand, such as blogs, posts or videos. This type of content is great in establishing the brand personality and tone of voice. There are two types of organic media: **owned media** and **earned media**.

Owned media is content generated by the brand and shared via its own digital and social-media channels. The brand does not need to pay for the right to share it in the same way as it would for advertising, but there may be a cost involved in creating the content – for example, hiring creatives or the salary of an in-house team. Ideas for owned content include meet-the-team posts, how-to guides, information on new collections and product drops, and behind-the-scenes videos, either in the office or during photoshoots and making-of videos.

Earned media is what could be termed digital word of mouth. This is when a brand's audience shares or reposts the branded content, mentions the brand themselves (such as showing an unboxing video when they receive the branded products), or gives a favourable review of the brand on their own personal social media. This is also known as user-generated content (UGC).

Search-engine optimization

Seach-engine optimization (SEO) helps people find a brand and its products or services more easily online. When customers search for particular products or services, they tend to check out brands that rank higher in the search results. The aim for a brand is to ensure the best visibility when people search online (usually through Google), and to get more traffic (people) to visit their website. This is known as organic search, and refers to the process of people finding a brand through an online search rather than via a paid advert. The aim of SEO is to get the brand to be seen at the top of the list generated by the search, on what is known as the SERP, or search-engine results page. To facilitate this process, it is important to ensure that when the searcher gets through to the brand website, it is easy for them to navigate and browse. If users spend more time on the brand website, Google picks this up and ranks the brand higher in the search.

SEO is all about keywords or key phrases. These are words and phrases added to the brand's online content that users are likely to type in when searching. Getting the right keywords helps to improve the ranking result for the brand. Generic keywords are less effective than what are known as long-tail keywords: more specific phrases made up of 3–5 words, and sometimes also known as 'search strings'. For example, if someone wanted to look for a handbag and just put that word into the search engine, hundreds of bags would show up. This is not good for the brand because there is more competition, and it is confusing for the searcher since many of the options listed will be irrelevant and not what they are looking for. A search for a leather cross-body bag, on the other hand, would provide a more focused result, making it easier for the potential purchaser and more likely that a specific brand or product might stand out. According to Klarna's 'Shopping Pulse' report 2023, 46 per cent of shoppers start their journey with an online search on Google. The way consumers searching for fashion enter their searches depends on what they are looking for. A Think with Google article in September 2019, 'What Fashion Fans Around the World Are Searching for on Google' by Jess Duarte and Stéphanie Thomson, highlighted the fact that '45% of dress searches contain a reference to an event, like a wedding or graduation. But when people are searching for bottoms, they're more likely to use gender-related terms, like "women's shorts", or a colour, like "black trousers".'

There are, of course, many social-media and marketing agencies that offer SEO among their services. For many people or businesses, employing someone to help them navigate the complexities of this area could be a good idea.

Timing and exposure

Having thought about the content and message of an advert or campaign, as well as the appropriate media channels for the target audience, the next issue to consider is the timing and exposure of an advert. This relates to when the advert will be released, and how long it will be viewable for. A company must balance the spread of media used with the time frame and cost of exposure. Traditionally, fashion houses released big advertising campaigns twice a year to coincide with the launch of the Spring and Autumn/Fall seasons, or launched special campaigns for specific seasonal festivities, such as the lunar New Year, Valentine's Day or the winter holiday season. Now, with social media, it is much easier to build awareness organically online and to advertise more frequently in shorter bursts to announce the launch of a new brand, product or service, promote an event or brand experience, or advertise promotions, such as limited-edition collections or reduced-priced products.

Digital content

Content marketing is the creation and sharing of digital content with the aim of promoting and selling a brand, product or service. The traditional channel for promoting new-season designs was advertising and editorial in a major magazine. Now, with an ever-increasing array of digital promotion options, fashion brands and retailers seek to provide consumers with a seamless digital media and shopping experience that means they can click and buy directly from branded content, including videos posted on social media. This is called shoppable content. The social shopping site Lyst.com has a tie-up with Pinterest. Consumers who 'pin' products straight from the catwalk will be notified when any of those products are available to purchase.

Video content is one of fashion's most successful modes of digital promotion. Gucci, Juicy Couture, Barneys, Neiman Marcus, ASOS, Valentino, Diesel and Kate Spade were all early adopters of the shoppable video. Smartzer is a live shopping and interactive shoppable video platform. It works with brands to help them produce shoppable campaigns. Valentino worked with Smartzer for a shoppable video campaign to promote and sell its 'Diary' collection for Spring 2021. The video featured clickable areas where viewers could find out more about the clothes. Interactive features created by Smartzer included clickable hotspots, a quick-buy function and a call to action to add items to the shopping bag. According to Smartzer, the video achieved a 44.67 per cent engagement rate and a 12.79 per cent click-through rate. Smartzer has also worked with Jacquemus, Mac, Sephora and Swarovski.

Live-streaming is growing in popularity as a sales channel. For *Emily in Paris* season 2 in 2021, ViacomCBS (now Paramount Global) partnered with Netflix and Saks.com to offer shoppable content. A shoppable link-up with Saks.com offered curated items from the show for viewers to purchase. Live-streaming for e-commerce is particularly strong in China. An article in the *South China Morning Post* by Jane Zhang in 2020 gives the details of a live-streamed pre-sales event for Singles Day held on Alibaba's Taobao Live. Sales hit US$7.5 billion in the first 30 minutes.

Creating digital content is now a major focus for those working in fashion marketing and branding. In the digital age, 'content is king', as Bill Gates wrote in an essay in 1996. It is a necessary tool, and brands themselves have to think not only about the products they sell, but also about how to be content creators and publishers. They must determine what type of content is suitable for their purposes, choosing between fashion films, video content (such as interviews, behind-the-scenes or sneak peeks), newsletters, blogs, podcasts and content about a forthcoming competition, product launch or special event.

↑ Lily Collins as Emily Cooper in the hit show *Emily in Paris*. Live-streaming for e-commerce was available for the second season, in 2021. Viewers could make use of a shoppable link-up with Saks.com, where curated items from the show were available for purchase.

RELATIONSHIP BETWEEN 4Cs OF CONTENT AND AIDA

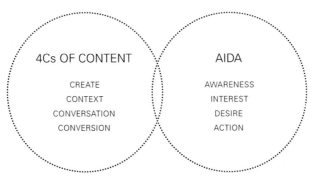

4Cs OF CONTENT
CREATE
CONTEXT
CONVERSATION
CONVERSION

AIDA
AWARENESS
INTEREST
DESIRE
ACTION

CONTENT CAN **CREATE AWARENESS** THAT AT THE RIGHT TIME IN THE RIGHT **CONTEXT** CAN GENERATE **INTEREST** THAT ENCOURAGES **CONVERSATION** THAT CAN LEAD TO **DESIRE** AND PROMOTE **CONVERSION** AND CONSUMER **ACTION**

You may have realized by now that marketers love to create marketing models, such as the 7P Marketing Mix (see page 41). We now come to the four Cs of content: Create, Context, Conversation and Conversion. The four Cs are a good complement to the AIDA model used in advertising (see page 164), and present a logical flow from the creation of content through to consumer conversion or action. The diagram below shows the interrelationship between these Cs and AIDA. There is also the Honeycomb Model of Social Media (opposite), which has seven building blocks that can be used to plan social media and digital content.

Digital storytelling

Digital content is great for telling a powerful story. By combining a range of media, including video clips, images, text, animation, illustration, music and audio recordings, it is possible to develop captivating digital content. This can be used, for example, in translating a print magazine article into a much more engaging digital storytelling piece better suited to online content. The *Vogue* feature 'Rihanna Wears the First Durag on the Cover of British *Vogue*' by Funmi Fetto in March 2020 was available in print and a standard digital format. However, a digital storytelling version was also produced. When clicked on, the title and hero image of Rihanna fade in subtly, and the image expands and contracts for added dramatic effect. Each paragraph of the article rolls up gently as the viewer scrolls down, allowing easy reading. There are images throughout the piece, some presented in carousels. Film footage miraculously appears and fills the screen, as if Rihanna herself were right there. A feature video, *When Rihanna Met Edward Enninful*, is available to click and watch. All this provides a significantly enhanced visual experience compared to the print or standard digital versions.

It is worth thinking about how to translate content from platform to platform, considering how a story can be told through video, written text, animation or still image. It is important to choose the right type of content for each platform, and to consider how a variety of content formats could be combined to produce a more interactive digital story, as described above.

Social-media influencers

The concept of influencers gained momentum around 2009, when bloggers and YouTubers became a more well-known phenomenon. An influencer is described as 'someone with the ability to influence potential buyers of a product or service by promoting or recommending the items on social media'. They have the power to affect the purchasing decisions of others because they have built up a reputation of authority

THE HONEYCOMB MODEL OF
SOCIAL MEDIA

The Honeycomb model of social media was created in 2011 by Jan Kietzmann, Kristopher Hermkens and Ian McCarthy, with the purpose of gauging social-media effectiveness. The idea is that a brand can use this in a similar way to the marketing mix or promotional mix, by reviewing which of the seven key building blocks might be most relevant for its social-media strategy. This can be used as a checklist for the planning and review of campaign effectiveness.

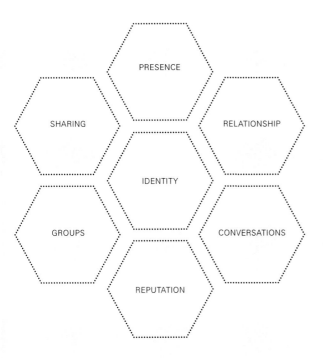

The seven areas of the model are:

IDENTITY The amount of information shared by users. For example: name, age, gender, location, profession, purchasing behaviour. The aspects of identity that are revealed help a brand to target its approach to social-media content and advertising.

SHARING Management of digital content. Make sure that users are engaging with brand content. How do users receive brand content, and how much do they share it?

PRESENCE To what extent is a person or business present on social media, and how aware are other users of this?

RELATIONSHIP How and how much do users relate to one another? Social-media users could be total strangers who follow each other, or groups of friends or family who use group messaging functions on social media.

CONVERSATIONS How are users communicating via social, and to what extent?

REPUTATION The brand's and its users' standing and reputation on social media. This can be seen via number of followers, numbers of likes, blue ticks, positive comments and reposts.

GROUPS How are people using social media to form communities and groups?

The key to using this model is to work through the building blocks and ask questions, for example: *What are our audience's social-media sharing habits, and how could we factor this into our strategy? What conversations are our users having on social about us as a brand or with each other? What's our plan for building our reputation on social?*

and made a connection with their followers. Using influencers for social-media marketing really took off with the rise of Instagram, when savvy brands recognized how powerful an endorsement an influencer could make on the brand's behalf. Influencer types are bloggers, YouTubers, Podcasters and those who do social posts. Influencers can also be categorized by number of followers:

» Mega-influencers (often celebrities)
1 million-plus followers on at least one platform

» Macro-influencers
500,000–1 million followers

» Mid-tier influencers
50,000–500,000 followers

» Micro-influencers
10,000–50,000 followers

» Nano-influencers
1,000–10,000 followers

In the early days of social-media marketing, brands wanted to partner with the influencers who had the largest following, but there has since been a shift. It is now not about how many followers, but rather about the quality of the content. An article by Rumble Romagnoli in *The Drum* in 2021, 'Are Genuinfluencers the New Influencers for Niche and Luxury Brands?', explained that concerns about fake accounts and the practice of buying followers and not declaring sponsored content had given rise to a growing fatigue at the use of influencers for luxury fashion campaigns. The antidote is the 'genuinfluencer', a name coined by the trend-forecasting agency WGSN. These influencers 'often identify as creators … and would rather be noticed for their high-quality content than their follower count'. Nano- and micro-influencers may have a smaller following, but they usually have a much more engaged audience than macro-influencers.

The rise of social-media influencing brought with it the establishment of influencer agencies and platforms. They give advice and help to broker deals between influencers and brands, matchmaking brands with influencers who are appropriate for the brands' target market. Among them are Tribe, The Blogger Programme, Zine, Takumi, Buzzoole, Goat and Komodo, to name a few.

Luxury fashion brands generally work with celebrity influencers or those who are famous influencers in their own right, such as Tanya Burr, who posted a picture on Instagram of herself wearing Dior Spring 2022 in Paris. Chanel works with Lily-Rose Depp, who at the time of writing has 8.5 million followers on Instagram, and

TIMELINE OF SOCIAL MEDIA

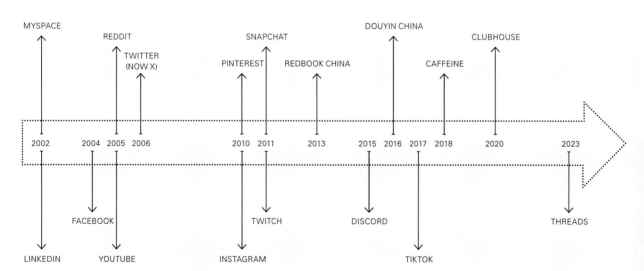

we have already seen that Gucci has worked with the TikTok star Francis Bourgeois.

A growing area within the influencer market is computer-generated virtual influencers. One of the best-known is Lil Miquela, a Brazilian-American singer and influencer with more than three million followers on Instagram. A computer-generated or CGI avatar created by Trevor McFedries and Sara Decou, she has worn Chanel, Burberry and Fendi. Although she appeared in a list of the top 12 CGI influencers, published by Koba Molenaar for Influencer Marketing Hub at the end of 2022, Lil Miquela was ranked second, below Lu do Magalu – another virtual influencer from Brazil. Often known only as Lu, she was created to be the face of Magazine Luiza, a collection of Brazilian companies that includes Magalu, Brazil's largest retailer. Third on the list was Barbie.

In March 2022 the Influencer Marketing Factory surveyed more than 1,000 Americans aged 18–55+, looking into their engagement and interest in virtual influencers. It was found that 58 per cent follow at least one virtual influencer. Of the 42 per cent who did not follow any virtual influencers, 51.4 per cent were not interested, 24.1 per cent did not know they existed, and 24.5 per cent preferred real human influencers.

The Swedish watch brand Daniel Wellington is among the brands working with nano-influencers. It offers a watch to influencers in exchange for a sponsored post on Instagram. Southern Gents, an American menswear brand, works with Kalan Laws (@senorguapo713), who has just under 11,000 followers on Instagram. He is a model, athlete, actor and fashion influencer who promotes himself as 'The Style Professor'.

Sales promotion

Sales promotion, also known as below-the-line marketing, works to increase demand and boost sales of specific products or services. The aim of a sales promotion is to make a brand and its merchandise or services more attractive to customers by offering additional inducements to purchase, such as a price reduction, a free product, an extra benefit or service with a purchase, or the chance of a prize. Promotions usually run for a limited and very specific time frame, and there may be conditions attached, such as a minimum spend. Sales promotions directed at the end-consumer are termed **consumer sales promotions**; those aimed at retailers, wholesalers or manufacturers are known as **trade sales promotions**. Trade sales promotions by apparel and textile wholesalers or suppliers

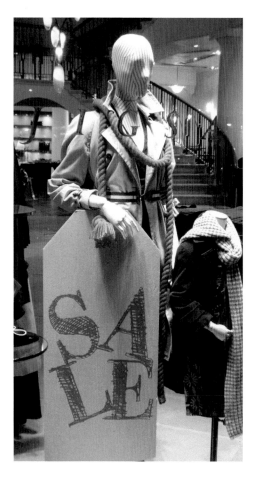

↑ Store windows can be used to advertise seasonal sales or special promotions.

and manufacturers are offered to encourage business customers to purchase or place forward orders.

Promotions directed to the ultimate consumer employ what can be termed **pull strategies**, the idea being that the offer creates demand and entices or pulls the customer in, encouraging them to visit the store or website and ultimately make a purchase. **Push strategies** are geared towards trade distributors and retailers and are designed to encourage them to promote or push a brand or particular product and sell it on to the end-consumer.

The key types of consumer sales promotion are discussed below, with indications as to how each might be used. The advantages of each technique and its benefit to consumers are given, as well as points to consider when planning sales promotion campaigns. Information outlining the essentials of trade sales promotions is given on pages 258–9.

Consumer sales promotions

The purpose of sales promotions directed at the end-consumer is to generate an increase in the volume of sales in the short term, with a positive effect on overall business in the long term. Promotions generally appeal to one or more of several basic consumer instincts: to save money, get something for free, buy something unique – ideally for a reduced price – or win a prize. For retailers, the motivation for sales promotions is to increase the number of consumers visiting the store or website, and increase the conversion rate (the number of visitors converted into purchasers). The advantage of sales promotion campaigns is that they achieve results quickly and usually cost less than high-profile advertising.

Fashion brands and retailers use a variety of promotional activities, the most common being:

> » Price reductions

> » Special offers

> » Gift with purchase

> » Coupons, vouchers and discount codes

> » Competitions and prize draws

Price reductions

Price reductions are most commonly used to shift slow-selling stock. The aim is to boost sales volumes as quickly as possible by reducing the price of selected merchandise. This helps to sell stock through, brings cash into the business and frees up retail space for new product. A price reduction should help to increase volume sales, but it will also reduce the margin and affect profit. Price reductions employed during seasonal sales are normally planned as part of the buying and merchandising strategy. Most reductions are in the region of 10–30 per cent, but in a harsh trading climate retailers may be forced to offer reductions of 50–70 per cent.

Special offers

The main objective of special offers is to increase sales, but they can also be employed as a technique to create desire for a brand or product, or as a way to develop or reward customer loyalty. Special offers can be designed in a variety of formats; the exact nature will depend on the situation to be addressed and the market level of the retailer. Offers such as 'two for the price of one' (known as a 2-4) and 'buy one get one free' (BOGOF) are typically used by mass-market or volume retailers as a way to move old-season stock or lower-priced merchandise that is underperforming. For example, the promotion 'Buy a camisole and get one free' could be used to shift camisoles in old-season colours so that fresh stock can be brought into the store. Another option is for retailers to offer customers a discount on a specific item when they make a purchase. A men's retailer might, for example, offer certain slow-selling tie designs at half price when a customer purchases a shirt. The advantage of this kind of

↓ A Levi's store in Bangalore, India. The US jeans brand is offering Indian shoppers the opportunity to purchase a $30 pair of jeans by paying in three instalments. This age-old sales promotion technique is more commonly used to sell white goods, such as washing machines, but Levi's has embraced the concept to tempt Indian customers with limited budgets.

promotion is twofold; it should help to improve sales of both the ties and the full-price shirts. In-store sales can be maximized if the offer is accompanied by clear signage and an eye-catching display. This will alert customers, inform them which items are being promoted, and give details of prices and time frames. Promoted merchandise can be featured on mannequins, presented on a selling table or highlighted through the use of in-store posters, banners, display boards or marketing materials. In-store, **point-of-sale** displays placed by till points (cash registers) can be used to encourage customers to purchase a special offer before they leave the store. Online, special offers can be promoted using appropriate social-media advertising tools, as discussed on pages 229 and 238–41.

Special offers can also be used to promote a specific brand. A department store, boutique or online marketplace site, such as Matches.com, might run a campaign to introduce a new brand or create an offer to push a brand that is not performing as well as expected. An option in this instance would be to run a cooperative promotion where the retailer and the fashion brand develop a campaign together and share the costs. Special offers may be used to encourage customers to shop in-store rather than online, to tempt customers to purchase online or sign up to a loyalty scheme, or to reward loyal customers who spend over a specified amount.

Gift with purchase

Gift-with-purchase promotions are widely used by the cosmetics and perfume industry, where trial-size make-up or skincare items are given away when a customer purchases a specified number of products. Women's fashion magazines also give away free gifts with a particular issue. These promotions can be a useful tool for fashion retailers, but it is vital to factor in the cost of the gift item relative to how much a consumer must spend before they are entitled to receive it. Referring to the example of the slow-selling men's ties above, a retailer might consider a gift promotion of a free tie when a customer buys a high-priced item, such as a suit, or spends over a certain amount. Giving a gift with a purchase could also be an effective promotion to use when launching a new brand, such as a perfume. In this instance a small sample of the fragrance could be given away. Overall a gift must be desirable and in keeping with the brand or retailer's image, and the scheme must have the potential to increase sales.

Coupons, vouchers and discount codes

Promotions using physical coupons, vouchers or digital discount codes that offer a discount to customers are another option.

Traditionally, such schemes have been operated between a magazine or newspaper and a fashion retailer. Customers usually receive a discount in the region of 10 or 20 per cent when they redeem their coupon in a participating store. This type of promotion benefits both retailer and magazine, with the potential of boosting circulation for the magazine and increasing sales for the retailer. Nowadays most discounts are activated with a digital discount code. This is most usually promoted when someone lands on a brand site and a pop-up announcement offers a 10 or 25 per cent discount on a first purchase if the potential purchaser signs up to the brand newsletter. Consumers can also sign up to special discount sites, such as Groupon, Voucherbox or Wowcher, that provide voucher codes or discounts on designer fashion and high-street brands. Consumers can also register to have **text codes** or mobile barcodes sent to their phone. The latest schemes allow consumers to scan **QR codes** or photograph barcodes on swing tickets, print ads or store windows. Barcodes or QR codes can also be sent straight to a consumer's smartphone, to be scanned by a retailer when the shopper wants to make a purchase or claim a promotional discount. Such promotions also offer a retailer or brand the possibility of direct communication and interaction with consumers, and the opportunity to gather useful data. This supports future direct-marketing possibilities (see the section on direct marketing on pages 259–60).

Competitions and prize draws

Prize draws can be operated online or via a printed entry form available in-store, in a magazine or newspaper, or by direct mail. Basic competitions usually ask entrants to answer a simple question about the brand or company, but much more interesting and engaging contests can be developed – inviting consumers to customize or redesign garments, for example. In 2012 the Nudie Jeans Empowerment Challenge invited customers to design a T-shirt print to illustrate the idea of 'empowerment'. A donation of €10 from every T-shirt sold was made to Amnesty International. Winners were rewarded with €1,000 and the honour of supporting Amnesty International and having their T-shirt produced.

The key point about a competition is to ensure that the prize is enticing enough; consumers must feel that it is worthwhile entering. Also consider the value and number of prizes on offer. Will customers believe they have a reasonable chance to win, and is the prize worth winning?

There is one last important point to mention. Legal regulations govern advertising and promotions, and prize draws and competitions in particular are subject to specific restrictions.

THE EMPOWERMENT *challenge*

BY NUDIE JEANS FOR
THE BENEFIT OF AMNESTY
INTERNATIONAL

www.nudiejeans.com/empowerment-challenge

AMNESTY
INTERNATIONAL

↑ The Nudie Jeans Empowerment
Challenge, 2012.

Sales promotional schemes should therefore be created with care to ensure that all aspects comply with relevant law. Professional bodies, such as the Institute of Sales Promotion, the Chartered Institute of Marketing and the American Marketing Association, can assist with information on legal matters.

Limited editions

One way a designer, brand or retailer can increase their kudos and create desire for their merchandise is to offer customers the opportunity to purchase limited-edition product. For many consumers it can be an attractive proposition to know that only a restricted number of people will have the same item. There are several ways to approach the concept of limited editions. One way is to develop a special one-off item that is available in limited quantity for a short time. Another is to create a limited-edition collection, rather than just one item.

Limited-edition capsule collaborative collections are now commonplace. In 2023 Netflix teamed up with Lacoste to produce a limited-edition genderless collection inspired by Netflix series, including *Bridgerton*, *Stranger Things* and *Sex Education*. This included adapting the iconic crocodile logo; for *Stranger Things*, for example, the crocodile face is embroidered and flocked, transforming it into a terrifying Demogorgon. In homage to Queen Charlotte in *Bridgerton*, the famous croc wears an oversized Georgian-style wig. While these collections are promoted as limited editions, meaning they are a special collection outside the main range, it is not always easy to detect exactly how many pieces are produced. The Lacoste x Netflix collection launched on 12 April 2023, but by June there were many pieces selling at reduced prices online, indicating that it may not have been so limited as to be very exclusive or desirable. To achieve this, it is best to really limit the number produced, or even have the number of the edition printed or stitched on to the product. In 2021 F/CE, in collaboration with the unisex fashion brand Stof, released only 100 of a special-edition backpack. F/CE stands for 'Functionality. Culture. Exploration', and the company is the brainchild of the designer and musician Satoshi Yamane. The backpack was printed with a story, 'Oku no Hosomichi' (The Narrow Road to the Deep North, 1694) by the Japanese poet and traveller Matsuo Bashō, translated into English. This, with the Japanese character for 'word' and the Arabic word for 'love', was integrated into the design of this highly functional rucksack.

Brand collaborations

Collaborations have become a mainstay of fashion marketing and promotion, and are regularly used season after season. The range of collaborations seems to be ever growing, from mass-market retailers teaming up with a high-profile designer to luxury fashion houses collaborating with musicians and artists. The permutations of collaboration types include:

» Fashion designers and retailers

» Fashion designers or fashion brands with celebrities (actors, musicians, artists, sports stars)

» Fashion designers or fashion brands with social-media influencers

» A fashion brand with another fashion brand

» Fashion designers or fashion brands with a brand from another industry

Designer and retailer collabs

This type of collaboration is not a completely new phenomenon; the UK department store Debenhams pioneered the idea in the 1990s with its 'Designers at Debenhams' collections. The collaboration concept really took off in November 2004, when the Swedish fast-fashion giant H&M teamed up with Karl Lagerfeld to produce the 'Lagerfeld for H&M' collection, consisting of womenswear, menswear, a fragrance and accessories. The collection was limited to 20 out of the 32 global markets in which H&M operated at the

↑ The British handbag and accessory brand Radley produces regular limited editions. Each season it designs and produces a unique bag featuring an illustrated scene incorporating its signature little black dog. These bags have become collectors' items, and many customers return season after season to purchase the latest version. To celebrate the coronation of King Charles III in 2023, the brand released a small collection of limited-edition bags featuring colourful bunting and royal corgi dogs running along with Radley's signature Scottie.

time. Now the retailer collaborates roughly once a year. Designers have included Stella McCartney, Viktor & Rolf, Roberto Cavalli, Marimekko, Comme des Garçons, Matthew Williamson, Maison Margiela, Lanvin, Isabel Marant, Erdem and Simone Rocha. For 2023, H&M released a collaboration with the French fashion label Mugler, providing customers with access to the luxury label's signature figure-hugging look at a more accessible price point.

Another retailer that collaborates with designers is the US discount store Target. The brand promise is, 'Expect More. Pay Less.®' Target delivers on this promise with its 'Design for All®' concept. The rationale is that good design should be available for all. The store wants to be able to offer customers designer products at affordable prices, and to that end it works with some of the most famous names in fashion for its Design for All® products. These include the accessory designer Anya Hindmarch and the fashion designers Isaac Mizrahi, Phillip Lim, Peter Pilotto and Prabal Gurung. In September 2019 a book entitled *Target: 20 Years of Design for All: How Target Revolutionized Accessible Design* was released. This and an accompanying documentary series took a deep dive into the concept of design for all in terms of inclusive and accessible design.

The collaborations discussed so far have been short-term activations either between a designer and retailer or between a celebrity and a retailer. Collaborations of this kind can attract massive crowds that gather outside the store before the launch, and stock sells out in hours or days. However, there are also more long-term brand partnerships, such as the one between Adidas and the Japanese designer Yohji Yamamoto. This gave rise to the 'Y-3' collection, which was launched in 2003 and has been a long-standing alliance between the two brands. A key purpose of this partnership was to establish a strong fashion element within the Adidas brand, giving it a distinctive platform for differentiation; the sports brand went on to develop a partnership with Stella McCartney to launch the fashion-directional sports collection 'Adidas by Stella McCartney'.

Designer/brand and celebrity collabs

A variation on the collaborative theme is for a retailer to team up with a celebrity. H&M has done this with the pop icons Madonna and Kylie, and the singers Lana Del Rey and Vanessa Paradis. In 2011 the brand worked with the superstar model Jerry Hall and her daughter Georgia May Jagger, and in 2012 it teamed up with David Beckham to launch a range of Beckham-branded underwear and bodywear. For Spring 2022 H&M broke the mould, working with the 101-year-old style icon Iris Apfel on a collection of dresses, coordinates and accessories. In the same year the jewellery brand Tiffany & Co. launched a collab with Beyoncé.

A celebratory special offer

DIESEL DIRTY THIRTY

Fashion companies develop limited editions as a way to differentiate them from competitors and to offer exclusive product to their customers. To celebrate its thirtieth birthday, the Italian jeans company Diesel developed an exclusive special offer to thank fans for their loyalty to the brand. The Diesel Dirty Thirty campaign offered customers the chance to purchase a pair of limited-edition jeans in the Heeven style for men or Matic for women. Only 30,000 pairs were made available in 160 stores worldwide. Priced at £30 (€30 or $50), the premium jeans were affordable and highly desirable. Designed with several distinctive features, each pair came with a commemorative xXx back patch (the Xs representing 30 in Roman numerals), a handmade repair patch and an embroidered 'Dirty Thirty 1978–2008' stitched on the side seam. They were finished with a special 'dirty' wash treatment. The promotion also had a limited and very specific time frame: one day only, from 10 am. As an added incentive, the first ten customers purchasing the jeans at each store were invited to attend one of the Diesel xXx global parties that took place simultaneously in 17 locations around the world. The Dirty Thirty promotion illustrates several important elements of creating a successful special offer:

» A desirable product with unique features

» Limited availability

» A limited and specified time frame

» A promotional price reduction

When developing a special offer, it is important to ensure that the offer is in keeping with the ethos and market level of the brand or retailer. Great special offers, such as the Diesel Dirty Thirty promotion, raise the profile of the brand and achieve a sales boost in the short term, but must not undermine or cheapen the brand's image and drive customers away in the long term.

↗ The limited-edition jeans included such unique design features as a leather back patch with the distinctive Diesel xXx sign, a handmade repair patch and embroidery celebrating Diesel's thirtieth anniversary.

→ Daisy Lowe models the women's Matic style Dirty Thirty jeans.

→ A promotional image for the high-street/designer collaboration between H&M and the French fashion house Mugler, which launched on 11 May 2023. Casey Cadwallader, creative director at Mugler, said: 'The collaboration includes many of our signatures, from catsuits and bodycon dresses to tailoring, denim and beautiful, bold jewellery and accessories.'

From 2007 the fashion retailer Topshop developed an ongoing relationship with the globally famous model Kate Moss. Moss worked closely with the in-house design team so that they could interpret her individual, eclectic fashion sensibility, translating it into the desirable and commercially successful 'Kate Moss for Topshop' collection. It is understood implicitly that the celebrity does not design the garments themselves, merely providing the inspirational style and lending their name to the enterprise. There is a risk to this kind of arrangement, since celebrity status can be fickle; a chosen personality can go out of fashion, lose favour with the public or make a misstep that means they will be dropped by the brand. Key to celebrity collaborations is to ensure that the face fits, that the celebrity enhances the profile of the brand, and that target consumers connect with that person's style.

Fashion and art are another mix for collaborative cross-fertilization, as evidenced when the artist Damien Hirst designed a range of scarves with distinctive kaleidoscopic prints for Alexander McQueen in 2013. Another very prominent collab has been that between Louis Vuitton and Yayoi Kusama (see page 217). Louis Vuitton described this as 'a creative dialogue'. This commercial conversation has been activated twice: in 2012, when the brand was under the stewardship of Marc Jacobs, and ten years later, in January 2023, with Nicolas Ghesquière as creative director.

Designer/brand and influencer collabs

Influencer marketing (see pages 238–41) is the most common tie-up between a brand and an influencer. However, a brand and an influencer can also work together to produce a new brand or collection. An example is provided by Prableen Kaur Bhomrah, a digital creator promoting body positivity, who documented her struggle to find affordable jeans that fit. To solve this problem, she teamed up with the direct-to-consumer jeans brand Freakins on a capsule jeans collection with more inclusive sizing and shaping.

Brands band together

Examples of brands banding together to collaborate are numerous, and this form of marketing and promotion does not appear to be going away any time soon. Here are just some of the collaborations that occurred in 2022 and 2023:

Axel Arigato x Mulberry The Swedish lifestyle brand Axel Arigato teamed up with the British heritage brand Mulberry to create a 35-piece capsule collection featuring clothes and accessories.

Puma x Fenty In March 2023 it was announced that Puma would again collaborate with Rihanna. The Puma website and social media teased the public with the message: 'She's Back.' This was accompanied by the Fenty and Puma logos.

Sézane x Farm Rio This is a collaboration between the French cult online brand and one of Brazil's best-known fashion labels, Farm Rio from Rio de Janeiro.

Nike x Tiffany & Co. This one took many people by surprise, and there were mixed feelings as to its outcome: Nike Air Force 1 Low sneakers in black suede featuring the iconic Tiffany blue for the Nike swooshes. The shoes came in a Tiffany blue box with a white Nike swoosh.

Levi's x Supreme The denim brand and streetwear brand created a collection of clothing and accessories, the idea being to give signature Levi's pieces a Supreme twist.

Heidi Klein x Temperley London The luxury swimwear label Heidi Klein released a swimwear collection designed in collaboration with Temperley London. The pieces combined Temperley's distinctive patterns with Klein's classic swimwear silhouettes.

Mr Porter x Arket This pairing resulted in an exclusive unisex childrenswear collection. Select pieces from this bold and colourful collection were sized up so that they could also be sported by parents alongside their kids.

↓ Boxie designs for O'Neill.

↑ The British luxury leather goods and stationery brand Smythson teamed up with Erdem to create notebooks lined with printed silk from Erdem's Resort 2010 collection.

Collabs outside the industry

Among the non-fashion brands collaborating with those inside the industry are the German luggage brand Rimowa, now part of the LVMH stable. It has collaborated with a raft of streetwear fashion brands, including Palace, Supreme, Anti Social Social Club, Off-White and Bape, and with Dior and Fendi. There have also been collaborations between fashion houses and car brands. In 2011, when Frida Giannini was the creative director at Gucci, she designed a custom Gucci Fiat 500 to celebrate the Gucci brand's ninetieth birthday. The special-edition car was available in black or white, with an interlocking G logo on the wheel hubs, a leather interior decorated with the Gucci logo, and the Gucci stripe in red and green on the doors. Other collabs include Bugatti x Hermès; Lamborghini x Versace; Porsche x Aimé Leon Dore; and Maserati x Ermenegildo Zegna.

Not all collaborations make obvious sense. The fashion brand Vetements teamed up with the courier company DHL in 2014, for example. Fashion brands collaborating with Barbie, on the other hand, does seem a great idea. In 2022 there was Barbie x Balmain. Olivier Rousteing, Balmain's creative director, created a 70-piece collection for the world-famous doll. Other fashion brands outfitting Barbie include the cult streetwear brand Kith in 2019, Moschino in 2015, and in 2017 a three-way collaboration between Barbie, the model Gigi Hadid and the fashion designer Tommy Hilfiger. The Gigi Barbie doll wore a Tommy logo T-shirt with cut-off denims, and sported a pair of rollerblades. With the release of the *Barbie* movie in 2023, more tie-ups between the doll and fashion are surely to be expected.

Fashion and the Metaverse

Not all collaborations are physical. Many occur in the digital realm, or **Metaverse**. This type of partnership first emerged in 2007, when H&M made digital clothes for the Electronic Arts game *The Sims*. The fashion retailer produced digital versions of some of the physical clothes sold in store, allowing players to dress their Sims characters as virtual versions of themselves. Since then there has been a significant increase in the number of fashion and gaming collaborations, a fact that comes as no surprise if you look at the size of the gaming market. According to the Statista report 'Global Video Game Market Value from 2020 to 2025' (2023), the global gaming market will account for more than US$268 billion in 2025, up from US$78 billion in 2021. In 2023 it was estimated that there were more than 3.2 billion gamers worldwide.

One of the most notable partnerships has been Balenciaga with Epic Games' *Fortnite*. This was *Fortnite*'s first ever luxury partnership. Players could acquire special Balenciaga 'skins' as in-game purchases. Research conducted by Anzu Virtual Reality into gamers in the USA found that 66 per cent treated themselves to luxury branded products. The study showed that 47 per cent claimed they had purchased Gucci items, 43 per cent Dior and 29 per cent Chanel. In 2022 Prada joined forces with Ubisoft, the French gaming publisher of *Riders Republic*®. The game invites players to experience the thrill of outdoor sports, such as skiing and snowboarding. Prada offered riders the opportunity to be seen wearing Prada Linea Rossa gear on the slopes. In the same year Ralph Lauren Polo released digital outfits on *Fortnite*, with physical versions available in-store, and Dior teamed up with the Sony Interactive Entertainment game *Gran Turismo 7*. In 2023 Louis Vuitton launched its first foray into NFTs (non-fungible tokens), with its VIA Treasure Trunk NFT. This 'phygital' (physical + digital) concept offered VIP customers the opportunity to apply to purchase one of a limited number of digital trunks that cost more than US$41,000 each. Customers had to apply, and only those selected were able to access a private homepage, where they were guided through an exclusive journey to acquire the coveted digital treasure trunk. Those who purchased one also received a matching physical version of the trunk and access to digital keys that would unlock new limited-edition products and experiences.

Research by Niko, a gaming intelligence agency, suggests that the Asian gaming market will reach US$41.4 billion in 2026. Bulgari tapped into this when it launched a virtual Bulgari world with pop-up store and café on Asia's biggest Metaverse platform, Zepeto, which has a particularly strong female following in South Korea and China. The digitally rendered Bulgari environment, designed to match the brand's physical store in the Parnas Hotel on Korea's Jeju Island, was opened by an avatar of the South Korean pop star Lisa (from the girl group Blackpink), who is a brand ambassador. When visitors to the game complete a quest, they receive signature accessory pieces from the Bulgari Resort collection to adorn their avatars.

Many fashion and gaming collaborations include both physical and digital elements. A host of fashion brands are following this approach. In Burberry's *B Bounce* online game, players can win garments both virtual and physical. Net-A-Porter collaborated with several Chinese fashion designers to create digital avatar skins for *Animal Crossing: New Horizons*, inspired by their real-life collections. Physical versions were available to buy via Tmall. Gucci partnered with Wildlife's *Tennis Clash*, again fusing the real and virtual worlds, where online players can wear exclusive Gucci virtual looks and buy physical versions of these outfits on the Gucci website.

↑ Smythson also worked with Giles Deacon to produce 300 boxes of couture correspondence cards embellished with exquisite, hand-engraved pen-and-ink sketches.

The benefits of collaboration

The general format for collaborations is for a large, well-known brand or retailer to join forces with a more exclusive design-led company, individual designer, celebrity designer, musician or social-media influencer. For the venture to work and be profitable, each partner must gain something from the relationship. It is also important to ensure that the association does not alienate existing customers. Collaborations between high-profile designers and high-street retailers provide considerable benefits to all parties concerned. The designer or brand gets wider exposure and should be able to attract a new audience that might previously have been excluded, usually because of the high price or exclusivity of the designer label. For the retailer, the arrangement allows it to offer increased choice, keep relevant and up to date, and attract new fashion-conscious customers. In short, the retailer gains prestige, the designer company is exposed to a new market, and consumers are able to buy designer fashion at an affordable price. Successful collaborative partnerships manage to build on the power and recognition associated with each contributor, merging their strengths to accomplish something unique that could not have been achieved by each partner on their own. Collaborations allow a brand or designer to:

» Attract new customers

» Gain credibility in a new market

» Enhance kudos and prestige

» Innovate and develop alternative creative approaches

↑↑ A Metaverse augmented-reality fashion show.

↑ A model wears the real-life version of an Autumn/Winter 2022–3 Balmain dress at Paris Fashion Week. The dress featured in the Balmain x *Need for Speed*™ Unbound collaboration. Inside the game, new racer Eléonore wears a digital rendering of this dress, and players were able to purchase digital versions of other real-life Balmain items.

» Generate new business opportunities

» Share resources

» Reduce the risk of going it alone

» Create a buzz and attract press coverage

As is clear from the variety of physical and digital collaborations featured, there is mileage in creative associations of this type, and more opportunity for other fruitful alliances to blossom. The growth of this phenomenon indicates that it is a beneficial strategy for brand awareness, promotion and product diversification.

Limit and hype: drop culture

An adjunct to brand collaborations is the idea of 'dropping' products. This refers to the moment the anticipated collection or merchandise becomes available in-store or online. The drop concept was originally conceived in Japan and activated within the streetwear market, but has since migrated to designer and mid-market fashion alike. The idea, which could be called 'Limit & Hype', has spread to the designer and luxury fashion sector, with such brands as Balenciaga, Burberry and Gucci all applying the tactic.

This approach has also become de rigueur for brands releasing limited-edition collaboration ranges. Apparently, when the Rimowa x Supreme suitcase collab went live in 2018, the product sold out in 16 seconds. Both brands announced the drop by posting a picture of the product on social media a mere three days ahead of the release date. The idea of Limit & Hype aligns with the basic concept of generating a sense of urgency by using scarcity as a driver for desire. It is also known as scarcity marketing. This taps into the psychological fear that people have of missing out, known as FOMO. The idea is that when supply decreases, demand will increase. Under-supplying the products and holding back information are key marketing tactics, meaning that there is a great deal of kudos for those customers who are in the know, and who are among the select few who get their hands on the coveted merch. As the sneakerologist – yes, that is a job title! – Matt Powell, vice president and senior industry advisor for the market-research company the NPD Group, said, 'If everyone can get one, nobody wants one.'

Queue culture: waiting in line

Another component of drop culture is the queue or waiting in line. Some of the most talked-about queues are those that form outside a Supreme store in advance of a product drop. Normally these are

→ Crowds flock to Louis Vuitton's Miami
store to purchase from the limited-edition
Supreme x Louis Vuitton collaboration in
the summer of 2017.

quite controlled, but in 2017, when the Supreme x Louis Vuitton collaboration dropped in London at 180 Strand, it was mayhem. According to an article by Hannah Keegan for *Stylist* magazine in 2019, the security firm managing the queue said this was one of the most intense events it had ever encountered. It feared things would get crazy since previously, when the collection had dropped in New York, there had been stabbings and people had been robbed of their items on leaving the store.

Queuing is not only the preserve of streetwear brands and major collaboration drops. The luxury luggage and accessory brand Goyard requires customers to wait in line before being admitted to the store. The reason for this, though, is slightly different: the concept is all about exclusivity. As Baya Simons pointed out in an article in the *Financial Times* in October 2018, 'You will never see a Goyard advertisement in print, nor find its wares on any ecommerce platform. It retails in just 19 locations around the world.' The queue in this instance operates as a system of controlled entry to ensure luxury service. Each person who enters the store gets superb one-to-one attention, since the number of customers allowed inside never exceeds the number of staff there to serve.

Goyard does not operate an e-commerce site, so waiting your turn is the golden ticket to purchase into the luxurious universe of this mysterious and exclusive brand. Interestingly, the YouTube video of the Supreme x Louis Vuitton drop at 180 Strand shows several people sporting Goyard crossbody shoulder bags with the distinctive signature all-over pattern.

Queue culture will be something to watch. Retail-industry insiders are talking about how brands might bring entertainment into the mix, so that standing in line becomes a branded experience and event.

Planning consumer sales promotions

One of the main advantages of sales promotional offers is that they have the potential to achieve results quickly. They can increase consumer traffic in-store and online and boost sales, and generally cost less than high-profile advertising. Campaigns can also be used to enhance consumer loyalty, often with the side benefit of collecting valuable data about consumers. Consumer sales promotions offer a company considerable scope, but they must be planned with care, since a company can cheapen its image if it relies too heavily on discounts or offers. Another problem, particularly in a tough trading climate, is that consumers cut back on normal spending and purchase only during a promotion. While this can be advantageous in keeping cash flowing through the business, it can devalue the overall financial position of the company. When planning a promotion, it is important to consider the following:

» Purpose of the promotion

» Target audience

» Most appropriate type of scheme

» How it will operate

» Time frame

» Range or reach of the offer

» How to inform customers about the promotion

» Costs

» Potential tie-ins, additional events and cooperative partners

The first consideration should always be purpose: what the promotion should achieve for the company and what it should offer customers. Tied to this is the next key issue, the target audience for the campaign. With these two points in mind, it should be possible to determine the most appropriate type of sales promotion and how it will operate. The time frame must be thought through with care. It is important to fix a viable time limit, long enough to allow the promotion to have an effect but not so long that consumers delay purchasing. The cut-off date must be communicated clearly so that customers appreciate the offer is limited. This should create desire and a sense of urgency. For a price reduction on slow-selling stock,

ADVANTAGES AND DISADVANTAGES OF SALES PROMOTIONS

ADVANTAGES

» Create desire and provide an incentive to purchase

» Short-term increase in sales

» Bring customers in-store or to the website

» Support consumer loyalty

» Improve conversion rate

» Can be used to target specific customer groups

» Cost less than advertising campaigns

» Can be used to collect valuable data on consumers

DISADVANTAGES

» Provide only short-term results

» Could negatively affect brand image

» Could negatively affect full-price sales

» Store might run out of promotional stock early and disappoint customers

» Must comply with government regulations

it is crucial to calculate how much to reduce the selling price in order to encourage customers to purchase while also ensuring the least damage to the overall margin and profit. For a special-offer promotion on a product designed or ordered in specifically for a promotion, the important issue is judging the correct quantity, particularly if it is a limited edition, such as Diesel's Dirty Thirty jeans in 2008. A fine balance must be achieved between limiting availability so that customers crave the product and ensuring that there is enough stock; running out too soon could disappoint loyal customers. Equally, over-ordering and having a large amount of unsold stock are counterproductive. The range or reach of the offer should also be determined: will it be available in every store or retail channel, or in selected channels or locations only?

Consumers must be alerted and informed about a promotion, so an advertising campaign may be required, or some form of public-relations activity, such as a teaser ad or video, or announcement on the website, blog or X feed. Information on a sales promotional campaign can also be disseminated in window displays or by using in-store and point-of-sale materials.

Finally, there is the ever-important issue of cost and available budget. Price reduction promotions used to shift stock are best handled with minimum extra costs, so promotional information is likely to be simple and informative point-of-sale or window signage. Planned special offers or limited editions that require a sizeable awareness campaign with possible advertising or PR support will have significant costs that must be budgeted for. There may, however, be cooperative partners or tie-ins that could extend the scope of the promotion and present the possibility of sharing costs.

Trade sales promotions

Much of the focus within fashion is on retail and the end-consumer, but business-to-business (B2B) trade and promotions are very important aspects of the industry. It is common practice for companies to offer promotions, such as discounts or extended payment terms, to business consumers as an incentive to purchase or place forward orders. Many companies offer special promotions at trade exhibitions, fairs or conferences to encourage customers on to a stand and to place orders at the show. It is also usual to provide incremental price reductions for purchasing higher volumes. Free point-of-sale materials in the form of literature, display visuals or swing tickets with product information may also be offered by manufacturers as part of the deal. Negotiations might also take place to discuss the possibility of cooperative advertising between the supplier and a retailer, perhaps as a special campaign to promote a new product, fabric or garment technology. Promotional schemes can be used to develop an ongoing relationship with a customer, or can be tailored to match the requirements of a specific customer. A promotional offer might help to finally close a sale with a customer who is wavering. Once again, it is important to consider the overall objectives of the company and its reasons for being at a fair or trade event, and to ensure that promotions are fair and ethical.

Direct marketing

The aim of direct marketing is to establish a direct link between the business and the end-consumer. It might not be considered as high profile as advertising, but it can be cost-effective and more easily controlled from within the company. Direct marketing covers such promotional activities as:

» Direct mail via post or email

» Mail-order catalogues

» Text-message alerts

» Magazine inserts

To carry out direct marketing, a company must have a customer database (although this is not necessary for magazine inserts). That is why brands offer a discount to sign up to a newsletter, or encourage customers to join a loyalty programme or voucher club. Once the customers are signed up, the brand can connect with them by email, text message or social media. Also of importance are purchases made online, since as part of the process the customer's information is automatically added to the database. Brochures or catalogues can be enclosed with monthly store card statements or sent out to customers who have ordered online. Magazine inserts are beneficial in communicating with potential customers who are not yet on the database; although not targeted at a specific person, they can be directed at the readership of particular magazines or newspapers. Uniqlo, for example, placed a ten-page insert in the weekend colour supplement of a major UK newspaper. The insert was used primarily to promote the Spring/Summer 2009 menswear collection, but it also informed readers that Uniqlo was due to open in Selfridges in February 2009, gave a useful list of all its other UK stores, and promoted exclusive offers and 'first chance to buy' opportunities online.

Direct marketing is also effective in B2B situations. Companies can send out new-season catalogues to existing trade customers, or send email information and updates. A business could pay to have

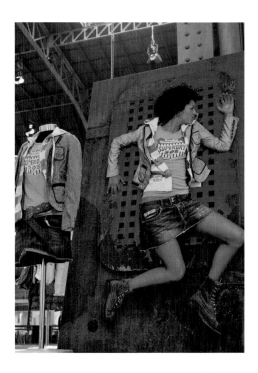

↑ A trade stand for the UK brand Superdry. Fashion brands that sell wholesale must market and promote their merchandise to the many fashion buyers who visit the fair. It is standard practice to offer discounts on larger orders if placed during the fair. This acts as an incentive to the buyer to place an order there and then, rather than leave the stand and perhaps purchase from a competitor brand. Trade discounts are usually incremental; in other words, the discount offered increases in line with the size of the order.

an insert placed in an industry paper or magazine, or carry out direct mailing. The London Edge trade fair, for example, sends out mailings to 30,000 international buyers to encourage them to visit the show.

Email marketing

Email marketing is one form of direct marketing. Emails can be sent to welcome a new customer if they have signed up to receive a newsletter or other service, for example. They can also be sent to alert an existing customer to a sales promotion or special offer, to invite them to an event, to share brand content with them, or to check in after a purchase.

It is important to consider the subject line carefully. You want the receiver to *want* to open it. Ensure that there is an engaging image that can be seen easily at the top of the message. Keep it clear and punchy to get your message across. Make sure there is a clear call to action and link to the appropriate place on your website when they click through.

Email marketing is reasonably cost-effective, since this is a channel already owned by the business and they have control over the content and messaging. HubSpot states that 79 per cent of marketers list email as one of their top three most effective marketing channels. Email is also highly targeted, since the marketer can select exactly who they want to send an email to. It is possible to see how many people opened the emails and how many clicked on any links or used a special offer code, so results are easily tracked and measured. Data from the email marketing platform Mailchimp shows that the average open rate for email is 20 per cent and the click-through rate 3 per cent. Email is also good for building a relationship with the customer. The main hurdle is to acquire the customers' email addresses in the first place. To summarize the benefits:

» Email marketing is highly measurable

» It is easy to create targeted messages

» It allows personalized messaging direct to the inbox

» Content can be highly branded

» It is suitable for informing and engaging in a range of purposes, such as events, product launches and competitions

Fashion PR and publicity

PR and publicity are a vital component of the fashion promotional mix. The overall aim of PR is to get media coverage and establish and generate a favourable image of an organization, brand or fashion label. Positive publicity and well-handled PR have a great advantage for fashion companies; not only do they have the potential to enrich the image, kudos or reputation of the company or brand, but also they can be cheaper than some forms of advertising. The rise of social media has lessened the division between advertising and PR and resulted in an increase in the number of agencies that handle both social-media advertising and online PR communications.

Depending on the requirement and the size of a company, it is possible to handle publicity and PR in-house. Small companies with low budgets may find they can manage most of the day-to-day aspects of publicity themselves via their website and social media. They may consider appointing a freelance PR person to help them get coverage in the press or to handle special projects or events. Large companies may employ a specialist PR or social-media agency, or they may be able to afford to run their own dedicated PR or press department. Some companies use outside PR agencies and employ a communications manager to oversee projects and liaise with the agency.

Basic PR techniques

The following section looks at a selection of basic techniques employed by fashion PR: celebrity endorsement, celebrity seeding, product placement, events and product launches, fashion shows and press days.

Celebrity endorsement and social-media influencers

Employing a celebrity to become the 'face' of a brand or campaign is a technique used by an increasing number of the world's most prestigious or high-profile fashion brands. Over the years a vast array of famous personalities from the worlds of film and music have signed deals to promote branded fashion, accessories, cosmetics and perfume. Beyoncé was the face of H&M, Rihanna featured in an Armani jeans campaign, and Lara Stone did the same for Calvin Klein Jeans. In 2023 the American actor Jenna Ortega from the Netflix series *Wednesday* (2022–) became the face of the Dior fragrance Gris Dior. In 2022 the British actor Jude Law and his son Raff Law became brand ambassadors for the Italian menswear brand Brioni. The duo, who are deemed to embody the elegance and class of

↑ Milla Jovovich presents a Tommy Hilfiger limited-edition bag in a window advertisement at the Coin store in Milan, Italy. The advert combines image and text to deliver its message.

When designing an advert or campaign, determine what will make it distinctive and how it will attract the consumer's attention. It is essential to decide on the message and understand how it will be relevant and meaningful to consumers. Will the advert provide a talking point, have a story to tell, communicate ideas directly or work more obliquely through a visual subtext? Should a celebrity be linked with the campaign, and will the budget allow this? Also consider the skills that might be required and the personnel needed; will there be a need for a stylist, photographer, art director or film director, or will a fashion illustrator have to be commissioned?

the brand, starred in a campaign shot by the fashion photographer Craig McDean. Other male celebrity endorsements include Garrett Hedlund as the face of Yves Saint Laurent's fragrance La Nuit de l'Homme, Romeo Beckham for Burberry, and Justin Bieber becoming a global style icon for Adidas.

The aim of celebrity endorsement is that the cachet and sparkle of the celebrity personality become directly associated with the brand, and that this reinforces the brand's image and position in the marketplace. It is crucial to choose the right celebrity. The Davie-Brown Index developed by the talent division of Davie Brown Entertainment helps advertising agencies and brands assess the suitability of a celebrity. Access to this system of evaluation costs a considerable sum, but if it is viewed as a percentage of the payment the celebrity receives, the actual cost could be considered relatively small. The index has eight criteria on which the celebrity is scored, and the result is analysed using a sophisticated database. The eight criteria are: appeal, notice, influence, trust, endorsement, trendsetting, aspiration and awareness. They are worth considering even without the addition of complicated number crunching or analysis, since they help to illuminate the essential factors that establish a celebrity's suitability to become a brand ambassador.

Appeal and notice relate to the celebrity's popularity, appeal and ubiquity within their specialist field and the media. Influence, trust and endorsement act as a measure of how strong the celebrity might be as a spokesperson or icon of the brand. Trendsetting and aspiration are concerned with how consumers might aspire to have the trendsetting lifestyle of the celebrity in question. Consumer awareness of the celebrity is, of course, essential for the endorsement to be effective.

The choice of celebrity can be varied and surprising. Gucci under Alessandro Michele featured the American rappers A$AP Rocky and Tyler, the Creator, and the music legend Iggy Pop as stars for the men's tailoring campaign in 2020. In 2022 Coach partnered with the hip-hop artist Lil Nas X. The campaign for that collection was entitled 'Courage to Be Real'. A statement on the Coach website said this was 'A call to action and belief in courageous self-expression. Because when you embrace every side of yourself with confidence, you inspire others to express themselves authentically, too.'

Celebrity seeding or celebrity product placement

The cult of celebrity and its relationship to the world of fashion is becoming increasingly important within fashion PR. Many agencies have had to add a dedicated celebrity division to handle 'buzz press', which refers to the new speed at which agencies have to pump out stories concerning a brand's links with celebrities or what clothing or accessory brands famous personalities are wearing. One consequence of all this interest in celebrities is the PR activity known as **celebrity seeding** or celebrity product placement. As we have seen, celebrity product placement occurs when a celebrity signs a contract to become the face of a brand. Seeding, on the other hand, is when a designer or brand loans or donates product to a celebrity so that they will be seen wearing the brand's products. This is usually handled via a PR agency. The aim of celebrity endorsement is, of course, to choose a suitable celeb with a personality and reputation that enhance the brand's status. Usually this is someone who is regularly in the public eye, has a large social-media following, and posts 'selfies' wearing the brand's products or is constantly snapped by the paparazzi; the result should be massive coverage on social media and in the press.

Product placement

A company can raise awareness of its brand and products by having them featured in a film, television show, music video or digital game. Known as product placement, this form of promotion can generate considerable desire for a particular product. One of the most notable examples of fashion product placement was in the *Sex and the City* (SATC) television show and films. The first movie, which came out in May 2008, featured clothing by Vivienne Westwood, Prada, Jimmy Choo, Louis Vuitton, Christian Lacroix and Chanel, to name but a few. The shoe designers Manolo Blahnik and Jimmy Choo became household names after their products first featured in the show. The association between the Blahnik and SATC brands became so integral to the concept that a link to the Blahnik website was included on the SATC movie website.

Product placement can have a dramatic effect on sales, as was evidenced when the movie *The Queen* was released in the United States in 2006. Immediately after the film opened in New York, visitor numbers at the Barbour by Peter Elliot store on Madison Avenue increased dramatically, as did demand for two classic Barbour jackets, the 'Beaufort' and 'Liddesdale', worn by Helen Mirren when she portrayed Queen Elizabeth II.

Product placement provides an important revenue stream for film financing, although companies do not always have to pay to have their products showcased. Karl Lagerfeld provided two custom-made white bouclé wool Chanel jackets with navy trim for Cate Blanchett to wear in the Woody Allen film *Blue Jasmine* (2013). The costume designer Sandy Powell collaborated with Armani to create the power

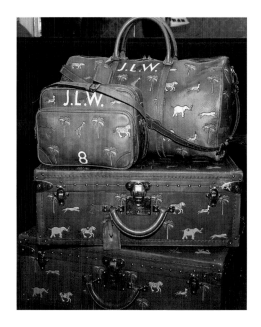

↑ This set of Louis Vuitton luggage featured in the Wes Anderson movie *The Darjeeling Limited* (2007). The luggage was designed by Marc Jacobs with the help of Anderson's brother Eric, who created the distinctive jungle pattern that decorated the surface of the cases. Not only did the luggage feature in the film, but also it became the centrepiece of a window display at the Louis Vuitton store in New York.

suit worn by Leonardo DiCaprio in Martin Scorsese's *The Wolf of Wall Street* the same year. In both cases, the outfits became talking points and were much written and blogged about.

Concave Brand Tracking is a UK company that provides a data-driven measure of how often and in what way brands are portrayed in entertainment. Featured at number eight on its list of top ten product placements in film for 2021 was the Panther Vision Powercap worn by Timothée Chalamet in *Don't Look Up*. The cap, with the brand name prominently featured, gained nearly five minutes of screen time. With an audience of 230 million worldwide, Concave Brand Tracking calculated this to be US$22.5 million in exposure. The firm also gives data on dark glasses by the British designer Tom Davies. These gained 15 minutes of screen time in *The Matrix Resurrections* (2021). All the main cast wore them, including Keanu Reeves and Carrie-Ann Moss. Tom Davies's glasses were also prominent in Disney's *Cruella* in the same year, again gaining 15 minutes of airtime worth US$31 million.

Special events

Special events can be designed to suit a variety of situations, including:

> » Product launches
>
> » Charity events
>
> » Sponsorship events
>
> » Fashion seminars and style clinics
>
> » Fashion shows
>
> » Private shopping evenings
>
> » Designer guest appearances

Special events can be aimed either at the press, industry professionals and business customers, or at the end-consumer. They are organized by a PR agency or an in-house events office or press office. With product launches, the product need not be apparel or accessories, but could be a trade initiative. For example, in 2008 an evening drinks event was held in a prestigious hotel in the centre of Colombo, Sri Lanka, to promote the Apparel South Asia Conference and two trade exhibitions, the Apparel Industry Suppliers Exhibition and the Fabric and Accessory Suppliers Exhibition. Another example is the Hermès Festival des Métiers in 2011–13. This travelling exhibition toured cities in China, Europe and the United States, giving visitors a chance to meet and watch artisans as they crafted Hermès leather goods, jewellery and watches. Special events aimed

Luxury fashion houses are continually searching for novel ways to create experiences and engage an audience. Gucci has presented two interactive touring exhibitions: 'Gucci Garden Archetypes' in 2021, to celebrate its centenary, and 'Gucci Cosmos' in 2023.

← 'Gucci Garden Archetypes' presented past Gucci campaigns set in a series of themed rooms and corridors. Here, the Gucci Beauty lipstick campaign #GucciBeautyNetwork, featuring the punk singer Dani Miller, is presented as a multi-screen installation.

↙ Visitors to the 'Gucci Garden Archetypes' exhibition in Shanghai take selfies in front of a feature wall.

at end-consumers can be used to draw in new customers, offer something engaging and extra-special, reward loyal customers, or promote sales or specific designers and brands. On top of this, many special events include a charitable element, such as a percentage from sales made at the event going to a not-for-profit organization.

At London Fashion Week in September 2023 *Vogue* held its Vogue World event. The entire net ticket proceeds were dedicated to supporting the performing arts in the United Kingdom, including the National Theatre, the Royal Opera House, the Royal Ballet and the Rambert dance company. The Vogue World concept had debuted the previous year in New York City with a high-fashion parade down West 13th Street, featuring the tennis legend Serena Williams, the dancer Mikhail Baryshnikov, 112 models, and performances from

Lil Nas X, plus marathon runners and drum majorettes. According to *Vogue*, there was a street party with cookies provided by Gucci, sandwiches from Michael Kors x Katz's Deli, and baguettes by Fendi.

Organizing a special event will require a press release, announcements via social media and, if necessary, invitations to be sent to potential guests.

Press days and press write-ups

PR agencies and in-house press offices organize press days to showcase next season's collections to the fashion press. Magazines work on long lead times, so press days are held well in advance of the season so that editors can request samples from designers and start developing ideas for fashion shoots and editorial. Press days can be held to promote trade fairs or a group of designers; the British Fashion Council, for example, held a press event to promote Estethica, its trade initiative for sustainable fashion, showcasing 23 ethical labels. Press events can also be held to launch a new brand or product, or to announce the appointment of a celebrity brand ambassador.

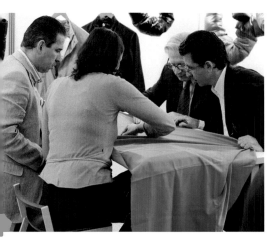

↑ Fabric buyers meet face to face with sales representatives from a textile company at Première Vision.

Personal selling

The last element of the Promotional Mix, personal selling refers to promotional or sales activities that take place face to face. There are two key interfaces for personal selling in the fashion industry. The first, most obviously, is in-store, where sales personnel interact directly with customers. The customer experience in-store can be a make-or-break factor in terms of whether customers purchase or not, so this element of personal selling is vital. This topic was discussed in Chapter 1 in terms of 'process' within the marketing mix (see pages 28–29). That concept views the entire process of purchasing from the consumer's point of view, of which personal selling is a part. Many boutique owners know their customers intimately; they often purchase items directly from design houses and fashion retailers with a specific customer in mind and call their most loyal customers to inform them that they have an item especially for them. There is a report of a personal stylist ordering three Balenciaga cocktail dresses priced around £3,000 each for her various clients at a Harrods pre-season trunk show.

The other important area for personal selling is in B2B situations. Much of the global fashion and textile industry operates at manufacturing and wholesale level, requiring sales representatives and agents to foster and develop profitable business relationships

Bringing the brand to life

FASHION EVENT ILLUSTRATION

One way to bring a brand to life and engage customers is to hold a live fashion illustration event, or invite illustrators to draw behind the scenes or from the front row at a fashion show. The British fashion illustrator Jo Bird has had many commissions from fashion brands. For Red Valentino, she was invited to work in Valentino stores in London, Rome and Milan. The loyal customers and influencers invited to the event were encouraged to dress up in the collection, and had their picture hand-drawn by Bird. Each customer who participated was allowed to take home their unique illustration, or, as Jo liked to call them, 'style portrait'. The illustration served as a nice memento of the event and encouraged the customer to forge a deeper connection with the brand. Bird says, 'It was a dream job to work on!' She loves working in watercolour but is also happy to draw using a tablet and i-pencil. Her other fashion clients include Tory Burch, Ralph Lauren, Chanel, Kate Spade, Liberty and Harrods.

Connie Lim, who is from Los Angeles but currently living in London is another professional fashion illustrator and designer. She also illustrates at fashion shows and live events, and has managed to merge her two loves – illustration and fashion design – to create unique, striking images with a strong personal vision. Lim's fashion and beauty clients include Guerlain, Bulgari, Louboutin, Alexander McQueen and Revlon. Her illustration work has featured in several publications, including *The Illustrator: 100 Best from Around the World* (2019), edited by Steven Heller and Julius Wiedemann.

↙↓ Connie Lim drawing live, and her illustrations for VIP clients at the Alexander McQueen store on Bond Street, London.

↖↑ Jo Bird's illustrations of customers wearing the latest designs for the Red Valentino Pre-Spring collection, along with the invitation to the Valentino Red event.

It's Never Too Late:
A brand product launch event

ADIDAS NITE JOGGER

The Midnight Club, a creative agency based in Shoreditch, east London, was briefed by the team at Adidas to create a launch event for the brand's Nite Jogger (2019). This new silhouette was based on the original product from 1977, the first sports shoe to feature reflective 3M material for visibility at night. A team of concept leads and event producers were responsible for devising the whole concept and orchestrating the build. A celebration of all night-time activity, the concept was centred on a pop-up petrol station in Peckham, south London. On arrival, guests received their own currency, which they could spend on experiences during the night, including sneaker customization in the late-night internet café, airbrushing Adidas apparel in the mechanics' garage, and developing film photographs in the custom-built darkroom. The project was turned around in just 15 days, from briefing, initial brainstorming, moodboards and rough sketches, to location-scouting and 3D renders, followed by a rigorous production schedule and budget management leading up to the live date.

The results? Positive traction for the brand, and full attendance by the target Gen Z audience, wholesale partners and VIP talent.

↗ Scenes from the Adidas Nite Jogger product launch in 2019, produced by the creative agency The Midnight Club.

with appropriate buyers. Personal selling occurs at a variety of industry trade fairs for fabric, trimmings, apparel, accessories and other industry resources. Fibre manufacturers must sell their products to textile manufacturers, who in turn need to capture the imagination of, and sell fabrics to, fashion designers and retailers. Each of these businesses will use personal selling as a key promotional tool.

The advantage of B2B personal selling is that it affords customers a high level of personal attention. Sales representatives can tailor their message and information to suit specific customers. Personal selling presents the opportunity to build a long-term business relationship, offer good technical advice and background information on products and services, and solve the numerous problems that occur within fashion design, manufacturing, supply and retail.

Creating campaigns

As with all aspects of marketing, thorough research, planning and clarity of purpose are essential when developing a promotional initiative or large campaign. The first step in the planning process is to set objectives. Is the purpose to inform about something specific, such as a sale, special promotion or product launch? Is it to maintain brand awareness and keep the brand in consumers' consciousness? Or is it to persuade a new target audience to adopt the brand? Will it be first and foremost an advertising campaign, or will it include sales promotion, require PR or have any direct selling components?

It is also essential to identify the target audience or audiences, understanding their behaviours, needs and wants, so that the right choice of media channel or social-media platform can be made. It is important to weigh up the advantages and disadvantages each channel or platform offers. For example, for a D2C fashion brand that wants a highly visual campaign, Instagram, Facebook or Pinterest might be suitable. TikTok, on the other hand, would be a better fit for a brand that wants to attract a young audience and share its sense of fun via video advertising. Aligned to the choice of media are decisions on the tone of voice and the exact messaging for each advert or communication within the campaign, as well as its style and content. It will also be necessary to calculate a budget and decide if the campaign can be carried out in-house or if an agency must be appointed. A simple advert or direct email campaign might be handled in-house on a limited budget. For a multimedia campaign, the brand will need a large in-house team or require the services of a specialist advertising or social-media agency.

In summary, the steps of the planning process are:

> » Set campaign objectives
>
> » Determine strategy and tactics
>
> » Identify suitable channels and media platforms
>
> » Decide who will devise the campaign
>
> » Set budget and time frame
>
> » Confirm who will create the content
>
> » Confirm content, style and advertising or communication message
>
> » Decide on and confirm appropriate talent for the campaign, if required

» Set key performance indicators (KPIs) and agree what measures will be used to gauge effectiveness

» Launch campaign

» Review success and return on investment (ROI)

Each advert or campaign should be considered with reference to the following:

Target audience Which media are most suitable to attract the desired consumers

Reach or coverage The total number of people or unique users online who have seen a piece of digital content or an advert, or have been exposed to an advert over a specific period

Frequency How many times the people see the advert. For example, if the reach is 100 people and there were 200 impressions, the frequency would be 2, with the assumption that everyone saw the advert twice

Impressions The total number of times an advert is viewed, regardless of whether it was viewed by the same user several times

Impact Which media or combination of media will provide the most impact when targeting specific audiences

Exposure The total amount of time (in milliseconds) an advert is seen by users on a website, app or social-media platform

Measuring effectiveness

Measuring the effectiveness of an advertising or promotional campaign is important to determine the extent to which a campaign has met its objectives and ascertain whether the financial investment has been worthwhile. It is not always easy to gauge results. There may be several criteria by which the campaign can be evaluated in terms of its ability to:

» Stimulate an increase in sales

» Build brand awareness

» Change consumer image and perception of a brand and product

» Target new consumers

» Increase customer loyalty

Sales increases may result from a combination of factors, such as pricing compared to competitors, or whether the product is also available online. The campaign could trend on social media, or a celebrity seen wearing the brand might boost sales. Product placement in a popular TV show or film could also create demand. Determining if an advertising campaign has increased consumer awareness requires research to test consumer awareness before and after a campaign; similarly, detailed consumer analysis will be required to determine if an ad campaign was effective in changing consumer image of the brand. Measuring a campaign also depends on the medium used. There are several metrics by which the effectiveness of an advertising campaign can be measured:

Cost per thousand Used for print and digital advertising, and can be abbreviated to CPT or, more usually, CPM (which stands for cost per mille, *mille* being Latin for a thousand). CPM is the average cost of reaching 1,000 of the target audience. This is calculated by taking the total cost of advertising, dividing by the number of impressions and multiplying by 1,000 (CPM = cost/impressions × 1,000). The cost of a full-page colour advert in American *Vogue* varies depending on its position within the magazine, but it will be upwards of US$100,000. To calculate the CPM, divide the cost by the circulation number and multiply by 1,000. So if the circulation were 1.2 million, the CPM would be just over US$83 per thousand. If a website publisher charges US$2 CPM, that would mean that an advertiser pays US$2 for every thousand impressions of its advert.

Return on advertising spend (ROAS) A metric that measures revenue earned per dollar spent on advertising. ROAS can be calculated for a single ad, a one-off campaign, a regular monthly campaign or an entire year. To calculate it, the revenue attributed to the ad campaign is divided by the cost of the campaign. For example, if the income achieved through a campaign is calculated to be US$10,000 and the cost of the campaign was US$2,000, the ratio is 5:1, meaning that for every dollar spent, five were returned. This can also be represented as a return of 500 per cent. The challenge is working out exactly what revenue was achieved as a direct result of the advert or advertising campaign. This requires access to data that shows how to attribute the value of the sales to the specific advert or campaign. Advertising agencies and social-media agencies can help with this.

Advertising impacts Used to measure the impact of an advert. For film, TV or radio, it refers to the total number of separate occasions when the commercial is viewed or heard by a target audience. If an advertising campaign airs 100 times over four months and each time the advert is on air it achieves an average of one million viewers, the campaign can be said to have received 100 million impacts, with a monthly impact of 25 million.

The clip report The traditional method of monitoring the number of press articles (called press clippings) published as a result of a PR campaign. Clip reports give details of which publications covered the story, the topic of the article published and the circulation of the publication. Measuring the number of column inches printed can refine this information.

Advertising value equivalent (AVE) Measures the benefit to a client of a PR campaign. AVE compares the cost of the column inches printed with how much the equivalent space would have cost as advertising.

Share of voice Compares a company's press results with those of its main competitors and determines who got the most coverage.

Opportunity to see (OTS) A traditional metric for measuring a multimedia campaign. It represents the frequency of exposure of an advert. Average OTS gives a figure to indicate how many people from a target audience had an opportunity to see, hear or read an advert. OTS is a rather blunt instrument, since it calculates only 'opportunities' to see, rather than the exact number of people who actually see an advert. Also, it does not compare like with like – viewing an advert as a film or video is different from seeing it as a static print advert in a magazine. **Gross OTS** is a cumulative figure for a campaign, derived from adding results from different adverts within the campaign and from the various media, such as TV, cinema, magazines, internet and outdoor channels. OTS figures were originally gathered using surveys, face-to-face interviews and self-reporting, such as diaries kept by members of the target audience. Now sophisticated digital tools are used by tracking companies, such as the global firm Nielsen.

Media Impact Value™ (MIV®) A proprietary algorithm owned by Launchmetrics. On its website Launchmetrics states that the algorithm is used to 'measure and benchmark the impact of all media placements and mentions across different Voices in the Fashion, Luxury, and Beauty industries'. This means that it is possible to compare the impact for each post shared across print, online and social-media channels so that 'brands can view (in monetary terms) the buzz generated by celebrities and influencers wearing their creations, and compare the success of strategies from one market to another.' Launchmetrics publishes useful articles and reports on its website; one, for example, explains that in 2020 the company used MIV® to highlight the top social posts in China, Europe and the United States. For Europe, 'the top social publication by MIV® was Millie Bobby Brown's Instagram post for Moncler which accumulated US$1.4m MIV® from October to December 2020.'

After reading this book you will have some insight into the theory
and practice of fashion marketing, branding and promotion. Many
aspects of these disciplines are interrelated and highly specialized,
but they still constitute a fascinating element of fashion. It is
a rapidly changing field that plays a key strategic role in shaping
the creative impetus at the heart of this challenging, ever-evolving
industry. An understanding of these principles provides a crucial
framework for the commercial basis of fashion, as well as the ethical
and sustainable requirements for its future.

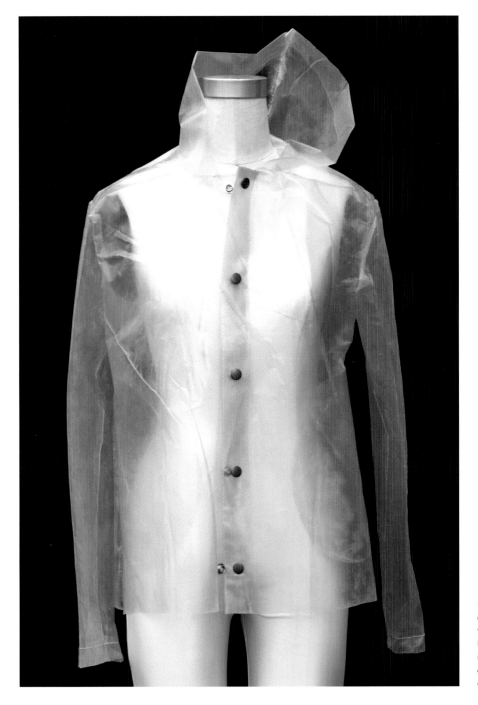

← A carbon-negative raincoat made with
an algae-based plastic material. The 'fabric'
was developed in the lab of Charlotte
McCurdy, an award-winning designer and
researcher who works at the intersection
of emerging technology, futures and
existential threats.

References

1: Marketing Theory

page 7, Philip Kotler: *FAQs on Marketing*, Marshall Cavendish Business, 2008

8, Philip Kotler: *Principles of Marketing*, Financial Times/Prentice Hall, 2008

9, Martin Butler: *People Don't Buy What You Sell: They Buy What You Stand For*, Management Books 2000 Ltd, 2005

10, Seth Godin: *Purple Cow*, Penguin Books, 2005

12, 'Exactitudes': www.exactitudes.com

15, Mark Hughes: *Buzzmarketing: Get People to Talk about Your Stuff*, Portfolio, 2005

17, Neil H. Borden: 'The Concept of the Marketing Mix', *Journal of Advertising Research*, Cambridge University Press, 1964
    Theodore Levitt: *The Marketing Imagination*, Free Press, 1986

24, Joseph DeAcetis: www.forbes.com/sites/josephdeacetis/2021/04/07/the-new-face-of-seersucker-cool

32, Robert F. Lauterborn: 'New Marketing Litany: Four Ps Passé, C-words Take Over', *Advertising Age* 61/41 (1990), p. 26

33, Anne Lise Kjaer: www.kjaer-global.com/wp-content/uploads/2019/02/02_19-PURE-The-Future-is-Now-Kjaer-Global_.pdf

33–4, Olga Mitterfellner: *Fashion Marketing and Communication: Theory and Practice across the Fashion Industry*, Routledge, 2020

34, Mark Ritson: www.marketingweek.com/mark-ritson-stop-reinventing-four-ps

38, Butler: as above
    Al Ries and Jack Trout: *Positioning: The Battle for Your Mind*, McGraw-Hill Professional, 2001. The concept of positioning was developed by Ries and Trout and first took hold in 1972 with a series of articles entitled 'The Positioning Era', published in *Advertising Age*.

2: The Fashion Market

page 47, Sinéad Burke: quoted in www.theguardian.com/fashion/2023/apr/25/i-have-an-invisible-disability-myself-edward-enninful-and-sinead-burke-on-their-fashion-revolution

59, Srishti Kapoor: www.appareIresources.com/business-news/retail/rise-gender-neutral-segment-fashion
    www.businessoffashion.com/articles/retail/the-state-of-fashion-2023-report-gender-neutral-fluid-fashion-gen-z-consumers

60, Umesh Bhagchandani: www.scmp.com/magazines/style/celebrity/article/3220352/meet-xin-liu-diors-androgynous-new-brand-ambassador-chinese-pop-star-shot-fame-through-girl-band

61, *The National*: www.thenationalnews.com/lifestyle/fashion/fashion-forward-dubai-shop-what-you-see-on-the-runway-1.860217

62, British Fashion Council report: 'Direct-to-Consumer: A New Model for British Fashion?', June 2019, www.britishfashioncouncil.co.uk/uploads/files/1/Direct to Consumer.pdf

71, Amy de Klerk: www.harpersbazaar.com/uk/fashion/fashion-news/a36810362/secondhand-clothing-boom
    www.fashionunited.uk/news/business/online-fashion-rental-market-to-grow-over-10-percent-annually/2021111859406

73–4, Elizabeth Paton: www.nytimes.com/2022/09/30/fashion/fashion-laws-regulations.html

76, Ellen MacArthur Foundation: www.ellenmacarthurfoundation.org

77, Good on You: www.goodonyou.eco

80, *Sourcing Journal*: www.sourcingjournal.com/footwear/footwear-business/coblrshop-footwear-repair-cobblers-artificial-intelligence-secondhand-resale-uber-441698
    United Nations Environment Programme: www.unep.org/resources/publication/sustainable-fashion-communication-playbook, 19 June 2023

81, www.scmp.com/magazines/style/celebrity/article/3220986/inside-angelina-jolies-new-fashion-collective-atelier-jolie-former-un-reps-project-allows-customers

3: Research & Planning

page 85, Faith Popcorn: Faith Popcorn's Brain Reserve, www.faithpopcorn.com. Faith Popcorn is a futurist and author of *The Popcorn Report*.

86, Philip Kotler: cited in G. Lancaster and P. Reynolds, *Management of Marketing*, Butterworth-Heinemann, 2005

97, Douglas Cordeaux: *Mail on Sunday*, 5 November 2012. Fox Brothers is a British manufacturer of woollen, worsted, cashmere and flannel cloth.

102, Brian Wilson: www.stornowaygazette.co.uk/business/the-queen-of-fashion-and-a-tale-of-two-orbs-3978494

104, Nordstrom/Mango: www.reuters.com/business/retail-consumer/retailers-lose-love-asia-snarled-supply-chains-force-manufacturing-exodus-2021-11-09

110, Stuart Rose: quoted in Patti Waldmeir, 'M&S Admits Shanghai Errors', *Financial Times*, 9 February 2009, www.ft.com/content/2bac61ae-f6e2-11dd-8a1f-0000779fd2ac

115, Bain & Company: www.bain.com/insights/the-future-of-luxury-bouncing-back-from-covid-19

117, Ganni: http://fashionunited.in/news/retail/ganni-expands-into-china-with-tmall/2021061629420

118: www.goodonyou.eco/degrowth-the-future-fashion

118–19, Lauren Rees: www.fashionrevolution.org/degrowth-in-the-fashion-industry

119, Bella Webb: www.voguebusiness.com/sustainability/degrowth-the-future-that-fashion-has-been-looking-for

4: Understanding the Customer

page 137, Erdem Moralıoğlu: quoted in *Elle* magazine, 2007

139, *Women's Wear Daily*: www.wwd.com/fashion-news/fashion-features/gen-z-wants-two-way-communication-with-brands-product-co-creation-1203377198

143, Norstat: www.the7stars.co.uk/original-misunderstood-generation

145, Bosanquet and Gibbs: www.bl.uk/collection-items/class-of-2005-the-ipod-generation–insecure-pressured-overtaxed-and-debtridden
    Fitch: www.slideshare.net/FITCH_design/gen-z-fitch

146, UNiDAYS: https://corporate.myunidays.com/fashion-report-2021
    Vogue Business: www.voguebusiness.com/consumers/gen-z-shopping-trends-uncovered-pay-pal
    Karen Reyes: bookstr.com/article/dark-academia-how-the-genre-turned-into-a-subculture

147, Paige Leskin: www.businessinsider.com/e-girls-definition-tiktok-e-boys-anti-influencer-teen-gamers-2019-9

148, Hugh Fletcher: www.wundermanthompson.com/insight/gen-alpha-how-children-shop-differently
    Nidhi Pandurang: www.businessinsider.com/young-adults-living-home-luxury-boom-usa-morgan-stanley-2022-12
    Dan Latu and Kelsey Neubauer: www.businessinsider.com/gen-z-millennials-live-at-home-to-buy-luxury-items-2023-2

156, David C. Edelman: www.hbr.org/2010/12/branding-in-the-digital-age-youre-spending-your-money-in-all-the-wrong-places

165, Joan Kennedy: www.businessoffashion.com/articles/luxury/where-did-luxurys-aspirational-shoppers-go

170, Hannah Jennings: information taken from Khabi Mirza, 'Portas Says Future Is Bright for UK's Indies', *Drapers*, 24 November 2007

5: Introduction to Branding

page 182, Allen Adamson, chairman of Landor Associates North America: www.landor.com

185, Walter Loeb: www.forbes.com/sites/walterloeb/2022/05/09/private-labels-are-flooding-retail

194, Chitose Abe: www.anothermag.com/fashion-beauty/7448/sacai-a-brand-of-feminist-empowerment

197, Elizabeth Schofield: posted in an article by Kayla Hutzler on *Luxury Daily* (www.luxurydaily.com), July 2011

6: Fashion Promotion

page 213: This famous quotation is usually attributed to John Wanamaker, who opened Philadelphia's first department store, Wanamaker's, in the second half of the nineteenth century. He developed the first ever copyrighted store advertisements in 1874.

215, Piers Butel: www.mintel.com/retail-market-news/is-digital-live-streaming-the-future-of-fashion-shows

223, Yiling Pan: www.jingdaily.com/dolce-gabbana-racism
    Tiffany Ap: www.wwd.com/feature/ynap-retailers-distance-dolce-gabbana-china-1202911885
    Danya Issawi: www.thecut.com/article/what-to-know-about-the-balenciaga-ad-scandal.html

223–4, Nike lawsuit: www.thefashionlaw.com/nike-deceptively-markets-sustainable-wares-per-new-lawsuit

225–6, Danny Parisi: www.glossy.co/fashion/fashion-brands-are-experimenting-with-linear-and-connected-tv-advertising

226, James Davey: www.reuters.com/business/retail-consumer/retail-media-ad-revenue-forecast-surpass-tv-by-2028-2023-06-12

227, Nielsen: www.meadowoutdoor.com/assets/deeper_reading/Nielsen-OAAA-Digital-OOH-Advertising-Report-2020.pdf
    Business of Fashion: www.businessoffashion.com/articles/media/a-survival-strategy-for-fashion-magazines

229, Kepios: www.datareportal.com/social-media-users
    Statista: www.statista.com/statistics/1254990/united-states-leading-social-networks-apparel-fashion-shopping
    Facebook: https://blog.hootsuite.com/facebook-statistics

231, TikTok Pulse Premiere: https://newsroom.tiktok.com/en-eu/tiktok-announces-new-european-publishers-to-join-pulse-premiere

235–6, Jess Duarte and Stéphanie Thomson: www.thinkwithgoogle.com/intl/en-gb/consumer-insights/consumer-trends/what-fashion-fans-around-the-world-are-searching-for-on-google

237, Jane Zhang: www.scmp.com/tech/e-commerce/article/3107667/alibabas-taobao-live-hits-us75-billion-first-30-minutes-presales

238, Funmi Fetto: www.vogue.co.uk/fashion/article/rihanna-first-durag-british-vogue-cover

240, Rumble Romagnoli: www.thedrum.com/opinion/2021/06/25/are-genuinfluencers-the-new-influencers-niche-and-luxury-brands

256, Hannah Keegan: www.stylist.co.uk/fashion/supreme-streetwear-sell-out-competitive-shopping/251297
    Baya Simons: www.ft.com/content/d8c5e164-c0ca-11e8-8d55-54197280d3f7

Further Reading

Allen P. Adamson. *The Edge: 50 Tips from Brands that Lead*, Palgrave Macmillan, 2013

D. Adcock, A. Halborg, C. Ross. *Marketing: Principles and Practice*, Financial Times/Prentice Hall, 2001

Teri Agins. *The End of Fashion*, HarperCollins, 2000

Michael J. Baker. *The Marketing Book*, Financial Times/Prentice Hall, 2001

Malcolm Barnard. *Fashion as Communication*, Routledge, 2nd edn, 2002

J.A. Bell. *Silent Selling: Best Practices and Effective Strategies in Visual Merchandising*, Fairchild, 2006

Wendy K. Bendoni. *Social Media for Fashion Marketing: Storytelling in a Digital World*, Fairchild, 2017

Sandy Black. *Eco-chic: The Fashion Paradox*, Black Dog Publishing, 2008

——. *The Sustainable Fashion Handbook*, Thames & Hudson, 2012

Ghalia Boustani. *Ephemeral Retailing: Pop-up Stores in a Postmodern Consumption Era*, Routledge, 2019

Evelyn L. Brannon. *Fashion Forecasting: Research, Analysis, and Presentation*, Fairchild, 2nd revised edn, 2005

Michael Braungart and William McDonough. *Cradle to Cradle: Remaking the Way We Make Things*, Vintage, 2009

Martin Butler. *People Don't Buy What You Sell: They Buy What You Stand For*, Management Books 2000 Ltd, 2005

Leslie de Chernatony and Malcolm McDonald. *Creating Powerful Brands*, Butterworth-Heinemann, 3rd edn, 2003

Michel Chevalier and Gerald Mazzalovo. *Luxury Brand Management*, John Wiley & Sons, 2008

Peter Chisnall. *Marketing Research*, McGraw-Hill Education, 2004

Jon Cope and Dennis Maloney. *Fashion Promotion in Practice*, Bloomsbury, 2016

Pamela N. Danziger. *Let Them Eat Cake: Marketing Luxury to the Masses – As Well as the Classes*, Dearborn Trade Publishing, 2005

Scott M. Davis and Michael Dunn. *Building the Brand-driven Business*, Jossey-Bass, 2002

Scott M. Davis and Tina Longoria. 'Harmonizing Your "Touchpoints"', March 2011, http://barradeideas.theobjective.com/wp-content/uploads/2011/03/Harmonizing-Your-Touchpoints.pdf

David C. Edelman and Marc Singer. 'Competing on Customer Journeys', *Harvard Business Review*, xciii/11 (November 2015), p. 88, www.hbr.org/2015/11/competing-on-customer-journeys

Rosie Findlay and Johannes Reponen. *Insights on Fashion Journalism*, Routledge, 2022

Mary Gehlhar. *The Fashion Designer Survival Guide: An Insider's Look at Starting and Running Your Own Fashion Business*, Kaplan Publishing, 2005

Malcolm Gladwell. *The Tipping Point: How Little Things Can Make a Big Difference*, Abacus, 2000

Seth Godin. *Purple Cow: Transform Your Business by Being Remarkable*, Penguin Books, 2005

Julia L. Freer Goldstein and Paul Foulkes-Arellano. *Materials and Sustainability: Building a Circular Future*, Routledge, 2024

Dario Golizia. *The Fashion Business: Theory and Practice in Strategic Fashion Management*, Routledge, 2021

Helen Goworek. *Fashion Buying*, Blackwell Science, 2001

Barbara Graham and Caline Anouti. *Promoting Fashion*, Laurence King, 2018

Kaled K. Hameide. *Fashion Branding Unravelled*, Fairchild, 2011

Joseph Hancock. *Brand/Story: Ralph, Vera, Johnny, Billy, and Other Adventures in Fashion Branding*, Fairchild, 2009

Eric von Hippel. *Democratizing Innovation*, MIT Press, 2005

Jeff Howe. *Crowdsourcing: Why the Power of the Crowd Is Driving the Future of Business*, Crown Business, 2008

Neil Howe and William Strauss. *Millennials Rising*, Vintage Books, 2000

Mark Hughes. *Buzzmarketing: Get People to Talk about Your Stuff*, Portfolio, 2005

Tim Jackson and David Shaw. *Mastering Fashion Buying and Merchandising Management*, Palgrave Macmillan, 2001

—— and David Shaw. *The Fashion Handbook*, Routledge, 2006

Richard M. Jones. *The Apparel Industry*, Blackwell Publishing, 2nd edn, 2006

Sue Jenkyn Jones. *Fashion Design*, Laurence King, 3rd edn, 2011

Jean-Noël Kapferer. *Strategic Brand Management*, The Free Press, 1992

—— and Vincent Bastien. *The Luxury Strategy: Break the Rules of Marketing to Build Luxury Brands*, Kogan Page, 2009

Yuniya Kawamura. *Fashion-ology: An Introduction to Fashion Studies*, Bloomsbury Academic, 2018

Kevin Lane Keller. *Strategic Brand Management*, Prentice Hall, 2003

Philip Kotler. *Marketing Management: Analysis, Planning, Implementation and Control*, Prentice Hall, 1994

——. *FAQs on Marketing*, Marshall Cavendish Business, 2008

—— et al. *Principles of Marketing*, Financial Times/Prentice Hall, 2008

Myles Ethan Lascity. *Communicating Fashion: Clothing, Culture, and Media*, Bloomsbury Visual Arts, 2021

Gaynor Lea-Greenwood. *Fashion Marketing Communications*, John Wiley & Sons, 2013

Suzanne Lee and Warren du Preez. *Fashioning the Future: Tomorrow's Wardrobe*, Thames & Hudson, 2007

Martin Lindstrom. *Buyology: How Everything We Believe about Why We Buy Is Wrong*, Random House Business, 2008

Malcolm McDonald. *On Marketing Planning: Understanding Marketing Plans and Strategy*, Kogan Page, 2007

Naresh K. Malhotra, David F. Birks and Peter Wills. *Marketing Research: An Applied Approach*, Pearson, 4th edn, 2012

Toby Meadows. *How to Set Up and Run a Fashion Label*, Laurence King, 2nd edn, 2012

Geoffrey Miller. *Spent: Sex, Evolution and the Secrets of Consumerism*, William Heinemann, 2009

Safia Minney. *Naked Fashion*, New Internationalist Publications, 2011

Olga Mitterfellner. *Fashion Marketing and Communication: Theory and Practice across the Fashion Industry*, Routledge, 2020

Gwyneth Moore. *Fashion Promotion: Building a Brand through Marketing and Communication*, AVA Publishing, 2012

Tony Morgan. *Visual Merchandising: Window and In-store Displays for Retail*, Laurence King, 2nd edn, 2011

Bethan Morris. *Fashion Illustrator*, Laurence King, 2nd edn, 2010

Uche Okonkwo. *Luxury Fashion Branding: Trends, Tactics, Techniques*, Palgrave Macmillan, 2007

Wally Olins. *Wally Olins: The Brand Handbook*, Thames & Hudson, 2008

Faith Popcorn. *EVEolution: The Eight Truths of Marketing to Women*, HarperCollins Business, 2001

Martin Raymond. *The Trend Forecaster's Handbook*, Laurence King, 2010

Al Ries and Jack Trout. *Positioning: The Battle for Your Mind*, McGraw-Hill Professional, 2001

Everett Rogers. *Diffusion of Innovations*, Free Press, 1995

Lon Safko and David K. Brake. *The Social Media Bible: Tactics, Tools and Strategies for Business Success*, John Wiley & Sons, 2009

Zubin Sethna and Jim Blythe. *Consumer Behaviour*, Sage, 4th edn, 2019

Sophie Sheikh. *The Pocket Guide to Fashion PR*, Preo Publishing, 2009

Michael R. Solomon and Nancy J. Rabolt. *Consumer Behaviour in Fashion*, Prentice Hall, 2008

Michael R. Solomon and Mona Mrad. *Fashion and Luxury Marketing*, Sage Publications, 2022

Don Tapscott. *Grown-up Digital*, McGraw-Hill, 2009

Mark Tungate. *Fashion Brands* [2005], Kogan Page, 3rd edn, 2012

Rosemary Varley. *Retail Product Management*, Routledge, 2002

—— and Mohammed Rafiq. *Principles of Retail Management*, Palgrave Macmillan, 2004

Diana Verde Nieto. *Reimagining Luxury: Building a Sustainable Future for Your Brand*, Kogan Page, 2024

Alina Wheeler. *Designing Brand Identity*, John Wiley & Sons, 4th edn, 2013

Nicola White and Ian Griffiths. *The Fashion Business: Theory, Practice, Image*, Berg, 2000

Judy Zaccagnini and Irene M. Foster. *Research Methods for the Fashion Industry*, Fairchild, 2009

Trade publications, magazines and blogs

10 Magazine	*Flaunt*	*Purple*
Adbusters	*GQ*	*Retail Week*
Advertising Age	*Harper's Bazaar*	*Selvedge*
Adweek	*Highsnobiety*	*Sneaker Freaker*
AnOther	*Hypebeast*	*SOMA*
Auxiliary Magazine	*i-D*	*Sublime*
Dansk	*InStyle*	*VMagazine*
Dazed Digital	*Luncheon*	*Visionaire*
Drapers	*MacGuffin*	*Vogue*
The Economist	*Marketing Week*	*Women's Wear*
Elle	*Numéro*	*Daily* (*WWD*)
Encens	*Nylon*	
Fantastic Man	*L'Officiel*	

Useful addresses

United Kingdom

British Fashion Council www.britishfashioncouncil.com
Provides support to emerging British fashion designers, with schemes ranging from business mentoring and seminars to competitions and sponsorship. Organizes the annual fashion awards and supports initiatives such as estethica, Fashion Forward and NEWGEN.

Fashion Awareness Direct www.fad.org.uk
A charitable organization committed to helping young designers succeed in their careers by bringing students and professionals together at introductory events.

UK Fashion & Textile Association www.ukft.org
Advises members on running a business and supplying clothing and knitwear to the global marketplace.

Walpole www.thewalpole.co.uk
Official membership association for UK luxury.

United States

American Apparel and Footwear Association www.aafaglobal.org
A national trade association representing apparel and footwear companies and their suppliers.

Council of Fashion Designers of America www.cfda.com
A not-for-profit trade association whose membership consists of more than 400 of America's foremost womenswear, menswear, jewellery and accessory designers.

United States Small Business Administration www.sba.gov
Assists with the start-up and development of small businesses.

Marketing, advertising and promotion associations

Advertising Research Foundation www.thearf.org

American Marketing Association www.ama.org

Chartered Institute of Marketing www.cim.co.uk

European Association of Communications Agencies www.eaca.eu

Institute of Direct Marketing www.theidm.com

Institute of Practitioners in Advertising www.ipa.co.uk

Institute for Public Relations www.instituteforpr.org

Institute of Sales Promotion www.theipm.org.uk

Internet Advertising Bureau www.iabuk.net

Licensing International www.licensinginternational.org

World Advertising Research Centre www.warc.com

Trend forecasting and fashion intelligence

BrainReserve (Faith Popcorn) www.faithpopcorn.com

Committee for Colour and Trends www.colourandtrends.com

The Future Laboratory www.thefuturelaboratory.com

Geraldine Wharry www.geraldinewharry.com

Li Edelkoort www.trendunion.com

Nelly Rodi www.nellyrodi.com

Pantone Inc. www.pantone.com

Peclers Paris www.peclersparis.com

Promostyl www.promostyl.com

Trend Atelier www.thetrendatelier.com

Trendstop www.trendstop.com

Trendwatching www.trendwatching.com

WGSN www.wgsn.com

Fashion and textile market and industry information

Business of Fashion (BoF) www.businessoffashion.com

Doneger Tobe www.donegertobe.com

Euromonitor International www.euromonitor.com

Fashion United www.fashionunited.uk

Fibre2fashion www.fibre2fashion.com

Mintel Reports www.mintel.com

Verdict Research www.verdict.co.uk

Marketing, branding, advertising and retail information

Campaign www.campaignlive.co.uk

Fashion Windows www.fashionwindows.com

The Gallup Organization www.gallup.com

Market Research Society www.mrs.org.uk

Prophet www.prophet.com

Retail Week www.retail-week.com

Unity Marketing www.unitymarketingonline.com

Wolff Olins www.wolffolins.com

World Luxury Association www.worldluxuryassociation.org

Sustainability and eco-fashion

Better Cotton Initiative www.bettercotton.org

British Association for Fair Trade Shops and Suppliers www.bafts.org.uk

Common Objective www.commonobjective.co

Eco Fashion World www.ecofashionworld.com

Ellen MacArthur Foundation www.ellenmacarthurfoundation.org

Ethical Trading Initiative www.ethicaltrade.org

Environmental Justice Foundation www.ejfoundation.org

Fair Wear Foundation www.fairwear.org

Fashion Revolution www.fashionrevolution.org/tag/uk; www.fashionrevolution.org/north-america/usa

Futerra www.futerra.co.uk

Global Organic Textile Standard www.global-standard.org

International Labour Organization www.ilo.org

New Economics Foundation www.neweconomics.org

OEKO-TEX www.oeko-tex.com

Pesticide Action Network www.pan-uk.org

Soil Association www.soilassociation.org

The Sustainable Angle www.thesustainableangle.org

Sustainable Cotton www.sustainablecotton.org

United Nations Global Compact www.unglobalcompact.org

World Fair Trade Organization www.wfto.com

Company profiles and data

Dun & Bradstreet www.dnb.co.uk

Census and trade data

UK Office for National Statistics www.statistics.gov.uk

US Census Data www.census.gov

Information on starting a fashion business

Design Trust www.thedesigntrust.co.uk

Fashion Angel www.fashion-angel.co.uk

Fashion Capital www.fashioncapital.co.uk

United States Fashion Industry Association www.usfashionindustry.com

Glossary

Advertising channel The medium by which an advert reaches the public, for example, cinema, magazine, internet or newspaper.

Advertising exposure The length of time an audience is exposed to an advert.

Advertising impacts The total number of separate occasions that a television or radio commercial is viewed or heard by a target audience.

Advertising message The message conveyed by an advert.

Advertising reach The number of people within a target market exposed to an advert over a specific length of time.

Advertising value equivalent (AVE) Measurement to compare the cost-effectiveness of PR against that of advertising.

Brand A **trademark** name that distinguishes a product or brand company from others in the market.

Brand architecture The way a company structures and names its brands.

Brand awareness The number of customers or potential customers with awareness of a particular brand.

Brand equity The extra value to the brand as an asset, contributed by the power of the brand name and any accumulated goodwill towards the brand.

Brand essence The essential nature of a brand; the core or heart of the brand expressed in clear and simple terms.

Brand experience An individual's perception of and response to a brand's action. It can be direct, through the individual's own interaction, or indirect, by the filtering and sharing of the experience of others. All interactions therefore come together to shape the consumer's experience of a brand.

Brand extension Expansion of a brand by developing and selling new products in a broadly similar market. The term 'brand stretching' is used if a brand takes its name into a very different, unrelated market.

Brand identity The elements of a brand that define its identity, for example, identifying colours, logo, product, window displays and advertising. The brand's identity is its fundamental means of consumer recognition, and symbolizes its **differentiation** from its competitors.

Brand image The consumer's view and perception of a brand and its **brand identity**. For users of a brand, this will be based on practical experience. For non-users it will be based on impressions gathered from media sources or the opinion of others.

Brand licensing The leasing of the use of the brand name and logo to another company by the brand owner. A licensing fee or royalty rate will be agreed for the use of the brand name.

Brand loyalty How loyal consumers are to a brand. In the fashion market it is possible for consumers to be loyal to several brands simultaneously.

Brand management The strategic management of a brand. Brand managers ensure that **brand identity** and **brand values** are maintained.

Brand message The message a brand organization wishes to communicate about the qualities and ideas behind the brand and its product. The message can be communicated via the logo, **strapline**, **slogan** and advertising, as well as via the press.

Brand personality The idea that a brand has a distinct personality and that it is possible to attribute human personality traits to a brand.

Brand positioning Both the strategic management of a brand's position relative to competitors in the market, and the perception of the brand's position in the mind of consumers. Positioning strategy is a key component of marketing and branding strategy.

Brand proposition A statement encapsulating what the brand offers its customers. It defines the brand benefits and what makes the brand unique.

Brand repositioning The process of redefining a brand's identity and position in the market.

Brand strategy The strategic plan used to enable the development of a brand so that it meets its business objectives. The brand strategy should influence the total operation of a business and be rooted in the brand's vision and values.

Brand touchpoint A point of interaction between a brand and consumers, employees or stakeholders.

Brand values The code by which a brand operates. Internally, the brand values act as a benchmark to measure behaviours and performance. They should be connecting and engaging, and can also be used to market and promote a brand to consumers.

Bricks-and-mortar retail Retail that takes place in-store as opposed to online.

Bridge line American term for **diffusion line** or a collection placed between designer and high-street fashion.

B2B (Business-to-business) Trading that takes place between one business and another.

B2C (Business-to-consumer) Trading that takes place between a business and the consumer.

Celebrity endorsement When a celebrity signs a contract to act as a brand ambassador and to be seen wearing and advertising the brand.

Celebrity seeding When a brand loans or donates product to a celebrity free of charge so that they are seen wearing the brand's products.

Circular economy An economic system that seeks to extend the life cycle of products by minimizing waste and promoting the sustainable use of natural resources. It can do this through disruptive technology and systems, reusing, repairing, refurbishing and recycling products and materials.

Clip report A report giving information on the effectiveness of a PR campaign. Indicates which publications covered the story, and their circulation figures.

Co-brand or **Partnership brand** A brand created when two brand names work together. Y-3 by Yohji Yamamoto and Adidas is an example.

Co-creation When a company designs and creates products with co-operation and input from consumers.

Comparative shopping (comp shop) Designers and fashion buyers researching the marketplace to compare products and prices from competitors.

Competitive advantage A specific advantage one company or brand may have over competitors within the market.

Concession When a store or department store leases space within it to another brand.

Consideration set The set of brand or product choices a customer considers when purchasing.

Consumer profile Description of a typical customer or targeted customer, derived from the analysis of **market research** data.

Consumer sentiment Audience opinion relating to a particular brand, advertising or PR campaign.

Content All communications material, in whatever form, generated by brands. Now that all content is available digitally, whether in written, visual, audio or video format, the creation and distribution of content are vital points of **differentiation** in brand building and **brand awareness**.

Conversion rate Measures the ratio of a website's visitors to conversions (sales or transactions, and successful downloads or subscription sign-ups). Conversion-rate optimization is a critical tool in online marketing, but can also be used in physical stores. In either case, it is a crucial mechanism for increasing sales and revenue.

Cost per thousand (CPT or CPM) The average cost of an advert reaching one thousand people within the target audience.

Country-of-origin effect (COO or COOE) The perception that products made in certain countries may be of better quality; for example, French perfume or Italian leather.

Crowdfunding A primarily web-based means of sourcing funding for a project, venture or business. Many individuals may contribute small amounts, so it can also help to build a community of engaged consumers.

Crowdsourcing When a company outsources design or other functions to the public, usually via the internet.

Customer pen portrait A written description of a typical or core customer.

Customer segmentation Analysis of customers, grouping them into clusters with similar characteristics.

Deadstock Fabric that remains unused by a manufacturer, or overproduction of garments that remain unsold. Can also refer to shoes that are still boxed and brand new. There is controversy over what is termed 'deadstock' versus available stock (extra fabric that a manufacturer might produce in the knowledge that it will ultimately be sold).

Demi-couture Luxury fashion positioned between **haute couture** and **ready-to-wear**.

Demographics The analysis of a population by gender, age, occupation and social class.

Differentiation A strategy used to ensure that a brand and its products are distinct from those of competitors.

Diffusion line A collection developed by a designer or brand to be sold at a lower price than the main collection; allows a wider range of customers to buy into the brand.

Direct marketing When a company markets directly to the **end-consumer** via mail-outs, direct emails or text messages.

Distribution channel The route by which product is distributed and reaches the market.

Eco-fashion Fashion designed, produced and marketed to minimize the environmental and social impact of the design, **sourcing** and production of the garments.

End-consumer The eventual user or wearer of the product. This is not always the customer; a baby may be the end-consumer, for example, but its mother might be the customer.

Endorsed brand A sub-brand endorsed by its parent brand. Obsession by Calvin Klein is an example.

Fad A short-lived fashion that does not survive long enough to become a trend.

Fashionability How fashionable a garment or brand is.

Flocking To add fine particles of natural or synthetic fibres to a surface to change that surface's texture, feel and look.

Focus group An invited group of people who are shown products or collections so that a company can hear their opinions, perceptions and attitudes, and use the feedback to improve the products.

Fourth cover The outside back cover of a magazine. Since it has a high visibility to readers, it typically carries a significant premium in advertising cost.

Geo-demographics A combination of geographic and **demographic** analysis used to classify customer types.

Greenwashing When a company or product aims to appear environmentally conscious without a real reduction in its environmental impact.

Haute couture French for 'high sewing', meaning the highest quality of made-to-order clothing created in a studio known as an 'atelier'. Only design houses approved by the Fédération de la Haute Couture et de la Mode in Paris may be classified as haute couture.

Impressions In digital marketing, the number of times a page containing a particular ad is visited. Whether or not the ad has been seen by the visitor is not known, so this is a rather crude assessment of the visibility of a digital advertising campaign.

Lead time The time between placing a fabric, component or garment order with a supplier or factory, and the delivery of that order.

Licensee A company purchasing the right to use a brand name.

Licensing A brand company selling the right for another company to produce and market branded product. Most commonly used by fashion brands wishing to create a perfume, cosmetics or hosiery.

Licensing in When a fashion company pays for the rights to use recognizable designs, images or intellectual property – such as a Disney character – on its garments.

Licensing out When a designer or brand grants a licence for their designs or logo to be used by a specialist manufacturer, or where the **licensee** operates in a territory where the **licensor** has no presence.

Licensor The company selling the right to use a brand name.

Like-for-like (LFL) product comparison Direct comparison of similar product sold by a range of competitive brands. Product can be compared in terms of price, quality, fabrication and design.

Likert scale A system for setting questions on a questionnaire using a five-point scale so that the answers can be analysed numerically.

Manufacturer brand Branded manufacturer goods, usually fibres or fabrics, such as Lycra® by DuPont.

Market research Research into a specific market, including the investigation of consumers.

Market segmentation A system of dividing a market into subsections, enabling a company to focus its marketing more accurately.

Market share The share a particular company or country has of a specific market, expressed as a percentage.

Marketing environment Factors that impact on an organization and its marketing.

Marketing mix Key elements that must be balanced in order to develop an organization's marketing. There are two versions: the 4P (product, price, place, promotion) and 7P (with additional criteria: physical evidence, process, people).

Marketing plan A formal plan outlining an organization's marketing strategy.

Marketing research The full range of aspects that must be researched to determine a marketing strategy.

Mystery shopping The process of researchers visiting stores anonymously to assess the quality of service and product on offer.

Non-Fungible Token (NFT) A digital object with a unique digital identifier that is used to certify authenticity and ownership. An NFT cannot be copied or substituted.

Online trunk show A means by which designers or brands allow consumers and clients to view and purchase new designs before they go on general sale or, in some cases, are produced.

Opportunity to see (OTS) Frequency of exposure of an advert; relates to how many people have the opportunity to see, hear or read the advertisement.

Own label (Own brand, Private brand, Store brand, Retailer brand) When a department store or retailer creates its own in-house brands. Marks & Spencer's Autograph and Macy's I.N.C. are examples.

Peer marketing The recommendation and promotion of products among consumers.

Perceptual map A map showing consumer perception of a brand in comparison to competitor brands.

PEST analysis The investigation and analysis of political, economic, social and technological factors affecting a business and its marketing.

Point-of-sale (POS) The actual place where product is sold to the customer, usually referring to the till point (cash register). 'Point-of-sale marketing' refers to material used within a store.

Pop-up store A temporary store set up for a limited time. Pop-up stores often include some kind of special event designed to create a buzz.

Positioning The position a brand or product occupies in the market relative to competitors.

Positioning map A **brand-management** tool used to indicate the current position or proposed future position of a brand in comparison to that of competitors in the market.

Prêt-à-porter French term for **ready-to-wear** clothing.

Price architecture The way a company structures pricing across a range, balancing the offer of low-, medium- and high-priced products.

Price point The price of an item, set according to type of product, quality or exclusivity.

Primary research Research conducted at first hand by collecting data through observations, surveys, interviews and **market research** techniques.

Product attribute The features, functions and uses of a product.

Product benefit How a product's attributes or features might benefit the consumer.

Product placement A process whereby a company raises awareness of its products by ensuring they are seen in films and television shows.

Promotional mix Key types of promotion (advertising, sales promotion, PR and personal selling) that must be balanced in order to develop an organization's promotional strategy.

Prosumer A consumer who also produces products or content. This can be for their own use or for others.

Psychographic segmentation Analysis of consumer type based on lifestyle, personality, motivations and behaviour.

Pull strategy Sales promotions directed towards the **end-consumer**, to create demand and entice the customer to the store or website.

Push strategy Sales promotions geared towards trade distributors or retailers, with the aim of encouraging them to promote the brand to their customers.

QR (quick-response) code A machine-readable code that allows rapid access to websites and digital data via a smartphone.

Reach A term used in a number of advertising contexts and increasingly referred to as a measure in digital marketing, with a common measure being the number of unique visitors per time period.

Ready-to-wear Fashion that is not couture or custom-made.

Relationship marketing Focuses on the relationship between a brand or business and its customers, with the aim of building long-term relationships and loyalty.

Sales channel The route by which a product reaches the market and is made available to consumers.

Sales promotion or **below-the-line marketing** Promotional offers designed to encourage consumers to purchase.

Secondary research or **desk research** The use of existing data that may have been gathered for other purposes and is available in the public domain.

Segmentation The process of subdividing and classifying a market and consumers.

Segmentation variables Criteria used to analyse and classify markets or consumers.

Sellsumer A consumer who no longer just consumes, but also sells their creative output to others.

Share of voice Comparison of a company's press results with those of its main competitors to determine which achieved most coverage.

Shoppable content Digital **content**, such as adverts, films and images, from which consumers can purchase products directly.

Showrooming Where consumers visit stores to examine items, then purchase online to get the best price. The opposite of **webrooming**.

Signature style A unique, identifiable style attributable to a particular designer, brand or label.

Situation analysis An audit of the situation within a company and analysis of the external market situation.

Slogan Words used as part of a promotional campaign to add to the message. The term is frequently used interchangeably with **strapline**, but most slogans are less permanent, used only for a specific campaign.

Slow fashion A socially conscious movement that aims to move consumers' approach from quantity to quality by offering high-quality, long-lasting items and producing clothes to trendless designs.

Sourcing The search for, and procurement of, fabrics, materials, trims and manufacturing at required prices and delivery time frames.

STP marketing strategy A strategy that makes use of **segmentation**, **targeting** and **positioning**.

Strapline or **tagline** A sentence or collection of words appearing under a brand logo or campaign title, such as 'Just Do It'. Generally used consistently as part of brand identity; changed only with a major rebrand.

Style tribe A group of individuals who share a distinctive style of dressing.

Supply chain The network of suppliers, manufacturers, agents and distributors involved in the process of producing a garment.

SWOT analysis Analysis of the strengths and weaknesses of an organization, and investigation of opportunities and threats in the marketplace, done as part of the development of a **marketing plan**.

Tagline *see* **strapline**

Targeting Developing products or services that are specifically aimed to appeal to a particular group of consumers.

Text code A code sent by text to a consumer's mobile (cell) phone, allowing them access to a promotional offer.

Tipping point The moment when a trend or idea crosses a significant threshold, after which it spreads exponentially through a population.

Total product concept A model created by Theodore Levitt to explain the tangible and intangible elements of a product.

Trademark A logo, symbol, brand name, **slogan** or design detail registered and protected by law.

Trend scout A person who seeks out and reports on emerging trends in fashion, street fashion, music, design and culture.

Triple bottom line An ethical accounting system that measures a company's success in economic, social and environmental terms.

Trunk show When designers or sales representatives go on tour to show or preview collections to buyers, invited guests and customers. Usually held in boutiques or hotels. See also **online trunk show**.

Unique selling proposition (USP) or **unique selling point** A distinguishing factor that differentiates one brand from another.

Upcycle To use old or discarded clothing or textiles as a basis for a new, refashioned garment.

Vertical supply chain When one company or conglomerate owns all the manufacturing resources within the **supply chain**.

Viral marketing Marketing campaigns where the message is spread by consumers on the internet.

Visual merchandising The promotion of fashion through window display, store layout and in-store product displays.

Webrooming When consumers research items online before visiting a retail store in order to have the ease and immediacy of purchase. The opposite of **showrooming**.

Index

....

Picture Credits

l = left; c = centre; r = right; t = top; b = bottom

Acknowledgements

Special thanks and gratitude go to all those who have contributed in so many different ways to the creation of this book. To Ursula Hudson for her years of friendship and for putting me forward for this project. To the team at Laurence King for their guidance and constant encouragement, in particular Liz Faber and Kara Hattersley-Smith for commissioning this third edition of the book, and for pushing me past a prolonged period of procrastination. Thanks also to Rosanna Fairhead for her detailed editorial eye, Sophie Hartley for the picture research, Alex Coco for the original design and Vanessa Green for updating the design for this edition.

I wish to acknowledge and thank all the individuals and fashion companies who have generously agreed to be interviewed and/or contribute quotations, case studies or material for this book: Monica Boța Moisin; Aashka Jadeja; Kuldip Gadhvi; Simone Simonato; Matthew Zorpas; Zeina Dakak; Oliver Keavey at Goral Shoes; Bert van Son at MUD Jeans; Josephine Philips at SOJO; Darren Glenister and Dora Lality at Material Exchange; Franceska Luther King from Restyle; Samanta Bullock; Michelle Lowe-Holder; Diane Wallinger; Sarah Angold; Parmis Beyzaei, Kelly Vero; Rachele Didero and Federica Busani; Katie Pope; Hannah Shakir, Geraldine Wharry; Rita Nazareno; Hannah Markham; Hannah Jennings; Charlotte Marsh-Williams; James Hayes and Aldo Kahane; Sophie Taylor; Laura Innes-Hopkins at Allbirds; Vincent Villéger; Timothy Rennie and Elizabeth Emanuel; Laura Winson and Emily Bloomer at Zebedee Talent; Jo Bird; Connie Lim; and Patrick Morgan.

Thanks to friends and colleagues at Condé Nast College of Fashion & Design, and to all the students. Your contribution and debates on fashion have helped to stimulate the topics and ideas for this book.

To all my friends and family who have cared enough to listen, been tough enough to push and kind enough to give me a hug when needed – thank you. Belinda Hill, thank you for offering me a place to stay as a writing retreat over the summer of 2023. And last, but in no way least, a very special thank you and mention to my husband, Mel, for your patience, support, guidance and love – I couldn't have done it without you.

First published in 2011
Second edition published in 2015
This edition first published in Great Britain in 2024 by
Laurence King
An imprint of Quercus Editions Ltd
Carmelite House
50 Victoria Embankment
London EC4Y 0DZ

An Hachette UK company

TPB ISBN 978-1-52942-032-6
Ebook ISBN 978-1-52942-033-3

10 9 8 7 6 5 4 3 2 1
Design concept by Alexandre Coco
Design for this edition by The Urban Ant Ltd
Commissioning editors: Liz Faber and Kara Hattersley-Smith
Editor and project manager: Rosanna Fairhead
Picture research by Harriet Posner and Sophie Hartley

Cover: Dior A/W 2023 RTW show in Mumbai; see p.117 (photo: Shutterstock)
Frontispiece: An illustration by Connie Lim of a look by MADbyMAD at London Fashion Week, 2023.

Printed and bound in China by C&C Offset

Papers used by Quercus are from well-managed forests and other responsible sources.